AF540508

GANDHI, NEHRU
AND
GLOBALIZATION

About The Editor

Harish K. Thakur, a renowned Indo-Anglican and Hindi poet, critic, storywriter and essayist is currently working as Associate Professor in the Department of Political Science in Government College Theog, Shimla. He is also Editor of a literary journal *Conifers Call : Shimla Journal of Poetry and Criticism;* Executive Editor of *Kafta Intercontinental*, a journal published from Chandigarh; and Associate Editor of *Asia Pacific Panorama*, a Journal of Political Science published from New Delhi. Mr. Thakur has so far authored six books in poetry i.e., *Candle in the Storm: 1999; In the Kingdom of the Dead: 1999; The Sun Lyre: 2001; Confessions: 2002; Silent Flows Danube : 2008* and *Raat Ki Qalam Se : 2007.* Two more poetry volumes are in press. He has also authored two volumes in politics entitled *Alienation and Integration in Jammu & Kashmir: 2000* and *Globalization and Human Rights: 2007.* Mr. Thakur has written more than 60 research papers, review articles and essays for different edited volumes and journals.

GANDHI, NEHRU AND GLOBALIZATION

Edited by
Harish K. Thakur

CONCEPT PUBLISHING COMPANY PVT. LTD.,
NEW DELHI-59

© Authors

All rights reserved. No part of this work may be reproduced, stored, adapted, or transmitted in any form or by any means, electronic, mechanical, photocopying, micro-filming recording or otherwise, or translated in any language, without the prior written permission of the copyright owner and the publisher. The book is sold subject to the condition that it shall not, by way of trade or otherwise, be lent, resold, hired out, or otherwise circulated without the prior publisher written consent in any form of binding or cover other than that in which it is published.

The views and opinions expressed in this book are author(s) own and the facts reported by him/her have been verified to the extent possible, and the publishers are not in any way liable for the same.

ISBN : 13-978-81-8069-684-8

First Published 2010

Published and Printed by

Concept Publishing Company Pvt. Ltd.
Regd. Office:
A/15-16, Commercial Block, Mohan Garden
New Delhi-110059 (India)
Phones : 25351460, 25351794, *Fax* : 091-11-25357109
Email : publishing@conceptpub.com,
Website: www.conceptpub.com

Editorial Office:
H-13, Bali Nagar, New Delhi-110 015, India.

Cataloging in Publication Data-- *Courtesy:* D.K. Agencies (P) Ltd. <docinfo@dkagencies.com>

Gandhi, Nehru and globalization / edited by Harish K. Thakur.
p. cm.
Contributed articles.
Includes bibliographical references (p.).
Includes index.
ISBN 13: 9788180696848 ISBN 10: 8180696847

1. Gandhi, Mahatma, 1869-1948--Political and social views. 2. Nehru, Jawaharlal, 1889-1964--Political and social views. 3. Globalization. 4. India--Politics and government. I. Thakur, Harish K. (Harish Kumar), 1968-

DDC 954.035 22

Dedicated

to

Col. R.C. Katoch
For Nicely Coalescing
The Sternness of Uniform
With the Suppleness of Khadi

PREFACE AND ACKNOWLEDGEMENTS

In the globalized era the voices that feel gravely estranged belong to all the hues except the capitalist mercantilist cult. The advent of the cyber-revolution and the consequent contraction of the world into communication-miniscule leaves multiple of life-strands uprooted and to be swept by the wind of uncertainty. In such a scenario there has emerged an urgent need to reread the history and grapple with the factors and forces which have triggered the current phase of events.

The onslaughts of globalization have not only marginalized and enfeebled the liberalist, socialist, and the nationalist forces in India but also the humanitarian schools of thought which largely designed the national political structures and policies and set the ideals of just and humane order. Here arises the exigency to rekindle the flames of the thought and vision of the duo of Gandhi and Nehru, the perennial source of inspiration and light.

The ostensible line of difference between the ideas of Gandhi and Nehru wanes into the eternity of the stream of humanism. The spirituality of the two comprised the finest expression of love, peace, fraternity and humanism. Whereas Gandhi construed a loose federation of local self-dependent autonomous units with least scope for capital and power regimentation. Nehru conceived a more vigorous power structure and planned economy to establish a just and egalitarian society. The mindscapes of the two perceived the issues of poverty, illiteracy, unemployment, economic development, and political instability alike but with distinct designs engineered into the realm of a just and virtuous society.

The current volume offers a humble dedication to the thought and vision of the two with special emphasis over the significance and relevance of their ideas in the globalized world of the day. In all there are fourteen papers presented by academicians and scholars from different disciplines and this makes the volume richer by all means.

Here I would like to express my thanks to all the contributors of the volume for sparing their precious time and contribute papers. My special thanks are due to Prof. Rajinder S. Chauhan (Chairman, Department of Political Science, HPU Shimla), the incessant source of inspiration and energy to carry out such endeavours. I would also thank Prof. Jai Narain Sharma, Dr. Mohammed Khalid, and Prof. Narinder K. Gupta for being ever benevolent to my calls.

Harish K. Thakur,
Shimla

CONTENTS

Preface and Acknowledgements *vii*
List of Contributors *xi*
Abbreviations *xiii*
Introduction *xv*
-Harish K. Thakur

PART-I

1. Gandhian Vision of Democracy 3
-Relevance in the Twenty-First Century
Vijay Sharma
2. Globalization, Culture of Peace and Gandhian Philosophy : A Gendered Perspective 23
-Usha Bande
3. Self-Reliance in the Globalised World 37
-Jai Narain Sharma
4. Gandhian Economics in the Globalized Era 57
-Raj Kumar & Kulbhushan Chandel
5. Globalization and Environmental Crisis : Gandhian Perspective 79
-Amit K. Singh
6. Globalization and Gandhi 93
-Anil Arora
7. Gandhi in the Globalized World 105
-Harish K. Thakur
8. Human Rights in the Globalizing World 115
-Ashu Pasricha
9. Globalization : Myth or Reality 137
-Manoj Rajan

PART II

10. Nehru and Globalization 159
–Mohammed Khalid
11. Nehru, NAM and Globalization 179
–A Decadal Reference Running into Centuries
–Rajinder S. Chauhan
12. Nehru in the Globalized World 191
–Harish K. Thakur
13. Nehru's Internationalism 207
–Narinder K. Gupta
14. Nehru's Perspective on Globalization 213
–Dasarathi Bhuyan
Bibliography 225
Index 235

LIST OF CONTRIBUTORS

Jai Narain Sharma, Professor, Chairman & Honorary Director, Gandhi Bhawan, Department of Gandhian Studies, Punjab University, Chandigarh.

Rajinder S. Chauhan, Chairman: Department of Political Science, H.P. University, Shimla, Himachal Pradesh, 171005.

Ms. Vijay Sharma, Reader, Department of Political Science, H.P. University, Shimla, 171005.

Usha Bande, Senior Fellow, IIAS, Shimla, Wexlow, Lower Kaithu, Shimla, 171001.

Mohammed Khalid, Department of Political Science, Evening Studies, Punjab University, Chandigarh.

Ashu Pasricha, Department of Gandhian Studies, Punjab University, Chandigarh.

Anil Arora, Department of Gandhian Studies, Punjab University, Chandigarh.

Amit K. Singh, Senior Lecturer, Department of Political Science, R.S.M. P.G. College, Dhampur, Bijnor, U.P.

Raj Kumar, Associate Professor & Head in the Department of Commerce, Government Degree College, Theog, Shimla.

Kulbhushan Chandel, Assistant Professor, Department of Commerce, H.P. University, Shimla, 171005.

Manoj Rajan, Senior Research Fellow, Department of Gandhian Studies, Punjab University, Chandigarh.

Narinder K. Gupta, Professor, Department of Laws, Himachal Pradesh University, Summer Hill, Shimla-171005

Dasarathi Bhuyan, Head in the Department of Political Science, Bellaguntha Science College, Distt. Ganjam, Orissa, India-761 119

Harish K. Thakur, Associate Professor, Department of Political Science, Government College Theog, Shimla, H.P. -171001

LIST OF ABBREVIATIONS

ASEAN	Association of South East Asian Nations
BIFR	Board for Industrial and Financial Reconstruction
CEDAW	Covenant on Elimination of All forms of Discrimination Against Women
CENTO	Central Treaty Organization
CNN	Cable News Network
COE	Council of Europe
CSIR	Council for Scientific and Industrial Research
EEC	European Economic Council
EXCOM	Executive Committee of the High Commissioner's Programme
FAO	Food and Agriculture Organization
FCCBs	Foreign Currency Convertible Bonds
FDI	Foreign Direct Investment
GATT	General Agreement on Tariff and Trade
GDP	Gross Domestic Product
HDI	Human Development Report
ICAR	Indian Council for Agricultural Research
ICMR	Indian Council of Medical Research
IGCR	Inter-Governmental Committee for Refugees
ILO	International Labour Organization
IMB	International Maritime Bureau
IMF	International Monetary Fund
INA	Indian National Army
IOR	Indian Ocean Region

IPCC	Inter-Governmental Panel on Climate Change
IPRs	Intellectual Property Rights
MNCs	Multi-national Corporations
MODVAT	Modified Value Added Tax
NAFTA	North American Free Trade Area
NGOs	Non-governmental Organizations
NHRC	National Human Rights Commission
NIEO	New International Economic Order
NSSO	National Sample Survey Organization
OCB	Overseas Corporate Bodies
PCR	Protection of Civil Rights
SAP	Structural Adjustment Programmes
SEATO	South East Asian Treaty Organization
STR	Statutory Liquidity Ratio
TINA	There Is No Alternative
TNCs	Trans National Corporations
UDHR	Universal Declaration of Human Rights
UNCHR	United Nations Commission for Human Rights
UNESCO	United Nations Educational, Scientific and Cultural Organization
UNHCR	United Nations Commissioner for Refugees
UNHR	UN Habitat Report
UNICEF	United Nations Children's Fund
UNO	United Nations Organizations
UNRRA	United Nations Relief and Rehabilitation Administration
UNSCOP	UN Special Committee on Palestine
WB	World Bank
WCP	Women and Culture of Peace Programme
WHO	World Health Organization
WTC	World Trade Centre
WTO	World Trade Organization

people against the one that relied on machines and huge industries minimizing the space for man. Today this net seems to be overwhelmed by the advent of economic globalization with the invasion of franchises and giant institutions. Man has been pushed into the backseat and commodity takes the preference. This also led E.F. Schumacher to bring "the economics as if people mattered"[1] into discussion. Therefore, a redesigning of the same keeping man in mind requires attention which necessarily doesn't go against the former. Rather a keen and rational adjustment in structuration of the emerging configurations might lead to the desirable goals.

The Gandhian alternative that was largely misconstrued and ruled out even for slightest of possibility by liberalists, nationalists, chauvinists and leftists still evokes attention as history boomerangs to the era of *laissez faire*, a model so dear to classical liberalists. At least in one respect there is a large resemblance between the current developments and the one Gandhi spoke against—the advent of gigantism of machines and the corporate world. The two have benefited the mankind a lot and there can be no controversies over that. However, the shift in preferences from man to material, value to profit and concern to commodity has made a huge difference and the splintered world governed by business conglomerates and capital corporatism leaving the poor majority far behind urges for genuine redressing.

The voices today that feel gravely estranged and subdued mostly belong to the socialist ilk. With the break up of the stringent state regimentations and the free flow of goods, capital, investment, technology and the world's becoming a battleground of the competing trans-national groups and multi-nationals the ideas of protectionism and welfare have suffered the most. In the current surge of events if the states are to witness immense increase in production and income the marginalized ones are to be further alienated and this is a matter of grave concern for the protagonists of the poor and the marginalized. Nehru who configured a 'socialism unique' to cater to the needs of majority of Indians while keeping national interests in mind would have enough to suggest against the wider sweep of the events.

This is but distressing that Gandhites and Nehruites have today established separate churches to raise voices with vested interests. The two might have different blueprints designed for economic structuraion and social harmony but at the core of their arguments lie the same thread of humanism and general welfare.

"The Gandhi-Nehru nexus needs to be restored today. The life, work and thoughts of the two are indissolubly linked together and constitute an interacting and integrated system. Gandhi articulated the imperatives of the moral and spiritual universe. Nehru articulated the imperatives of the rational and scientific universe. But the two together constituted the entire universe of mind and spirit of our national movement dedicated to the search for a new identity for our country. The spirituality of Gandhi and Nehru constituted the finest expression of humanism. The essence of this humanism lay in the vision of a society where love and compassion transcend hatred and violence; where, as Tagore said, 'the clear stream of reason has not lost its way into the dreary desert sand of dead habit'; and where the only justification for acquiring wealth is that it is held in trust for the poor and the deprived".[2]

The dynamic fluidity of Gandhi's ideas are expressed in his statement when he remarks "We can try to canalize economic trends, we can't run against them in a head-on collision".[3] This simply meant that Gandhi was not totally against the emerging trends in economics and consequently in society rather he would suggest to wade through successfully keeping in mind the larger interests of mankind.

The post modernist vein of the current times is characterized by its questioning of matters we commonly take as good, natural, or right in the modern era and it endeavours to unsettle and decenter the premises that moderns hold to. It also shows how the constructedness of the modern world favours some over others and often leads to practices of domination and legitimizes disciplinary practices. In many ways, holds Ronald J. Terchek, "this approach parallels the problematizing proclivities of Gandhi who continually questions much that has been taken for granted in the modern world. He means to show that modernity is not neutral or objective but carries extraordinary costs, even though many of its products provide welcome goods. Gandhi extends his argument to claim that what the modern world has constructed is not the culmination of a universal rationality but a particular rationality that legitimizes disciplinary networks that deprive modern men and women of their autonomy, some more severely than others".[4]

In this phase of modernity and post-modernity we have reached the pinnacles of heights so far as science and technology is concerned. This is some thing that the mankind should be elated over but the newer heights of economic splits and distances leaving the traditional ones far behind land us in troubled waters. The turning of the globe into a battleground of trans-national groups and business conglomerates driving the poor states and ordinary man to the backseat makes the revival and rethinking of the thought and vision of those who dreamt for the well-being of mankind imminent.

Vijay Sharma in her paper **Gandhian Vision of Democracy: Relevance in the Twenty-First Century** presents the Gandhian narrative of democracy that encompasses the larger objectives of a just and welfare society. For Gandhi true democracy is not merely reflected through representative democracy rather it depends upon the element of morality attached to it.

Gandhi links freedom to responsibility because in his opinion, freedom without responsibility is a contradiction. From his perspective, a person who does not account for his actions cannot be free. The liberal formulation of freedom is also defective from his perspective because it is self-maximizing and refuses to recognize the social basis of human life. According to Gandhi, what we do affects others, we are affected by them, and we cannot make claims for ourselves at the expense of others. He insisted that rights and responsibilities are reciprocal, without the one, the other is impossible to justify. In his words, "Every duty performed confers upon one certain right, whilst the exercise of every right carries with it certain obligation. And so the never-ending cycle of duty and right goes ceaselessly on." Gandhi insisted that people needed to be aware of the consequences of their own actions. Only when they realized that they are responsible for what they did and what they tolerated could they be said to be free. Democracy, for Gandhi, was not merely procedural but also substantive. Democracy, to him meant that the weakest should have the same opportunity as the strongest. He advocated equality which meant for him fulfilling the basic needs of life of everyone. Here he lands somewhere near socialism but would argue against it as it means inviting centralizing tendency leading to curtailment of individual freedom. For Gandhi, equality should enhance individual freedom, not retard it. Accordingly, he wanted the range of economic differences significantly narrowed. Gandhi envisaged trusteeship as a post capitalist arrangement in order to transform the capitalist order of society into an egalitarian one. Unlike utilitarian thinkers who talked of the greatest happiness of the greatest number, Gandhi believed that the doctrine of real, dignified, human doctrine is the greatest good of all, and this can only be achieved by uttermost self-sacrifice.

Gandhi, in fact, through his philosophy, and in great resemblance with the idea of "Golden Means' of Confucius, offered guidance in transforming what he called the nominal democracy, of the modern western type into a truer or fuller democracy. This he refers to as *Purna Swaraj* (complete or integral democracy), *Ramrajya* (sovereignty of the people based on pure moral authority), or *Sarvodaya* (a social order promoting the good of all), leading to total and integrated progress of the individual ultimately leading to the progress of the whole society.

According to Vijay Sharma another area of concern in the contemporary world that Gandhi addresses is violence, as democracy, according to Gandhi, as mentioned earlier, was instrumental to achieve the larger goal of non-violence. His concept of non-violence becomes more relevant today in the context of intensification of the traffic in weapons and unabated armed conflicts. In Terchek's opinion, in this setting, Gandhi is a clear voice about the dangers of accepting violence as inevitable, whether local or international. However, Trechek is afraid that the metaphors of the future are likely to be revolved around globalization, the market and consumerism. In his opinion, Gandhi's walk into the twenty-first century may be a lonely one.

Pantham also draws parallels between Gandhian and Habermas's critique of the late capitalist society in his book *The Legitimation Crisis* where he suggests the relevance of Gandhian vision of democracy in the present century. Both Gandhi and Habermas have criticized the late capitalist society. They believe that the claims of the state that they are democracies are not true, rather these western liberal democracies have imperialist and fascist manifestations. In order to prove their claims of democratic legitimacy these states impose state intervention in the economic, social and cultural spheres in support of the private appropriation of public wealth. Their utilitarian ethics are offset by the political and administrative considerations, which under state-managed capitalism, determine the social production and private appropriation.

The second paper of Usha Bande entitled **Globalization, Culture of Peace and Gandhian Philosophy : A Gendered Perspective** brings forth the deep nexus between the concept of culture of peace and the Gandhian philosophy which is more a way of life than a self-disciplined mode.

The concept of culture of peace entails harmony, and as peace-activist Elise Boulding avers it stands for "peaceableness". Culture of peace is the guiding principle of any society or country which helps it to promote the quality of life and it includes life-ways and patterns of belief, value, and behaviour that endorse peaceful relationships and peace building. Coming to "Gandhian Philosophy", one acknowledges that it is both deep and broad-based, covering almost all aspects of life: politics, sociology, economics, culture, humanitarianism, education, spirituality and religion, and even literature. It is a perspective on life—a perspective to make life happy and to enable an individual to be a better human being. At its basis is the Indian concept of "Sarva Bhavantu Sukhina", achieved through peace, non-violence and love.

According to Usha Bande, Gandhi might have spoke against industrialization and mechanization of culture but he was never against the Globalization as he once remarked, "I do not want my house to be walked in from all sides and my windows to be stuffed. I want the cultures of all the lands to be blown about my house as freely as possible. But I refuse to be blown off my feet by any".

According to Usha Bande, Gandhi never took peace as a negative concept as it was taken by Greeks defining it as 'absence of war'. Gandhi took the word in its positive sense and added that negation of justice cannot vouchsafe peace because peace is also presence of justice. According to him an oppressive society, even if it lacks violence cannot be termed a peaceful society, because oppression itself is unjust. In Gandhi's vision of peace, justice is inherent in the process. Today when people are at war with nature, women, children and poor and 'new slavery', 'new holocaust' and 'new apartheid' are the buzz words.

The present era, marked by the concepts of globalization and the mind-boggling progress in science and technology, is also tarnished by hatred and violence, fear and passion, and the constant tension of uncertainty. On the cultural side, there is rapid degeneration of values—those perennial values that sustain humanity. In this scenario, Gandhian thoughts have great relevance. Peace means the harmonious balance between the human and the natural world. Here Gandhi's voice for the poor, deprived and women is more relevant than ever.

The paper that nicely presents the abstract of the centuries compressed into phases of waves and transfixes the idea of '*Swadeshi*' in the consequent scenario is the one entitled ***Self-Reliance in the Globalised World*** by Jai Narain Sharma, leaving aside the first wave and the initial phases of the second wave Sharma holds that 'the post-colonial counter attacks by global corporations' mark the third phase of the second wave, a periodical depiction where Alvin Toffler might have problem as he defines it as the beginning of the 'Third Wave'. Many states despite having freed themselves from the colonial yoke have lost much of their economic sovereignty to corporate-controlled international institutions such as the International Monetary Fund (IMF), the World Bank (WB) and the World Trade Organization (WTO).

The postcolonial powers were industrial countries in their late stage, when capitalism had developed further, combining industrial and financial capital into huge monopolistic conglomerates in continual search for new acquisitions, sources of cheap raw materials and labour, and markets. The third wave of Globalization is marked by the emergence and eventual dominance, within the most advanced industrial countries, of the information sector the sector that produces, manipulates, processes, distributes and markets information products. The increasing dominance of the information sector in what had been industrial economies is turning them into information economies. These emerging information economies-principally the U.S. and to lesser extent some countries of Europe—are at the core of the third wave of Globalisation. Because of the way these economies are so closely interconnected, they are better seen as a single emerging global information economy.

The basic conflict within the information sector is the incompatibility between the highly monopolistic forms of information ownership and the social nature of information. The socializing tendency emanates from the nature of information itself, and can therefore, never be suppressed. The monopolizing tendency emanates from the potentially high profit margins in selling information and the economic and political power concentrated in information monopolies. The conflicts arising from these two opposing tendencies will drive the historical development of the third wave of Globalisation. The present situation of economic imbalance is generally due to evolution of institutions, which are one-sided because these institutions had been the brain child of developed countries.

The developed countries, because of their edge over the developing nations, played an important role in international scene. The countries hailing from the South were kept at a low profile as they were considered late comers on the international fora. And this leads to 'Economic Darwinism' which is a new form of international order and a threat to the poor nations. What we call Darwinism is nearer to Galbraith's 'Second Imperialism', which deals with the core nations behaviour vis-à-vis others. In such a state of affairs, holds Sharma, the idea of *Swadeshi* propounded by Gandhi still holds good.

According to Gandhi, "*Swadeshi* is the spirit in us, which restrict us to use of the service of our immediate surroundings to the exclusion of more remote. I should use things that are produced by my immediate neighbours and serve these industries by making them efficient and complete where they might be found wanting". However, here Gandhi does not intend to target the remotest rather its a hierarchy of duties based on the degree of proximity. It is this nearness that multiplies from a narrow point to the universal with having ethical accountability at the base. Gandhi might look protectionist here but he adds the element of morality into the idea of consumption that only provides the way out for the domestic industry. Economic revival is an exciting proposition. It has to be invigorating, self-generating and mass based and herein lies the test for the nation's nerves.

Raj Kumar and Kulbhushan Chandel in their well researched paper **Gandhian Economic Order in the Globalized Era,** hold that the globalization is not a panacea for the world economic crisis, rather globalization is deepening this economic crisis. Globalization is not only a threat to the economic sovereignty of states but also a challenge to the political and cultural sovereignty. The agenda of globalization is controlled by multi-national corporations of United States, Europe and Japan and implemented by World Bank, International Monetary Fund and World Trade Organisation. The entire process of globalization is based on exploitation and violence which is against the basic principle of Gandhian economic order. The remedy lies in the deglobalisation of the dehumanized trade, investment, information technology and aid schemes. The globalization is pushing the world into dangerous direction which breeds violence, exploitation, poverty, inequality, corruption, unemployment, injustice, crime and discontentment in the society. Hence, the Gandhian economic model is the only worthwhile alternative for man's peaceful, purposeful, successful and happy existence. In fact we want culture of peace and harmony and therefore, we must have the technology of peaceful co-existence. The rehumanisation of science, technology and industry, the main stream of Gandhian vision, is the ardent requirement of twenty first-century. The globalization is widening the gap between individual and society, rich and poor, city and village, local and global whereas the only solution to bridge this gap lies in the Gandhian Economic order.

Amit K. Singh in his paper **Globalization and Environmental Crisis : A Gandhian Perspective,** tries to highlight the deep concern of Gandhi for the global environment that he had foreseen decades back with the advent of industrialization. Besides the alarmingly rising gap between the rich and the poor at global as well as states level there has been a tendency of imposition of global culture on the whole of the world perpetrated by the West especially United States. The process of Globalization discards villages and villagers. It is an urban-centric development process. In present consumer culture, the relationship between man and environment is at stake.

Gandhi was against this tendency of global homogenous culture when he remarks *"What is good for one nation seated in one condition is not necessarily good enough for another differently suited. One mans food is after another mans poison. Physical geography of a country has a predominant share in determining its culture. A fur coat may be necessity for the dweller in the polar region it will smother those living in the equatorial regime."*

Anil Arora in ***Globalization and Gandhi*** while differentiating between the older and the newer version of capitalism holds that whereas the first capitalism, or "liberalism", was constrained by governments, neo-liberalism or globalization subsumes governments and even the whole of society. It exploits freely, without any restraints, neither of governments nor of any moral order. The International Monetary Fund and World Bank invented at the end of Second World War to rescue and revive European and Japanese Economies, today prey on "Third World" governments in particular and bend them to their economic policies that are anti-democracy, anti-poor, anti-humanity, focused on securing giant corporations their monopolistic profits.

The capitalism and political freedom do not necessarily go hand in hand. Capitalism is very successful in creating wealth but it does not assure freedom, social justice and the rule of law. It is not designed to safeguard universal principles. While we can speak of the triumph of capitalism we cannot yet speak of the triumph of democracy. If we care about universal values such as freedom and democracy, we cannot leave them to the care of market forces. That is why Gandhi formulated his economic principles in the context of his design of an ideal social order : a non-violent non-exploitative, humanistic and egalitarian society. Satisfaction of needs and moral elevation of individual were not anti-thetical for him. He was not averse to the inflow of ideas and values from the outer world but was against allowing one swept away with them.

For Gandhi, the principle of 'Trusteeship', though seems outdated today, provides a means of transforming the present capitalist order of society into an egalitarian one. It gives no quarter to capitalism, but gives the present owning class a chance of reforming itself. It is based on the faith that human nature is never beyond redemption. It does not recognize any right of private ownership except so far as it may be permitted by society for its own welfare.

He saw the capitalist as dispensable but the worker was the core of society. This is in sharp contrast to globalization which weakens the worker and makes him dispensable and replaceable with technological innovations and which strives to eliminate his bargaining power by getting rid of trade unions if possible. For Gandhi, machinery and technology have no right to exist if they invade the rights of workers. Therefore, Gandhi's concern for the poor, workers, and welfare of all by founding an egalitarian society as also the ethical and normative upliftment of all are essential postulates for establishing a just society even today.

In yet another paper **Gandhi in a Globalized World** by Harish K. Thakur pleads for genuine understanding of the ideas of Gandhi and remarks that Gandhi had rightly advised to opt for a shift from the current disequilibrium in economics and go for a more fragmented, decentralized, and autonomous way of life. He had the foresight to peep into the forthcoming times and point out that we are moving ever more rapidly into a world dominated by the large-scale complexity and high capital intensity which eliminates the human factor and leads to violence. In order to ensure survival, he recommended new guidelines which point towards smallness rather than giantism, simplification rather than complexity, capital saving rather than labour saving - and towards non-violence. The profit motive throws humanity and the planet out of equilibrium. The emphasis has to be shifted back to the person rather than the product. Costs have to be measured in human terms by taking cognizance of happiness, beauty, health and the protection of the planet. Hence, the stress on the normative aspect of life and preference for the human element against the material progress has an intrinsic reference to the well being of majority against a few.

Ashu Pasricha in her paper **Human Rights in the Globalizing World** alarms that the consequence of violation of human rights lead to an increased feelings of deprivation and injustice among the populations of the different countries of the world which is enhanced by the rapid and unprecedented advance in communication and information technologies, which really turned the world in this respect into a global village, the deprived is exposed daily, if not every minute to images and evidences of the huge gap in standards of living between the rich and the poor. Manoj Rajan in **Globalization : Myth or Reality** elaborately discusses terminologies complexities, various dimensions of globalization as also its impact on the social and cultural stratificaion of the global society.

Thus, this is the time to ponder over the other alternatives and check the unhindered flow of developments into a more socialist and Gandhian mould of planning where the centre of the development will be welfare of man, of course one and all, and the capital saving for the good of more, labour increase to generate employment and economic concentration to eliminate poverty and economic disparities.

Mohammed Khalid in his paper **Nehru and Globalization** concedes that India is grappling with the challenges posed by Globalization and trying to find solutions within the framework of her democratic polity. In the Post-Cold War period India is charting its course in a globalizing world. Political parties in India are fully aware that globalization is a reality. The Indian National Congress, which harps on Nehru as builder of modern India has left his economic ideology behind to grab the opportunity, the globalization offers.

Nehru, a socialist at mind didn't opt for the ideology in principle rather he would be pragmatic. He inspired the industrialists to provide a fillip to India's economy. However, he had strict reservations on the question of foreign investment, an idea that lays at the bottom of the current scenario.. Although he did not officially decry the possibility of foreign investment in direct terms, he did stress that the sectors of foreign investment would be regularized, and the terms and conditions of investment and employment would be strictly controlled by government rules in case there were possibilities of a foreign investment. Moreover, Nehru emphasized that the key sectors will always be in government hands.

Nehru very much in line with Gandhi forged a policy that aimed at rural self-development of India. He tried to boost India's cottage industries and believed that the rural and cottage industries of India played a major role in the economic fabric of the country. He was also of the belief that small-scale industries and cottage industries were effective solutions to the massive employment problems that remained a perpetual issue of concern throughout his lifetime. Contrary to his efforts for rural development the lowering of tariff barriers under the WTO pressure has glutted Indian market with goods from outside especially China forcing a large number of small scale industries to shut down. Small scale producer has become trader of the foreign goods under the circumstances.

Khalid holds that though, the Congress continues to be the hub of Nehruvian thought-strands, yet under the force of globalisation his economic policies had to be abandoned or at least diluted. It can thus be said that Nehru's economic policies are far away from structural reforms and post Cold-War globalisation. Had he been there on the Indian political scene, he would have certainly devised a middle path as he did in the fifties in the form of mixed economy and non-alignment.

Another paper entitled **Nehru, NAM and Globalization: A Decadal Reference Running into Centuries** by Rajinder Singh Chauhan is a study of the initial phase of the Indian Foreign Policy, its formulation and the influences that worked upon it. The mindscape of Nehru, holds Chauhan represented the confluence of major global streams like idealism, welfarism, internationalism, socialism and cosmopolitanism. His presentation to the world the ideas of 'Panchshil' and 'Non-alignment' suggest that such policies are inherently superior–even politically and morally too, against the alternative of military alliances and confrontations that keep the fear of war alive. According to this perspective, non-alignment and panchshil may not always prevent wars, but may make it less likely through a spirit of tolerance and co-operation. Nehru concluded that military weakness did not necessarily imply diminished security or political influence abroad. Instead, greater security could be achieved through non-involvement in military blocks. His philosophy of Non-alignment that he made the basis of Indian Foreign Policy also paved the way for the growth of a wider global perspective of peace and cooperation.

No doubt, the current waves within globalization characterized by IT Revolution, Corporate Governance and Information Capitalism are turning the traditional thinking extraneous yet the middle path preached by Nehru based on dynamic rational understanding of the global developments and maneuvers would keep on haunting the minds of statesmen, policy-makers, and thinkers alike.

The paper **Nehru in the Globalized World** by Harish K. Thakur traces a parallel stream that is visible there in the contemporary welfare thinking and the vision Nehru professed. However, a big contrast is also discernible as Nehru's 'one world' was guided by his philosophy of socialism and humanism. He envisaged a world where all the states would be equal in status and would have the magnanimity for the poor and the needy of the world. He would advocate socialism but again never at the cost of individual freedom, a socialism of different creed. However, in this phase of globalization, holds Thakur, the ideas of Nehru have not lost their original gloss. His concern for the deprived and the ideas of a welfare state, state planning, and the state ownership of major sectors and natural resources still carry meaning. Globalization is good to the extent it is homogenizing in effect and works for the uplifting of the all but if it creates further rifts and cleavages among people chiefly on economic grounds the socialist mode with due honour to individual freedom would never loose its relevance and so would Nehru. To understand the ideas of Nehru and their relevance in the new world order it is necessary to assess him as a socialist, planner, policymaker, welfarist, humanist, internationalist and statesman.

Being a socialist, Nehru, unlike his international counterparts who turned states into socialist regiments, kept due space for the free breathing of the common nationals. In his own words even the complete nationalization of the industry unaccompanied by political democracy will lead only to a different kind of exploitation for while industry will then belong to the states, the state itself will not belong to the people. He never advocated total state protective policies rather the inflow of foreign capital was a welcome thing to boost economy unless it goes against the national interests.

Thus Nehru's ideas over international peace, cooperation and brotherhood together with his ideas on planning, non-alignment and mixed economy would remain relevant in times to come. In this globalized world where there have been emerging new lines of social diversity, barriers of capital monopolies, borders of economic corporatism, stringencies of information and technology transfer, and widening gaps between the two classes the Nehruvian vision that provides just space for the poor and the marginalized would never loose significance, at least until the normative stream of human thought doesn't loose ground.

Nehru's Internationalism, an essay by Narinder Kumar Gupta focuses on the cosmopolitan outlook and philosophy of Nehru. For Gupta Nehru would be remembered for his special qualities like his concern for genuine humanism, staunch patriotism, unorthodox internationalism, scientific temperament, immaculate secularism, love for the poor and the oppressed, his regards and sympathy for minorities, aversion to narrow chauvinism and obscurantism, his virtue of integrity and honesty, his tolerance against opposing ideas, his respect for the opposition, his understanding of incipient nationalism in many parts of Asia and Africa, his fearlessness, his attempt to synthesize the old and new, the material with the spiritual and traditional with the modern.

Thus Nehru represented a combination of ideas as dictated by the imminence of contemporary times and the necessities of national interests of India. He gave due place to the ideas of human welfare, peace, cooperation and universal brotherhood and at the same time preached a middle path via non-alignment–a rational and pragmatic way out to the ferocious currents of cold war. His alternative of mixed economy governed by the tenets of socialism and welfare of all would keep on working at the mindscapes of people in general and statesmen in particular.

Dasarathi Bhuyan in his essay **Nehru's Perspective on Globalization** sees a parallel between globalization and internationalism of Nehru, though there exist a big difference between the two. Globalization, no doubt, relates to the globe or world. But it is much more than this. This implies that in an ideal regime of globalization, there are no national borders. There is free flow of information, ideas, capital, products, services and even governance across the border. Nehru had also the same vision. According to him Internationalism demands that each country shall take an intelligent interest in world affairs and give up the desire to live in isolation from the rest. In this age of atomic weapons and sputniks the only way to avoid the destruction of human civilization is the free association of all the nations in some type of world federation. Nationalism and internationalism must be balanced and harmonized in the interest of world peace and world unity. The idea of NAM came to rescue the world from the clichés of power confrontations.

According to Bhuyan for Nehru the economic activity of the state aims at providing social services such as education, health, social security etc. to the people. It acts as a facilitator and co-coordinator and refrains from acting as an owner and regulator. It continues to be a welfare state performing all the protective functions as well as several social functions. Nehru's idea of mixed economy and the model of planning is not irrelevant in the process of globalization, which involves a change in the role of the state. Globalization constitutes a natural extension of the principles of international interdependence. It is a natural extension of the ideology of internationalism favoured by Jawaharlal Nehru.

Thus the fourteen papers by different scholars and academicians produced in this volume represent myriad of themes, shades and dimensions of the thought and vision of Gandhi and Nehru. We hope that they would provide better understanding of the complexities and crises India, and of course the world is faced with. The positives apart the alarming negatives being delivered by the process of globalization needs to be keenly observed and keeping the basic human civilizational values at the prime and the views expressed by prominent thinkers and philosophers in mind the answer is to be searched by mankind itself. This volume is a humble addition to the literature on the significance and relevance of Gandhism and Nehruism in the contemporary times and it is hoped that would be of help and interest to the readers, researchers and scholars alike.

NOTES

1. Schumaker, in Weber, Gandhi and Buddhist Economics, www.mkgandhi.org/budhist.htm
2. P. N. Haskar, http://www.mainstreamweekly.net/auteur131.html
3. D.G. Tendulkar, Vol. 7, 2nd Edn., (1960), Publications Division, Government of India
4. Ronald J. Terchek, *Problematizing Modernity: Gandhi's Decentering Impulse*, Gandhi Marg, April-June 2001, pp. 5-20.

PART - I

1

GANDHIAN VISION OF DEMOCRACY

Relevance in the Twenty-First Century

Ms. Vijay Sharma

> "Today in politics, democracy is the name for what we cannot have - yet cannot cease to want."[1]

Gandhi is best known for his theory of non-violence and freedom. Throughout his writings, he emphasized that every one must be respected as a free moral agent and that violence degraded both its objects and subjects. This does not mean that he did not have vision of other aspects of human life and society, rather, it can be said that Gandhi wrote and offered recommendations for a particular historical situation, the India of his time, while writing about spinning, rural economics, village democracy or the critique of modern civilization as such. The fact is that non-violence and freedom were the overall goals of his philosophy and democracy was instrumental to these larger goals.

The present article deals with his vision of democracy, the instrument that Gandhi wanted to use to achieve his larger goals. In this context an attempt has been made to place Gandhi's views about democracy in his normative framework. Whether his vision is applicable or relevant in the contemporary world with all its complexities is debated.

The conclusion that follows this debate is that Gandhian vision of democracy can neither be applied in totality nor ignored in totality. In fact, it needs to be contextualized according to the present circumstances. This conclusion has been substantiated by referring to few latest theories and concepts.

Gandhi considered arbitrary rule antithetical to the goals he had set for himself. He realized that democratic government coupled with an equitable society appeared to offer the greatest prospects to achieving his goals. According to him democratic rule fostered a diffusion of power and increased the prospects that equality and freedom would be pursued. Democracy, he believed, should be based on consensus and cooperation, which transcended the majority principle and pursued the welfare of all. In his words, "The rule of the majority has a narrow application, i.e. one should yield to the majority in matters of detail. But it is slavery to be amenable to the majority, no matter what its decisions are... Under democracy individual liberty or opinion or action is jealously guarded... what we want, I hope, is a government not based on coercion even of a minority but on its conversion."[2] According to him democracy as practiced in Britain, was bad because it believed in counting of heads, those who won 51 per cent votes carried the day. The minority had to submit to the majority. While he believed that consent was the basis of all good governments, he wished to conceive the ideal state as the rule of selfless individuals. He dismissed liberal democracy, in which people compete for their own self-interest.

Democracy, for Gandhi, was not merely procedural but also substantive. Democracy, to him meant that the weakest should have the same opportunity as the strongest. He complained that democracy had come to mean party rule, or to be more exact, rule in the hands of the Prime Minister who often lacked honesty of purpose. In it, he held, each party thrives in horse-trading and sensationalism which is blown out of proportions by the press.[3]

Gandhi placed his ideal democracy in the village, where life was simpler, power diffused and the economy decentralized. Consuming only what they produced themselves, the villagers would be self-sufficient. Work in the village would revolve around handspun cloth or *Khadi* and provide everyone with useful labour. Gandhi laid considerable emphasis on direct labour in the fields and handicraft industries and insisted that the worker must be able to control the machinery and not become so dependent on mechanized work that he could not earn his livelihood without it. He believed that distribution can be equalized when production is localized; or in other words, when the distribution is simultaneous with the production. By concentrating all activity in the villages, he believed that the means of production of elementary necessities would remain in the control of the masses. The villagers would work cooperatively, pooling their labour and goods and dividing their profits. He expected that the competition of capitalism would be replaced by the cooperation in an agrarian-based society in which each village would be largely economically and politically self-contained. The villages would be locally controlled by the panchayats (village council of five persons elected by the people).[4]

Gandhi distrusted the standard idea about democracy. He denied that voting and elections are sufficient either to assure a government based on popular consent or to safeguard the autonomy of everyone. Gandhi considered representative democracy important but argued that popular rule required even more. He wanted to promote a regime where significant economic, social and political inequalities have been reduced and where all forms of power are dispersed. For him ideal democracy protects and reflects plurality, most especially responding to those who have been excluded in the past. In this spirit, Gandhi says, "This age of awakening of the poorest of the poor is the age of democracy."[5] To make it a reality he urged democrats to struggle to make government simple and avoid hierarchy and domination. However, according to Gandhi, even ideal democracy can make mistakes, and he invests his citizens with civil disobedience to confront injustice.[6]

Related to the question of disobedience is the question of obligation, that is further related to the concept of freedom, that is the foundation of Gandhian democracy. Gandhi links freedom to responsibility because in his opinion, freedom without responsibility is a contradiction. From his perspective a person who does not account for his actions cannot be free. The liberal formulation of freedom is also defective from his perspective because it is self-maximizing and refuses to recognize the social basis of human life. According to Gandhi, what we do affects others, we are affected by them, and we cannot make claims for ourselves at the expense of others. He insisted that rights and responsibilities are reciprocal, without the one, the other is impossible to justify. In his words, "Every duty performed confers upon one certain rights, whilst the exercise of every right carries with it certain obligations. And so the never-ending cycle of duty and right goes ceaselessly on."[7] Gandhi insisted that people needed to be aware of the consequences of their own actions. Only when they realized that they are responsible for what they did and what they tolerated could they be said to be free.

Another important foundation of Gandhian democracy is equality. While talking about equality Gandhi did not mean absolute economic equality which applied to every one in the same way. At the economic level, according to Gandhi, equality "simply meant that everybody should have enough for his or her needs."[8] Although this kind of equality could be achieved through government ownership of all property, but Gandhi rejected such a solution because it rested on centralized power leading to curtailment of individual freedom. For Gandhi, equality should enhance individual freedom, not retard it. Accordingly, he wanted the range of economic differences significantly narrowed.[9]

Gandhi envisaged trusteeship as a post capitalist arrangement in order to transform the capitalist order of society into an egalitarian one. In his opinion, "Trusteeship provides a means of transforming the present capitalist order of society into an egalitarian one. It gives no quarter to capitalism, but gives the present owning class a chance of reforming itself. It is based on the faith that human nature is never beyond redemption. It does not recognize any right of private ownership of property, except in as much as it may be permitted by society for its own welfare."[10] This suggests that new Gandhian outlook was of declining to receive what all cannot get. Gandhi did not believe in the doctrine of the greatest good of the greatest number. In his words, "I do not believe in the doctrine of the greatest good of the greatest number. It means in its nakedness that in order to achieve the supposed good of 51 per cent the interest of 49 per cent may be, or rather, should be sacrificed. It is a heartless doctrine and has done harm to humanity."[11] Thus, in Gandhi's opinion the only real, dignified, human doctrine is the greatest good of all, and this can only be achieved by uttermost self-sacrifice.

Gandhian vision of democracy implies that Gandhi is for participative or substantive democracy and that state is perfect and non-violent where the people are governed the least. In Gandhi's words, "True democracy cannot be worked by twenty men sitting at the centre. It has to be worked from below by the people of every village."[12] He admitted the need of a central government administration but believed that it should not be modelled after the accepted western form of democracy. Central government administration should not become the bearer of the alienated political rights of the citizens. He said, "Under my plan, the state will be there to carry out the will of the people, not to dictate to them or force them to do its will."[13] Although, he did caution people against converting democracy into mobocracy, however, he insisted that democracy is an impossible thing until the power is shared by all. He said, "Most people do not understand the complicated machinery of the government. They do not realize that every citizen silently but nonetheless certainly sustains the government of the day in ways of which he has no knowledge."[14] He believed that real Swaraj will come not by the acquisition of authority by a few but by the acquisition of the capacity by all to resist authority when it is abused. In other words, *Swaraj* is to be attained by educating the masses to a sense of their capacity to regulate and control authority.[15]

Gandhi, thus, recognized the need for a central government administration but he suggested that it should be structured not as a pyramid but as an oceanic circle. In this structure composed of innumerable villages, there will be ever widening, never ascending circles. Life will not be a pyramid with the apex sustained by the bottom. But it will be an oceanic circle whose centre will be the individual always ready to perish for the village, the latter ready to perish for the circle of villages, till at last the whole becomes one life composed of individuals, never aggressive in their arrogance but ever humble, sharing the majesty of the oceanic circle of which they are integral units.[16]

Gandhi argued that electoral democracies of Europe and America are only "nominal democracies," belonging to "the same species" as fascism, both are exploitative systems and "resort to ruthlessness to the extent required to encompass their end."[17] The only differences he saw between liberal democratic and fascist systems were that the violence of the latter was much better organized than that of the former, and that these "have the backing of their peoples who imagine that they have a voice in their own government."[18]

Gandhi, in fact, through his philosophy, offered guidance in transforming what he called the nominal democracy, of the modern western type into a truer or fuller democracy, which he referred to as *Purna Swaraj* (complete or integral democracy), *Ramrajya* (sovereignty of the people based on pure moral authority), or *Sarvodaya* (a social order promoting the good of all), leading to total and integrated progress of the individual ultimately leading to the progress of the whole society.[19]

Gandhi sought to redeem individual freedom even in the political sphere without endangering social harmony. Gandhi wrote that social life "is not divided into water tight compartments, called social, political and religious" and that "every act... has its... spiritual, economic and social implications."[20] He referred to his ideal of true democracy as the "square of swaraj", whose four sides are the political, the economic, the social and *dharma* (i.e. universal morality).[21] He believed that the observance of social norms consciously and as a matter of duty not only was a more secure foundation for social order than their observance for reasons of legality or out of fear of external sanctions but was also conducive to individual freedom. Gandhi said that his conception of true democracy was one of the reign of the self-imposed law of moral restraint. He held that by learning to adjust his individualism to the requirements of social progress man would move in the direction of a truly democratic order.[22]

After having an overview of Gandhian vision of democracy the question that arises is that how far this vision is relevant in the contemporary scenario. In this context what is visible today is that the present democracies are based on competitive elections and interest group pluralism. Voters choose their representatives, who govern them for a period of time, and if satisfied, they return the incumbents; otherwise, they turn to alternative candidates. Between elections, the organized groups are expected to represent the interests of their members before various government agencies to influence their public policy. Gandhi departed from this model of democracy because he wanted a small setting with a relatively simple economy. Gandhi offers a view of politics that is local, simple and participatory. For Gandhi, self-governance is very important. The pluralists on the contrary have been concerned with the problems of representation in large and highly diversified societies. Pluralists hold that politics is based on pursuit of interests which invariably leads to disagreements and conflict. From their perspective, interests are individualistically generated and consequently not in some automatic harmony. Interests are natural and conflict is inevitable. Therefore, according to them, politics should be so structured that allows the freest expression of interests, and institutions should be devised in such a manner that they can hold conflict to manageable levels.

The pluralist thought leads to the politics of bargaining and compromise because of the by play of interests. The pluralists argue that policies based on compromise assure that no one is an absolute looser. Since everyone in the pluralist model is concerned about defending his own interests, little attention is paid to how this affects the rest of the society. Gandhi hoped to define political life in ways that emphasize the community rather than individual interests. He began from the premise that social life required both freedom and interdependence and this required the appropriate social setting to pursue these values effectively. He believed that needs could be differentiated from interests and politics should be institutionally structured to give priority to basic needs and in his opinion, from this perspective, interest group politics endangered the very purpose for which any government should be designed to serve – to provide for the common good.[23]

Regarding the relevance of Gandhian vision of democracy in actual practice, in the contemporary world, with all its complexities, there is difference of opinion amongst political scholars. Ronald Terchek, a Professor at the University of Maryland, who has done a seminal analysis of Gandhian philosophy, believes that Western democratic societies have become stronger. Their dangerous totalitarian opponents have been vanquished, technology today continues to move at a dizzying pace, their models of economy have become dominant and their culture is becoming globalized. The West has put its stamp on the world. Modernity and modernization provide the standards for understanding success and failure. According to Terchek, on the other hand, the themes of several books published in the West have started challenging the concept of liberal democracy such as Agnes Heller and Ferenc Feher's *The Postmodern Political Condition,* Jeffrey Goldfarb's *The Cynical Society,* Daniel Bell's *The Cultural Contradictions of Capitalism* Bobbio's, *Future of Democracy,* Ronald Beiner's *What's the Matter with Liberalism?,* David Marquand's *The Unprincipled Society* and Alan Bloom's *The Closing of the American Mind* etc.[24]

Rajni Kothari one of the authorities on Indian government and politics, in his book *Footsteps into the Future,* has tried to describe the complexities of the modern world, provide a design for an alternative to it and sketch out practical strategies for moving from the expected future to a preferred one. The perspective that guides such an effort is based on essentially Indian world view as it has evolved overtime. He opines that present trends indicate a scenario of growing inequity and violence in the world - between nation states as well as within a large number of them. There are other signs of trouble and discontent. Political participation is declining while cynicism is increasing; hard choices assert themselves between full employment and a generous state; drugs and crime climb to troubling levels; the family is under siege; people live longer but many seem neither secure nor satisfied; the world's population is increasing; and because of technology and fast-deteriorating nexus between man and nature, environment is degraded. Technology is generating forces that deny opportunities for a meaningful life to large numbers of human beings and condemns them to a state of dependence and indignity. They are forced to live under conditions of stress, overcrowding, and despair.

Special problems await the youth of the world especially in poor countries. A large proportion of this age group is expected to live in urban areas, acquire some education and skill, but be unable to find jobs, leading to unemployment or underemployment. They are likely to be socialized in modern and cosmopolitan ways of thought, more away from the traditions of their parents, and less deferential to authority. They are also likely to be more mobile and restless and less tolerant of inequalities. The upshot of these various converging trends is likely to be seething discontent, a certain rootlessness, and a widespread feeling of futility and rejection among millions of men and women.[25] All this may lead to unrest and violence and that may further lead to strong, disciplinary governments trying to check this unrest and violence with harsh police measures attacking the basic rights of human beings. The political leaders may manipulate the frustration of people into ugly, violent nativist movements. The poor may be intimidated and humiliated in the harsh realities of their urban slums.[26]

Under these complexities of the modern world assaulting the autonomy of the individual human beings, leading to the centralization of power in the hands of few i.e. the political leaders, the so-called representatives of people, application of Gandhian theory of democracy in totality seems impossible e.g. with respect to selfless individuals, truth, non-violence, decentralization of power, resistance to globalization and modern technology. But from Gandhian perspective such outcomes were inevitable. These are the outcomes of intense demands of individualism, decayed traditions and continued devaluation of persons in the economy.

Regarding the relevance of his vision of democracy one view is that this is true in the modern context that it is impossible to return to the period when Gandhi wrote and lived, by the complexities of the modern world can be avoided to some extent, if not completely, by attempting to apply ethical standards to contemporary practices and institutions. American president recently asked his senators to improve their ethical behaviour.

There is no doubt that there is need for greater diffusion of economic and political power, greater equality in social relationships and a wide concern for moral values. For example, regarding diffusion of economic power, in the Indian context, Prime Minister Dr. Manmohan Singh suggested that rural development should catch up with urban development. This is true that Gandhi's specific proposals like trusteeship may not be applicable in the crowded polity of the contemporary world, but his political critique signals what has traditionally been at the heart of the democratic project, namely, that people ought to govern themselves, decentralization of political and economic power, increased participation throughout society, and harmony in one's life and community. Even though, Gandhi's call to decline to receive what all cannot get and to limit wants may seem utopian today, because of narrow individualistic outlook of people, the urgency of his message becomes all the more pressing in today's consumer society in which people have little sense of obligation towards their fellow beings. Gandhi wanted to challenge this kind of moral apathy.

Another area of concern in the contemporary world that Gandhi addresses is violence, as democracy, according to Gandhi, as mentioned earlier, was instrumental to achieve the larger goal of non-violence. His concept of non-violence becomes more relevant today in the context of intensification of the traffic in weapons and unabated armed conflicts such as Iraq war, Afghanistan issue, America's so-called war against terrorism, India-Pakistan situation etc. In Terchek's opinion, in this setting, Gandhi is a clear voice about the dangers of accepting violence as inevitable, whether local or international. As per Gandhian philosophy not only conflicts should be settled without violence but civil society, with its patterns of domination and humiliation should also be reconstituted in order to avoid the conditions that give rise to violence in the first place. Terchek also believes that although, many support autonomy and decentralization, however, as the postmodernist impulse to question is extensive, these Gandhian concepts do not seem to be the priorities of the late modern world. According to him, this does not mean that the twenty-first century promises to be hostile to Gandhi's theory and his idiom, more likely, it will be unconcerned. The metaphors of the future are likely to be revolved around globalization, the market and consumerism. In his opinion, Gandhi's walk into the twenty-first century may be a lonely one.[27]

This is true that the modern temper is preoccupied with matters far removed from much that Gandhi wanted to promote and although some of his specific proposals are anachronistic in the present complex society, his legacy comes with the issues he raises about individual autonomy and social harmony, economic security, participatory communities and the non-violent resolution of the conflict. In this context Gandhian vision of democracy can neither be applied in totality nor ignored in totality. In fact it needs to be contextualized according to the present circumstances. M.P. Parameswaran's idea of the 'Fourth World' can be quoted here to prove that how he has tried to contextualize various ideas and philosophies in the present context including Gandhian philosophy in order to enunciate a new concept of a post-capitalist society. His concept can form the basis for Marxists, Gandhians, environmentalists, feminists, socialists, dalits and peace activists to work together.

M.P. Parameswaran is a leading thinker from Kerala, who quit his job, about four decades ago, as a nuclear scientist in the nuclear establishment of India soon after coming back from USSR after a three year stay. Since then he has been associated with various movements of social change. He was expelled from the Communist Party of India(M) for propounding an unmarxist concept of the 'Fourth World'. The concept of 'Fourth World' put forth in 1998, caused a controversy in 2003 in Kerala. There was a massive debate in the media and subsequently he was expelled. Post-expulsion, he elaborated and expanded his views and published a booklet in Malyalam, which has gone into number of prints. Now an English translation of this document, more than 40,000 words long *Thoughts about a Fourth World* is circulating on the net.

"Thoughts" is a major alternative vision document to come from within the Indian mainstream left in the aftermath of the breakdown of the USSR. The "Fourth World" aims to provide an ideological document which evaluates the failure of the socialist experiments and provide a sound foundation of economics, politics, and ethics for a new society. It identifies three important reasons for the break-up of the USSR: economic centralization, political centralization and a distorted view of progress. Its vision of the future world is based on the necessity of: participatory democracy, an alternative view of progress, and an alternative approach towards the progress of productive technology.

His vision of the future world based on the necessity of participatory democracy with economic decentralization at village level and political decentralization of a kind of direct democracy, is quite nearer Gandhian vision. He wants the economy of the Fourth World to be network of hundreds of thousands local communities which are increasingly becoming self-sufficient. Like Gandhi he seeks to localize material production as far as possible. The difference between Parameswaran and Gandhi is that he is not against modern technology. Rather, he wants that modern technology should be used to make "small powerful too". By the use of modern technology there will be continuous reduction in working hours and increase in leisure and this is how material progress is to be reflected in the Fourth World.

The political structure of the Fourth World is premised on citizens' ability and willingness to participate in socio-political activities. The political structure goes deeper than even panchayats. It is based on the neighbourhood groups consisting of 20-30 proximate households of 60-80 citizens (voters). In his opinion beyond the size of 60-80, direct democracy is viewed to be unwieldly. He has suggested the inversion of a power pyramid—where only delegated functions move up and residual powers rest with the grassroots.

Another aspect of Parameswaran's vision of Fourth World that has been influenced by Gandhian philosophy is the future action plan for achieving this vision, consisting of two components, direct and indirect struggles. The direct component includes economic boycott of not only multi-national corporation products, but the reactionary strength of national large-scale-manufacturers will also be checked by using the same techniques used against foreign trans-nationals—boycott and local substitutes, for the promotion of local products. In the Gandhian mode Parameswaran also suggests indirect mode of struggle, wherein employees of state institutions from panchayat to national government can use their own files as a weapon to fight the class enemies.

Parameswaran's vision, although, has been criticized for suggesting weak economic structure or being utopian, that is another debate, however, one thing is sure that he has contextualized Gandhian philosophy according to the changing socio-economic needs.[28]

A growing number of third world countries seem to be developing a kind of democracy that facilitates democratic procedures but fails to provide essential civil liberties. However, this is not a new phenomenon: states with such features have long been referred to as 'semi-democratic,' 'quasi-democratic', 'authoritarian' or worse. But for some commentators, such terms are no longer sufficient. Consequently, a new catch phrase - *Illiberal Democracy* - was coined by Farid Zakaria in 1997. The concept is rooted in the practice of allowing for political rights yet denying civil liberties. Now-a-days a new self-assured defence for restricted, illiberal, democracy is on the rise, particularly among the countries that have demonstrated an ability to combine illiberal measures with economic growth and social stability.[29]

Jeff Haynes has given another categorization of democracies in third world countries namely: façade, electoral and full or liberal democracy. In façade democracies rulers have few real pretensions to democracy, there are regular but heavily controlled elections and rulers always work closely with their armed forces. Electoral democracies have certain formal procedural criteria of democracy. There are meaningful rules and regulations determining the conduct and content of elections, which take place when the constitution demands and governments, most of the time, rule with at least some concern for the process of law. Beyond this these democracies are deficient in respect of societal freedom, such as poor civil liberties regimes, limited societal toleration and little citizen participation in politics. Full democracy extends the idea of democracy beyond the formal mechanisms of electoral democracy. These democracies give importance to individual freedom and the representation of interests through elected public fora and group participation. In such regimes there is a high degree of equity, justice, civil liberties and human rights; and the armed forces are unequivocally subservient to civilian rule. It is a kind of democratic regime that in its most developed state would offer citizens means of access to governmental processes and a real say in decision-making. In a full democracy there would be not only genuine participation in rule by the majority of citizens, but also consistently effective channels of accountability between ordinary people and public officials. Those traditionally lacking power - the poor, the minority ethnic and religious groups, women, young people—would have a say in the direction of a nation.[30]

These categorizations of democracies in Third World countries suggest that the basic difference in full democracies and facade or electoral or illiberal democracies is that the latter are only procedural and not substantial democracies, citizens have political rights but not civil liberties. There is similarity between this categorization and Gandhian categorization of nominal and complete or integral democracy. Gandhi too was for substantive democracy where the weakest had the same opportunity as the strongest and where individual freedom and opinion was, in his words, "jealously guarded." This suggests the relevance of his vision of democracy in the contemporary scenario too. Although, political analysts like Jeff Haynes believe that "full" democracy is an aspirational category and regimes with mixed characteristics, that is, electoral democracies are more prevalent, however, there should be a conscious effort to redress past imbalances, so that the mass of ordinary people come to believe that democracy is a better system than alternative ones, such as benign dictatorship. This is what Gandhi aspired for in his own times.

Pantham's attempt to find parallels between Gandhian and Habermas's critique of the late capitalist society in his book *The Legitimation Crisis*, again suggests the relevance of Gandhian vision of democracy in the present century. Both Gandhi and Habermas have criticized the late capitalist society. They believe that the claims of the state that they are democracies are not true, rather these western liberal democracies have imperialist and fascist manifestations. In order to prove their claims of democratic legitimacy these states impose state intervention in the economic, social and cultural spheres in support of the private appropriation of public wealth. Their utilitarian ethics are offset by the political and administrative considerations, which under state-managed capitalism, determine the social production and private appropriation. State is not promoting the greatest good of all in Gandhi's words or the generalizable interests of the people in Habermas's words.[31] To quote Habermas, "Genuine participation of citizens in process of political will formation, that is, substantive democracy, would bring to consciousness the contradiction between administratively socialized production and the continued private appropriation and use of surplus value."[32] Both of them believe that capitalist ethos and utilitarian principles militate against participatory or substantive democracy. Pantham's argument is that the untruth of the state's claims to democratic legitimacy, which Habermas saw in the advanced capitalist countries in the present context was seen earlier by Gandhi in the peripheral states of South Africa and India, which were the arena of his experiments with truthful or authentic politics. This argument itself suggests the relevance of Gandhian vision of democracy even today. The only need is to relate his vision to the present circumstances and keep striving for it. In Gandhi's words, "We should be sure of our ideal but know we shall ever fail to realize it, but never cease to strive for it. That constant striving, that ceaseless quest after the ideal represents the best of human conditions."[33]

NOTES

1. John Dunn, *Western Political Theory in the Face of the Future*, Cambridge: Cambridge University Press, 1979, p. 27.
2. Ronald J. Terchek, "Gandhi and Democratic Theory", in Thomas Pantham and Kenneth L. Deutsch (ed.), *Political Thought in Modern India*, New Delhi: Sage Publications, 1986, p. 308.
3. *Ibid.*, V.R. Mehta, *Foundations of Indian Political Thought*, New Delhi; Manohar Publishers, 1996, p. 219.
4. Ronald J. Terchek, "Gandhi and Democratic Theory", *Op. cit.*, p. 309.
5. Ronald J. Terchek, *Gandhi: Struggling for Autonomy*, New Delhi: Sage Publications, pp. 139-40.
6. *Ibid.*, p. 140.
7. Ronald J. Terchek "*Gandhi and Democratic Theory*," *Op. cit.*, pp. 314-15.
8. *Ibid.*, p. 316.
9. *Ibid.*
10. Pyarelal, *Mahatma Gandhi: The Last Phase*, Vol. 2, Ahmedabad: Navjivan Publication, 1958, pp. 633-34.
11. Thomas Pantham, "Beyond Liberal Democracy: Thinking with Mahatma Gandhi," in Thomas Pantham and Kenneth L. Deutsch (ed.), *Political Thought in Modern India*, *Op. cit.*, p. 330.
12. M.K. Gandhi, *Democracy: Real and Deceptive*, Comp. R.K. Prabhu, Ahmedabad: Navjivan Publication, 1961, p. 7.
13. *Ibid.*, p. 70.
14. *Ibid.*, p. 30.
15. *Ibid.*, pp. 4-5.
16. *Ibid.*, pp. 73-74.
17. *Ibid.*, p. 78.
18. *Ibid.*, p. 76.
19. V.R. Mehta, *Op. cit.*, p. 224; Thomas Pantham, "Beyond Liberal Democracy: Thinking with Mahatma Gandhi," *Op. cit.*, p. 335.
20. Thomas Pantham, *Ibid.*, p. 336.
21. *Ibid.*
22. Gandhi, *Democracy: Real and Deceptive*, *Op. cit.*, p. 32.
23. Ronald J. Terchek, *Gandhi and Democratic Theory*, *Op. cit.*, pp. 317-18.
24. Ronald J. Terchek, *Gandhi: Struggling for Autonomy*, *Op. cit.*, pp. 229-38.
25. Rajni Kothari, *Footsteps into the Future*, New Delhi: Orient Longman, 1974, pp. 90-94.
26. Ronald J. Terchek, *Gandhi: Struggling for Autonomy*, *Op. cit.*, p. 230.
27. *Ibid.*, pp. 231-37.
28. M.P. Parameswaran, *Another World is Possible: Thoughts About A Fourth World*, Circulated on Net; Rajinder Chaudhary, "Fourth World:

Marxian, Gandhian, Environmental…", *Economic and Political Weekly*, Vol. 42, Oct. 15-21, 2005, pp. 4504-06.

29. Jan Engberg and Svante Ersson, "Illiberal Democracy in the 'Third World': An Empirical Enquiry," Jeff Haynes (ed.), *Democracy and Political Change in the 'Third World'*, London: Routledge, 2001, pp. 35-54.
30. Jeff Haynes, "Introduction: The 'Third World' and the Third Wave of Democracy," Jeff Haynes (ed.), *Op. cit.*, pp. 1-20.
31. Thomas Pantham, "Beyond Liberal Democracy: Thinking with Mahatma Gandhi," *Op. cit.*, pp. 326-27.
32. *Ibid.*, p. 327.
33. Quote in Ronald J. Terchek, *Gandhi and Democratic Theory, Op. cit.*, p. 312.

2

GLOBALIZATION, CULTURE OF PEACE AND GANDHIAN PHILOSOPHY

A Gendered Perspective

USHA BANDE

> In around 2002-03, Belfast in Northern Ireland witnessed a unique spectacle when a large number of women gathered at the Ormean park in Anderson Town to reaffirm their right to live in peace. There were no fiery speeches or heated discussions, they created no problem to law and order situation; they just sang hymns, prayed and recited their charter reaffirming their faith in peace. They were reiterating their right to live, and love and build a just and peaceful society. This was the "end-the-violence-rally" with the motto "let's build peace, brick by brick". The women departed as peacefully as they had gathered leaving a favourable impression that women can be best peacemakers in the world. (Bande, 2003)[1]

Before we start the paper, let us consider briefly the three key words in the title "Globalization", "Culture of Peace", and "Gandhian Philosophy". Globalization is based on the concept that the globe is a single unit for decision-making and that it opens up tremendous possibilities for the world to reap the benefits of each others' knowledge and expertise. It thus purports to bring harmony and sharing in the world. The concept of culture of peace entails harmony, and as peace-activist Elise Boulding avers it stands for "peaceableness". Culture of peace is the guiding principle of any society or country which helps it to promote the quality of life and it includes life-ways and patterns of belief, value, and behaviour that endorse peaceful relationships and peace building. Coming to the third key word "Gandhian Philosophy", one acknowledges that it is both deep and broad-based, covering almost all aspects of life: politics, sociology, economics, culture, humanitarianism, education, spirituality and religion, and even literature. It is a perspective on life—a perspective to make life happy and to enable an individual to be a better human being. At its basis is the Indian concept of "Sarva Bhavantu Sukhina", achieved through peace, non-violence and love.

The first point that needs to be clarified is if Gandhi was anti-globalization as the proponents of this ideology aver. There is no denying the fact that Mahatma Gandhi was not in favour of industrialization, consumerism and mechanization of culture. He had abhorrence for reducing man to a thing and had a great faith in the power of the spirit as against the power of mammon. Some of his ideas may appear too idealistic or unrealistic for the modern world while others quite contrary to the ideology of globalization but in effect he was open to the new influences and wanted only the best out of the lot for his countrymen. In one of his article in 'Hind Swaraj', he puts it succinctly, "I do not want my house to be walked in from all sides and my windows to be stuffed. I want the cultures of all the lands to be blown about my house as freely as possible. But I refuse to be blown off my feet by any". (Gandhi: 1997)

Gandhi was not against India's having global contacts, or global collaborative enterprise. But he would not have favoured globalization in its present form. He might have rejected this model as it does not use indigenous resources commensurate with India's cultural and ethical traditions. The idea most foundational to his model was that neither development nor its implementation should be unethical. It may look utopian these days because a good number of people, both politicians and administrators/implementers, accept that some unethical practices are bound to creep in the execution of some scheme or project. The globalization has, despite its claim to the contrary, violence embedded in it is proclaimed by actvists like Vandana Shiva and Bharati Ray. Vandana Shiva points out that the world order of globalization is dictated by commerce, greed and profits and is giving rise to "new slavery, new holocaust, new apartheid". It is a war against nature, women, children, and the poor". (Shiva, 2001) Bharati Ray studies the impact of globalization on Indian women's life-situations and questions its efficacy for women already struggling with gender inequalities, poverty and poor health-care. In her article "Gandhi and Globalization", Aruni Mukherjee, a Professor at the University of Warwick tries to establish that Gandhi was not against globalization because he himself was its product in a way. What he rejected and resented was its corroding effect on culture. I quote the author elaborately to make my point:

> "It seems ironic the world-wide anti-globalization movements often portray Gandhi as someone who shared the same side of the ideological spectrum, when Gandhi himself was clearly a product of globalization. He was educated in London, started his political activities in South Africa before he joined the political arena in India and was greatly influenced by the western figures such as Jesus, Tolstoy, Thoreau and Ruskin. Gandhi himself identifies globalization as an ancient phenomenon, whereby he claimed that it was not a bigger threat to India as various races starting from the Greeks, Huns to the British had invaded India but ended up being a part of the nation. He believed that the mingling of the cultures in India would not

> be a threat to India's customs and culture. However, he did identify that the establishment of a global society would carry certain dangers for the sovereign nations such as colonialism, both cultural and political; industrialization and commercialization of the economy leading to class antagonism and environmental hazards. Today, we see many of those problems emerge clearly in our lives and hence, Gandhi's relationship with globalization remains extremely important and his ideas valid even today. (Mukherjee)

Gandhi's idea of development was all-around improvement of an average Indian's quality of life. The concept of quality of life is grounded on the belief that it is not to be assessed on the basis of quantitative measurement of nation's wealth but on qualitative changes. Thus standard of living does not mean the enhanced purchasing power of the individual but on the contrary it is to be evaluated on the basis of the existence of peace, harmony and mental happiness as the ultimate goal. Quality of life rests on the fulfilment of physical, psychological and ultimately the spiritual needs of the man.

Humanistic psychologist Abraham Maslow rates the spiritual needs of man as the highest in the hierarchy of his needs though he places it at the bottom of his chart precisely because in the hierarchy of basic needs the physical needs are the top human priority, followed by emotional needs. When Gandhi Ji propounded his theories, he too gave priority to basic needs. This is clear from the special attention paid to villages, the down trodden and the weak. Basic needs of people are security of food, shelter, healthcare, nutrition, drinking water, education and the right to employment; emotional-psychological needs are measured by psychological security, peace, compassion and sense of belonging and spiritual needs are the urge for self-realization, mental happiness and peace.

The notion of the culture of peace remains incomplete without reference to non-violence and to Gandhi precisely because living in a sub-culture of violence Gandhi's idea of non-violence and brotherhood are intrinsically connected to our life. Campaigns for non-violent action and peace have become a part of life in the millennia. Its proponents challenge abuses by authorities, spearhead social reforms and protest militarism and discrimination with peaceful means. The principles of non-violence are based on love, inner strength and intrinsic boldness. As Bhikhu Parekh points out:

> For Gandhi then *Ahimsa* meant both passive and active love, refraining for causing harm and destruction to living beings as well as promoting their well-being. *Himsa* was opposite of *Ahimsa*. Since the ancient Indian thinkers took *Himsa* to be positive concept, they defined *Ahimsa* in terms of it. Gandhi equated *Ahimsa* with the positive and self-contained concept of love and adapted the opposite approach of defining *Himsa* in terms of it. (Parekh, 1989, 116-117)

Our second question is : what is really meant by evolving a culture of peace? Culture manifests two contrasting features: the higher involves the cultivation of inner life of human beings and their spiritual elevation; in its lower aspect, it denotes man's aggressiveness, his invasive imposition on other people's rights and culture. Those on whom we impose our will tend to be resentful. This sows the seeds of future conflict. In its former aspect culture is conducive to peace, in the second, it is the cause of war. Nichola Roerich, the great creative artist define culture as the cultivation of the creative potential in man. He said, "positive creativeness is the fundamental quality of the human spirit. Let us welcome all those who, surmounting personal difficulties.... Propel their spirit to the task of peace-building, thus ensuing a radiant future".

Put in simple words, peace-culture is a culture that would include life-ways and patterns of belief, value, and behaviour which promote peaceful relationship and peace building. At the institutional level, it require arrangements that promote well-being, equality, stewardship, and equitable sharing of earth's resources. It present security to human kind—as individuals, families or nations. In other words, peaceableness is an action–concept, involving constant shaping and reshaping of understandings, situations and behaviours in constantly changing world. Dwight D. Eisenhower's words signify how in the strife-torn world, one has to think of the deprived to go a step further towards peace. "Each gun that is made, every warship launched, every rocket fired, signifies, in the final sense, a theft from those who hunger and are not fed and those who are cold and are not clothed."

The United Nations is dedicated to promoting peace and well-being. Its charter declares: "we, the people of United Nations, determine to save succeeding generation from courage of war, which twice in our life time has brought untold misery to mankind...reaffirm ... to promote the social practice of tolerance and live together in peace with one another..." The UN declares the year 2000 as the International Year of Peace and has designated the decade 2001-2010 as the International Decade of Peace and Non-Violence. This could have afforded a unique opportunity to mankind to transform the existing culture of war into a culture of peace, not mere passive peace but an active peace. But what has of late been happening in the world has given a strong blow to peace. When cultural imperialism, an ideology justifying the subjugation of others, becomes the dominant creed, the culture of peace gets a big jolt.

The term currently in practice is Cultural Internationalism that views culture as a vehicle for building cooperative relations across national boundaries and defusing the underline confrontation due to difference. Difference and distinctions are opposite to co-existence and they become threat because we fear those who are different. We exaggerate the difference to fail to see the common humanity of man. J. Krishnamurti often said in his dialogues that where there is fear there is violence and violence itself is anti-thesis to peace. Another thinker Felix Frankfurter opines that there can be no security where there is fear. The very basis of war is the psychologically damaging notion that says "once a looser, always a looser" and of course, no body wants to be looser, so the best way out of this psychological trap is to strike whenever you get a chance.

Today, man erroneously thinks of power in terms of knowledge and knowledge when superficial, exhilarates in the show of physical strength which leads to brute force and violence. But, as Elise Boulding, a renowned peace study scholar emphasizes, culture of peace are to be found in each individual's process tenaciously continuing peace-oriented behaviour. Peace is not something to be left to others in a distant place. It is something, which we create in our day-to-day efforts to create and cultivate care and consideration for others, forging bonds of friendship. Boulding also talks of women's contribution to peace in her "Feminist Invention in the Art of Peace-Making". She writes:

> The portrayal of woman's family roles and women's culture as symbols of nurturance and peace in war-making societies is an ancient theme in history. However, the rise of nineteenth century suffrage movement in Europe and United States meant for many women a narrowing of the historically broader focus on social ills to the wrongs suffered by women. This reduced the visibility of the women reformers who have been galvanized by evil effects of war, colonialism, an unbridled capitalism on the world as a whole....The contrasting effect on women of their relegation to the household and the private spaces of the society has been over stated. What tends to be ignored is the historical reality that women's work of

> feeding, raring and healing humans and building and rebuilding households and communities under conditions of constant change—including war, environmental catastrophe, plague, and continual push-pull migration—has produced resources and skills within women's cultures that have been critical not only to human survival but also to human development. My argument is not an essential one, not that women are biologically predisposed to nurturance and peace-making. It is rather that women's knowledge and experience worlds have equipped them to function creatively as problem-solvers and peace-makers in ways that men have not been equipped by their knowledge and experience worlds. This, obviously, can change. More sharing of experience worlds between women and men will be an important next step in human development."[2] (Boulding, 1955:409-12)

A strong character is, therefore, the first necessity if mankind wants to build a culture of peace. Such a person instead of trying to "reform" the world looks within and attempts to reform the self. According to Thich Nhat Hanh, a Vietnamese Buddhist monk and author of *From Love in Action:* "In each of us, there is certain amount of peace and a certain amount of violence and a certain amount of non-violence. We must work on ourselves if we want to have a real impact. If we work for peace out of anger, we will never succeed. Peace is not an end. It can never come about through non-peaceful means. When we protest against war or injustice, we feel that we are a peaceful person, but this is not always true. If we look more deeply, we will see anger, frustration, and the roots of war in ourselves also. To create a peaceful society, we have to transform the anger and defuse the bombs that are in us...Most important is to be peace, so that when a situation presents itself, we will create more suffering."[3] The above words are a pointer towards developing a strong character. Boulding writes : "Put in the simplest possible terms, a 'peace culture' is a culture that promotes peaceableness. Such a culture would include life-ways and patterns of belief, value, and behaviour that promote peaceful relationships and peace building, and accompanying institutional arrangements that promote well-being, equality, stewardship and equitable sharing of the earth's resources. It represents security for humankind-without the need to resort to violence. In other words peaceableness is an action-concept, involving a constant shaping and reshaping of understanding, situations, and behaviours in a constantly changing world, to sustain individual and collective well-being". (Boulding : "What is a Peace Culture?")

The culture of peace initiative is based on UNESCO's mission of creating peace in the mind of men. The UN General Assembly's Declaration and Programme of Action of Culture of Peace—2000 made the culture of peace a concern of the whole UN system. The document provides an elaborate definition of the concept emphasizing that the culture of peace would be fostered through the actions aimed at education, sustainable economic and social development, human rights, understanding, tolerance and solidarity, equality between men and women, actions to foster democratic participation, free flow of knowledge and information and promotion of international peace and security. During the International Year of Culture and Peace, more than 72 million of signatures were obtained from people. This is a clear indication of people's longing for peace. It means commitment to : respect all life, reject violence, share with others, listen to understand, preserve the planet and rediscover solidarity. (Manifesto, 2000, IYCP UNESCO, Paris).

The Women and Culture of Peace Programme (WCP) was established in 1996, as part of UNESCO's follow-up to the Fourth World Conference. The main aim is to promote women's participation in conflict resolution to build culture of peace. The UNESCO tends to explore in the context of the Women and Culture of Peace Programme, the social, cultural and economic conditions producing violence and practical strategies for reducing violence and finding out ways of raising boys that emphasize qualities such as emotional response and caring which are the forte of women. Women are by nature peacemakers and recognizing this fact, some feminist organizations brought to the fore the necessity to include women in the peace process and in policy-making. The positive aspects inherent in peace are love, fellow-feeling, understanding and empathy. Incidentally these are the very qualities intrinsic to women's nature and when given due recognition, these become the empowering influences transforming women's vulnerability and victim status into agency and women's power. Peace activists opine that peace can never be won through a military solution. What is required is to build a culture of peace in which women should be given the central role.

The basic premise of culture of peace mission is "peace is in your hand, cultivate peace". The initiative of UNESCO is, indeed, an attempt to build a vision that could be shared broadly by both men and women as it entails unlearning the codes of culture of war and violence—physical violence as well as the violence of economic and social deprivation, and replace it with inter-cultural understanding and solidarity. These norms and values constitute the basis of global ethic and show that these do not belong to any one culture but are common to all humanity. Given that women's basic nature, which is peaceful, they could save many situations from being blown up to violence. Women's absence in peacemaking has been mainly because of the gender stereotype. The idea of women as peacemakers appears outrageous in political circles. Since women by and large are not holding key top-positions they hardly get chances to sit across a negotiation table. An interesting episode during the 1996 peace talks on Irish problem reveals how women asserted themselves when relegated to the background and by their persistence earned a place at the negotiation table. The story runs thus: in 1996, peace activist Monica McWilliams and Mary Blood were told that only leaders from the ten top-ranking political parties would be included in the peace talks. These women leaders mustered public opinion, formed the Northern Ireland Women's Coalition and within six weeks gathered notes and got themselves on the ballot. They were voted into top ten and they got their place at the negotiation table.

There are women's organizations that have succeeded in raising their voice against violence. One such example is the success of the Pakistan-India People's Forum for Peace and Democracy. Setup in 1994, this women's organization has been able to bridge some of the differences between India and Pakistan by organizing huge rallies to unite the citizens of the two country. The Forum has also held annual convocations where citizens from the two countries can affirm their shared histories, forge networks and act together on specific initiative. Researchers in the field of psychology feel that women, because of, and in spite of, their status as second class citizens, have developed innovative strategies to cope with problems. Tackling smaller, everyday problems that keep people apart, women switch over to taking initiative in drafting principles for comprehensive settlement.

Gandhi was aware of women's coercive power and wanted them to be on the forefront in his *Satyagraha* movement. One of the revolutionary elements of his *Satyagraha* was the effort to make the extended family the model for society as a whole. The patriarchal societies have clear cut divisions between women's and men's sphere activities—the domestic sphere is for women and the public sphere for men; concomitantly, most power is vested in the male member. Gandhi refused to accept the private/public binary and tried to integrate the two as conducive to and instrumental in socio-political transformation.

Traditionally, we think of peace in relation to war and define it as absence of war. Some of the oft-repeated quote are, "if you want peace, be prepared for war". This is because the Latin word for peace is *pax*, which means *absentia belli* the absence of war. Gandhi took the word in its positive sense and added that negation of justice cannot vouchsafe peace because peace is also presence of justice. According to him an oppressive society, even if it lacks violence cannot be termed a peaceful society, because oppression itself is unjust. In Gandhi's vision of peace, justice is inherent in the process.

The present era, marked by the concepts of globalization and the mind-boggling progress in science and technology, is also tarnished by hatred and violence, fear and passion, and the constant tension of uncertainty. On the cultural side, there is rapid degeneration of values—those perennial values that sustain humanity. In this scenario, Gandhian thoughts have great relevance. Peace means the harmonious balance between the human and the natural world. Concepts like eco-feminism, peace feminism, and cultural feminism are greatly helping in the process of peace, and women, known and unknown, have contributed to a large extent to the peace culture which has become a main challenge for us in the process of building inter-cultural identity and respect, so vital for world peace. For, Gandhi, peace was self-fulfilling; it was a process, it was not a means to an end but an end itself. As he often said, "there is no way to peace; peace is the way". Every society has traditional practices of conflict resolution that have evolved over centuries. Women's culture in every society is at the core of the culture of peace. As Richard Johnson contends, "Globalization from below, including women and men in all these diverse societies, careful attention to non-violent theory, and listening to the actual experience of women are essential in the creation of women-affirming cultures of peace". (Johnson, 2000: 53) Peace, like non-violence, requires moral strength to stand up against injustice, to speak out and to counter without being offensive.

A man or woman of strong character need not always be the other worldly one; even being one of us he or she shows the characteristics of being what the Gita calls a "Slithapragya". It is only when a renewed awareness of our common humanity takes roots in individual thought that the phrase "universal humanism" becomes a reality. Our concept of "Vasudhaiv Kutumbakam" is not a mere slogan but a philosophy in which the creative synergy between the inner and the outer is integrated. The inner or internal synergy is introspective and spiritual; it tends to reform the individual; the outer or external one is legal, social and institutional, it reforms the society. It was Lord Buddha who could transform the dreaded robber and murderer Anguliman with his force of character, his inner strength, not by any outer force. It was Jesus Christ who when betrayed held his peace and advising his disciples said, "those who live by the sword, perish by the sword". Later, even when on the cross he uttered, "Forgive them, Lord, for they know not what they do". Such is the strength of character that exudes love and peace. Once a person learns to dissociate himself from the idea of personal misery, he sees much that is common in humanity.

NOTES AND REFERENCES

1. See Usha Bande, "Women and Peace", A paper widely discussed in academic circles, journals and new papers in 2003. Available on internet at http://www/pib.nic.in/feature
2. A phrase coined by Elise Boulding, Professor Emeritus of Sociology in Dartmouth College and former Secretary General of the International Peace Research Association. See "What is a Peace Culture?" http://www.globaleduc.org/whatisa.htm
3. These words of Thich Nhat Hanh appear in a box as part of the article in www.globaleduc.org/whatisa.htm)

3

SELF-RELIANCE IN THE GLOBALISED WORLD

JAI NARAIN SHARMA

We are all familiar with colonialism. The dates may have varied; the colonizing country may have been different; but the main features of our common colonial experience were basically the same.

Using superior military technology, the colonizing power forcibly imposed its rule over the peoples, at great cost to us in terms of human lives and suffering and in terms of human and natural ecology.

Military conquest was very often preceded—and most certainly followed—by the imposition of new religions and cultures, which facilitated subjugation by dulling the impulse to resist the clutches. The effects of such cultural implantation on our minds have lingered on and continued to do their damage, keeping us in mental bondage long after the last colonizing soldier had left our soil. Soon, the colonial mind started to take for real the masks worn by the colonizers and the words they used to deceive their victims, such as "we bring you civilization", "we will teach you democracy"; etc. As soon as resistance was quelled, the colonizing power setup a colonial administration, run at lower levels by people culled from local elites, many of whom decided to work hand-in-hand with their colonial masters to preserve their wealth and privileges. [1]

As the colonial bureaucracy was put in place, the process of drawing out our wealth began. Over the centuries, the colonizing powers enriched themselves immeasurably by drawing human and natural resources from our lands—human slaves, indentured labour, tributes, precious metal and other minerals, colonial crops cultivated on seized indigenous land, and so on. At the very foundations of the richest countries of today, are the broken remains of our own ancestors and the wealth plundered from their communities.

The colonizers brought with them the practices of plantation agriculture, large-scale logging, large-scale mining, and unsustainable technologies, which were meant for plunder and for maximizing exploitation and profits. These unsustainable practices replaced the sustainable indigenous practices our pre-colonial peoples had relied on for centuries.

The impact on the people and their communities was grievous. We lost our right to self-determination and our freedom. We lost our wealth through colonial plunder. Our best lands were seized for colonial tillage. Indigenous communities lost their rights to their lands. The impact on the people and their communities was grievous. The impact on nature was equally disastrous. Colonial occupation was invariably marked with plunder of our natural resources and the introduction of monoculture in direct contrast to the much more sustainable and ecological practices of our pre-colonial past.

During this period, the colonial powers that took over the globe were mercantilist and, later, early industrial powers. Often operating their own State monopoly corporations, they scoured the globe in search of slaves, tradeable goods or raw materials, and bases for their colonial operations. This period of colonialism may be called the first wave of Globalisation.

Where independence was won by arms in China, for example—the colonial economic and political interests had to beat a full retreat. They lost their territorial rights and their businesses, their properties confiscated and nationalized. Where independence was gained through non-violent means, the nationalists made efforts to regain control of their economy. These took the form of foreign ownership limits, profit remittances restrictions, local content requirements, exports quotas, and other attempts to regulate foreign businesses.

During this post-colonial period, the role of global capital expanded, partly due to internal developments in their home countries, and partly as a counter-response to independence movements and economic nationalism. Having lost direct control over their colonies, global capital sought and became better at indirect control; military aggression was replaced by cultural aggression and economic control. By this time, internal developments within the colonizing powers themselves had prepared their economies for this shift: many of them had reached the late industrial stage development. Huge private corporations in partnership with governments had accumulated vast amounts of financial wealth, turning money itself into a major commodity. These corporations needed new markets and investment areas, rather than colonial territories that were becoming more and more difficult and costly to retain politically and militarily.

We are also familiar with these post-colonial developments. Again, they masked their real intention of drawing wealth from our lands and communities with such pretexts as: "we bring jobs"; "we bring technology"; "we will lend you money for development"; we will protect you from communism"; and so on.[2] Instead of relying on military conquest, these global corporations worked closely with elite-led governments, particularly those local classes whose economic interests coincided closely with their former masters. Often, the local police and armed forces were flooded with aid, to win their loyalty and service.

The post-colonial bottom line was no different: the extraction of wealth. This occurred through: unequal trade (depressed prices for our agricultural commodities, monopolistic prices for their industrial manufactures); high interest rates on foreign loans; using loan conditionalities to exact further concessions, quick and massive profit repatriation; and low wages. By retaining post-colonial dominance and control in the economic and cultural spheres, post-colonial wealth extraction could proceed unabated.

Chemical agriculture was introduced to intensify the production of export crops, widespread poisoning and damage in the countryside. Exploitation of our natural resources intensified, and energy generation projects such as huge dams, coal and oil plants, and nuclear plants in some cases ravaged the countryside.

The development of a nationwide mass media infrastructure served to further strengthen the colonial hold on local minds, to create and expand markets, and to ensure a friendly environment for foreign investments and foreign products.

This post-colonial wave may be called the second wave of Globalisation, where industrial countries and global corporations would range across the globe for investment areas, industrial markets, trading partners, and sources of cheap labour and raw materials.

This wave has gone through several phases, reflecting the progress of an unequal contest between powerful countries strengthened by the immense wealth they had drawn from colonial victims on the one hand, and the newly-independent nations weakened by centuries of plunder and exploitation on the other hand.

The early-independence phase was often marked by intense economic nationalism, as local economic interests tried to mobilize their government to enhance their economic sovereignty while global corporate interest fought to retain their colonial privileges. This phase saw the adoption of economic protectionist measures meant to strengthen local capital *vis-a-vis* foreign capital.

The second phase saw a succession of crises that included the oil shocks of the 70s, the debt crises of the 80s, the socialist crisis of the early 90s, and the financial crisis of the late 90s, which is still going on. Socialism had earlier provided a counter-balance to global corporations and their governments, as well as a possible alternative path for independence movements. These crises weakened the capacity, the will, and the overall position of the former colonies and enabled global corporations to launch major counterattacks in order to regain much of the colonial power and privileges they had lost during the economic-nationalist phase.

The post-colonial counterattacks by global corporations mark the third phase of this second wave. Many countries, despite having freed themselves from centuries of colonial rule, then lost much of their economic sovereignty to corporate-controlled international institutions such as the International Monetary Fund (IMF), the World Bank (WB) and the World Trade Organization (WTO). Through loan conditional ties, structural adjustment programmes, and other means, many nationalist laws and provisions gained by earlier anti-colonial independence movements were undermined and dismantled. Some authors Chakravarty Raghavan, for example have called this phase a process of "recolonization", a return of colonial privileges for global corporations.[3]

The impacts of this wave of Globalization are no less destructive than the colonialism that preceded it. Our agricultural products consistently suffer from low prices; our workers from low wages. We are losing much of our capital due to profit repatriation and the debt crisis; chemical farming is taking away our food security and putting it in the hands of global chemical and seed conglomerates. We enjoy national sovereignty in name only. We are suffering from widespread ecological disasters, triggered by intensive resource extraction, disruptive energy projects, and toxic pollution. Our forests, mines and quarries are being quickly depleted; our air, water and soil heavily contaminated; and pervasive monoculture is seriously threatening our biodiversity.

This part of our history and current events should also be familiar to most of us.

We are still in the midst of the second wave of Globalisation, yet a third one has already emerged. The third wave of Globalization began to be felt worldwide in the last half of the 1990s and is expressing its overwhelming presence in full force at the dawn of the 21st century. This looming third wave is the global information economy.

Like the first two waves, the third Globalization wave arose from internal developments within the hearts of the global powers. It is important to look at these internal developments, because they will, as in the past, eventually impinge or the rest of the world-including our own- often shaping our destinies and steering our development in directions we never wanted to take.

The colonial powers were mercantilist and, later, industrial countries in their early expansionist stages. The postcolonial powers were industrial countries in their late stage, when capitalism had developed further, combining industrial and financial capital into huge monopolistic conglomerates in continual search for new acquisitions, sources of cheap raw materials and labour, and markets. The third wave of Globalization is marked by the emergence and eventual dominance, within the most advanced industrial countries, of the information sector the sector that produces, manipulates, processes, distributes and markets information products.

The increasing dominance of the information sector in what had been industrial economies is turning them into information economies. These emerging information economics—principally the U.S. and to lesser extent some countries of Europe – are at the core of the third wave of Globalisation. Because of the way these economies are so closely interconnected, they are better seen as a single emerging global information economy. The internet is perhaps the most visible portion of this economy—and certainly the one which has received the most media attention. This emerging global information economy includes the global infrastructure for telecommunications, data exchange, media and entertainment; the knowledge industries; the publishing industries; the computer hardware and software industries; the emerging financial systems that will support online transaction; the emerging global legal infrastructure based on the WTO, including the GATT and the agreements in information technology, telecommunications and financial services; and the biotechnology and genetic engineering industries.

Unlike the first two waves, the implications and consequences of the global information economy are an unfamiliar phenomenon to most of us there are so many new things, so many new possibilities, that it is quite difficult to separate the chaff from the grain, the hype from the substance.

The cost of reproducing information what the economist calls its marginal cost—is very low and oftentimes approaches zero. In the last analysis, this feature is due to the very essence of information itself. Information is non-material in its essence—a numeric measure of the uncertainty which it resolves. The non-materiality of information is the basis of its low reproduction cost, which may be driven lower and lower by adopting representations that can be manipulated at lower cost. With today's digital representations, the costs of reproducing and distributing information have reached historic lows—as low as the cost of copying a diskette or downloading a file from, an online server.

The low marginal cost of information has two major implications: one for those who use it and another for those who sell it. For users, it encourages sharing. Many cultures, in fact, see knowledge as social wealth a collective asset that is meant to be shared.

These cultures—including most Third World and indigenous cultures—are therefore in close harmony with the very nature of information. When we share software, for example, we are only being true to the nature of information and to our own cultures.

But there are other cultures, where private property concepts have become more absolute and where almost everything may be commodified. In these cultures-often with capitalism at their core information has become an object of commodification and privatization. Culture itself has become commodified, together with knowledge and life. They have become vehicles for profit-making.

Let us look more closely at the mechanism of profit-making through information. First, the seller turns information from a collective asset into private property. Then, copies are sold on the market, at prices set by the "owner"/seller. The near zero marginal cost of reproducing information now makes its selling price nearly pure profit. A diskette of software that may be copied for cents is sold for-fifty dollars. A CDROM that may be reproduced for three dollars is sold for three hundred.

To realize these extremely high profit margins made possible by the low marginal cost of information products, however, the seller must create an artificial scarcity of the product. We have seen that information can now be easily copied by users themselves at practically no cost, creating a natural abundance which drives prices down. To keep prices and profit margins high, this natural abundance that proceeds from the essence of information itself must be prevented. The seller does it by essentially prohibiting sharing among users and acquiring from the State a monopoly in using and making copies of the information product. This creates the artificial scarcity that drives prices up and realizes for the seller the potential profits from high margins.

It is monopoly that creates the scarcity. Such monopolies are euphemistically known as —intellectual property rights (IPR), the main form of ownership in an information economy. They are the mechanism for maintaining the high profit margins of those who control and sell information products. IPRs have two major forms: copyrights (historically, limited monopolies covering literary materials), and patents (historically, limited monopolies covering inventions). In recent years, as the information sector gained and increased their political and economic power, IPRs have been strengthened and extended to new areas.

IPRs are, in reality, statutory monopolies. They are monopolies over information granted through statutes, by the State. Those who control information through IPR are basically renters: they make money by charging monopoly rents from users, who are threatened by State action should they continue to practice information sharing.

Still, enforcing information monopolies is not simple. After all, information monopolies are incompatible with the social nature of information. The deeply ingrained cultural habits of information sharing and exchange continue to assert themselves, regardless of the will of monopolists and their State protectors.

This is the dilemma within the emerging global information economy. On the one hand, information itself is a highly social good; on the other hand, the forms of ownership are highly monopolistic. On the one hand, users tend to share information goods; on the other hand, IPR holders insist on their monopolies. On the one hand, developing countries need the widest access to various technology options at the least cost; on the other hand, rich and powerful information economies control almost 90 per cent of all the IPRs in the world today, and want to increase their control further.

The basic conflict within the information sector is the incompatibility between the highly monopolistic forms of information ownership and the social nature of information. This conflict is also expressed between users who want to share information freely and monopoly claimants who want to prevent free sharing of information. It is further reflected in the conflict between developing countries who need low-cost access to major bodies of information and information economies which have established virtual monopolies over information. Historically, these information economies are basically the same colonial powers that have exploited developing countries over the centuries.

The socializing tendency emanates from the nature of information itself, and can therefore never be suppressed. The monopolizing tendency emanates from the potentially high profit margins in selling information and the economic and political power concentrated in information monopolies. The conflicts arising from these two opposing tendencies will drive the historical development of the third wave of Globalisation.

Within the U.S., the high profit margins in the information sector is attracting more investment capital towards this sector, away from the agricultural and industrial sectors. This is the internal engine that is slowly transforming the U.S. economy into an information economy.

Within the emerging global information economy itself, monopoly concepts are already well-established and are even expanding their coverage. One item, for instance, is always non-negotiable in the U.S. diplomatic agenda: intellectual property rights (IPR). These concepts are increasingly dominating international legal system through bilateral negotiations with the U.S. and through the World Trade Organization (WTO). Thus, worldwide, pressure is increasing on countries with non-monopolistic attitudes towards information to adopt the same U.S. legal system that strictly protects IPRs.

However, the social nature of information continually asserts itself. Information abundance created through user sharing and exchange keeps breaking through the artificial scarcity created by information monopolies. The latest releases of population software, songs or video immediately find themselves being copied in every corner of the globe. In effect, information automatically globalizes itself regardless of the will of those who insist in monopolizing them. Ironically, information monopolists find their products better distributed in those parts of the globe where they could not enforce – their monopoly. Therefore, they insist on imposing monopolistic legal systems upon the rest of the globe, so they can realize the same profit margins they enjoy in their monopoly areas. Even one country that refuses to be part of this global legal system will pose a threat to their global monopoly, thus they will exert every effort to bring it in. These monopolists will never leave any country- or any community alone. They are the real engines of Globalisation's Third Wave.

This is also what makes the information sector qualitatively different from the industrial and agricultural sectors. It justifies why the emergence of the global information economy must be considered a distinct wave in itself, instead of simply a part of the second wave of Globalisation.

Information monopolies may be established not only by staking monopoly claims over information content through IPR, but also by controlling the hardware infrastructure for manipulating or distributing information. This infrastructure includes computer centers, voice and data switching centers, communication lines, television and radio stations, satellite networks, cable network, cellular networks, printing prosses, movie houses, etc. Like their software counterparts, the owners of the hardware infrastructure make money through monopoly rents, in the form of subscription fees or per-use charges.

Because they earn their incomes from monopoly rents, the propertied classes of the information sectors are rentier classes. They are the landlords, of cyberspace, or cyberlords. The content monopolies are owned by information cyberfords, and the infrastructure monopolies are kowned by industrial cyberlords.

The richest man in the world, as was several others among the ten richest is a cyberlord. The economic powers of cyberlords are immense, and these powers are increasingly being felt in the political and diplomatic arena. Among U.S. negotiators, for instance, IPR—the mechanism which gives software cyberlords their power—is invariably a non-negotiable item in their agenda. It is the partnership between information cyberlords, industrial cyberlords, and Finance capitalists which is at the core, the third, wave of Globalisation.

Thus an information economy is one whose information sector has become the main source of wealth, eclipsing its industrial and agricultural sectors. The products of industrial and agricultural economies are material goods; the products of an information economy, however, are non-material goods. The reproduction cost of information goods is very low. This has led to the widespread social practice of freely sharing and exchanging information. On the other hand, it also promises extremely high profit margins, if the seller can monopolize information. Information monopolies have become the main form of ownership in the information sector. The high profit margins that they realize have led to a continuous movement of investment capital towards the information sector, eventually making it the dominant sector of the economy and transforming the economy into an information economy. The products if this information economy spread worldwide, as people freely share and exchange information goods.

Thus as information economy needs a global system for enforcing its monopolies as well as for gathering information materials, tapping intellectuals and of course collecting payments worldwide. This leads to the Globalization of the information economy and is the engine of the third wave of Globalisation. The main propertied classes within the information cyberlords, who control information content, industrial cyberlords, who control information infrastructures, and finance capitalists, who control investment funds.[4]

The present situation of economic imbalance is generally due to evolution of institutions, which are one-sided because these institutions had been the brain child of developed countries. The developed countries, because of their edge over the developing nations, played an important role in international scene. The countries hailing from the South were kept at a low profile as they were considered late comers on the international fora. And this leads to Economic Darwinism.

Economic Darwinism is both a new form of international order and a threat to the poor nations. What we call Darwinism is nearer to Galbraith's 'Second Imperialism', which deals with the core nations behaviour *vis-a-vis* others. The will to national independence according to him, is the most powerful force in modern times. Therefore, its antithesis is not mere imperialism but, to use Kautsky's phrase, 'Ultra Imperialism' if the national leadership is strong, effective and well regarded, it will not tolerate foreign domination.[5] If the leadership is weak, ineffective, unpopular, corrupt and oppressive, it may accept foreign guidance, support and a measure of domination, to be ultimately marginalised. But then it may not be tolerated by its own people. This is the eroding effect of new imperialism.

It is universally recognized that the present international system is in some kind of crisis. Capitalism is in crisis, communism is in crisis, the Third World is in crisis and so on.[6] But talking about crisis has become an international industry. Those who control the international system or its sub-system and who enjoy its fruits, living in great luxury are most vocal about it. One of the techniques they have developed is to talk continuously about the urgency to help the poor. International organisation such as the UN, NAM and the commonwealth produce mountains of documents. This exercise creates the illusion that somebody is concerned about the world and its people. In reality this is a fraudulent exercise.

Since this exercise is conducted through top world leaders of the great powers, it becomes difficult to expose its real meaning in order to understand what is really happening behind the scene, and why the present highly exploitative and iniquitous international order as well as national orders are continuing.

No matter how one looks at its opponents or critics, the system is nothing but a well designed international dictatorship: political, economic and military. International economic monopolies buttress this dictatorship. Paradoxically this dictatorship is internally democratic and externally authoritarian. It has come to loom large in the perceptions of policy-makers, and adjustment to it in the form of economic liberalization and the shrinking of the state has moved to the forefront of their economic agenda, even when not imposed on them. The phenomenon of economic globalisation provides the widest possible context for the examination of economic policy reform. However, as a concept in contemporary social science, it appears in many variants. In one strong version, globalisation refers to the presumed emergence of a 'supra-national', borderless global economy with its own laws of motion, encompassing and subordinating the various local economics in a single worldwide division of labour, rendering national governments into municipalities. A softer version of the concept treats globalisation less as an end-stage and more as a process in which the 'international' economy becomes more closely integrated, with domestic economic agents increasingly oriented to the global market rather than to particular national markets, even as the state continues to remain central to national economic advancement.[7] Regardless, economic globalisation represents only one part of the equation. Equally necessary to the understanding of economic policy reform is the opposing social force in the form of economic nationalism. While diverse meanings go with the term, economic nationalism's core is constituted by the para-mountcy of national economic interest against the claims of other nations.[8]

Economic globalisation and economic nationalism are, then, the two fundamental forces that have been shaping the world's economic terrain over the last several decades.[9] The two forces are obviously related to each other, with globalisation opposing and provoking economic nationalism as well as transforming and transcending it, even as its own apparently inexorable path of expansion and possible eventual triumph has been continually interrupted and redirected by nationalism. Both contending forces are integrally linked with markets and states, for both have been fundamentally rooted in the rise of markets and states in the modern era. Indeed, economic globalisation is simply a fuller expression of the expansion of one or more markets to world scale, while economic nationalism is nothing but the manifestation in the economic arena of the consolidation of states in the international system. They thus simply represent another level of the working of markets and states. At the same time, each by itself as well as in interaction with the other generates pressures for economic policy reform, which, in turn, has principally to do with the roles of states and markets in economic affairs. One of the vital questions for the developing world at the dawn of a new century, therefore, becomes precisely the relationship of globalisation and nationalism to economic policy reform.

'Good economics is bad politics' as the saying goes, is an erroneously conceived garbling. Some spontaneous adverse responses may emerge as misplaced reactions to a good policy regime that may be aimed at long-range structural corrections of the growth path as well as the developmental course of the economy. These policy alternates are like a minor, and sometimes major, surgery that may be painful for a while. Yet if these pains persist too long and turn out to be too severe, the well intended surgical operation may ricochet to spell disaster. An effective and rational economic policy regime entails sensitive balancing process and amounts to walking on a tight rope of trade-offs between economic logic and political sensitivities of affected sections of society. Characteristically, in the context of political economics, if good economics is not viewed as good politics, it is no economics at all. It is the violation of logical politic-economic parameters that generate antipathy to the ruling authority.[10]

In such a scenario we can learn a lesson or two from Mahatma Gandhi. In a speech delivered before the Missionary Conference Madras on 14 February, 1916, Gandhi defined *swadeshi* (self-reliance) in the following terms, "After much thinking I have arrived at a definition of *swadeshi* that, perhaps, best illustrate my meaning. Swadeshi is the spirit in us, which restrict us to use of the service of our immediate surroundings to the exclusion of more remote. I should use things that are produced by my immediate neighbours and serve these industries by making them efficient and complete where they might be found wanting".[11]

While it is true, we have duties to all humankind, but the duties we own to all segments of it are nor of equal importance. There is a hierarchy of duties based on the degree of proximity: Proximity is the decisive elements in forming ties in terms of both closeness of feelings and knowledge of circumstances. Accordingly we must start with service to neighbours. An individual service to his country and humanity consists in serving his neighbours. One could not starve one's neighbours and claim to serve one distant cousin in Antarctica, for one must not serve one's distant neighbour at the expense of the nearest. This is not only the teaching of all the religions in the world but also the foundation of true and human economics.[12]

Asked it a man can serve the immediate neighbours and yet serve the whole of humanity. Gandhi replied that he can, provided the service of neighbours was not itself exploitative of others. The neighbours would in turn serve his neighbours and in this way the chain of service would be expanded to include the world, rather than shut it out. Gandhi was neither metaphysical not too philosophical for comprehension but just, good common sense, for it you love your neighbour as thyself, he will do likewise with you, and both would gain thereby.

There is no denying of the fact that Gandhi's doctrine of buying local products have some protectionist implications. In response to an interviewer's comment that no country was free from foreign competition, Gandhi observed that on contrary each sovereign nation tried to protect its infant industries by bounties and tariffs. However, the exercise of ethical preference by consumer was, he claimed a better solution, because it was voluntary and hence was in correspondence with the principle of non-violence and was more likely to benefit the poor. Consumption behaviour that corresponds to the principle of ethical preference, far from destroying the economic benefits flowing from foreign trade would be conductive to the healthy growth of nations and so promote both material and moral progress.[13]

If India is to emerge as a nation whose global relevance is commensurate with its image, it must establish its credentials by further multilateral economic and political relationship all around, and not remain hostage to the western global interests. Infect the linkage of India's economy with the global economy is such that India has no option but to grapple with the dynamics of globalisation. Whether to globalise India or not is not the question now because globalisation of the world financial system is a historical process. India is already hooked on to both the world financial economy and the ballooning flow of world information. It can not hope to remain half pregnant, and it can't abort it also but have to go all the way.

Economic revival is an exciting proposition. It has to be invigorating, self-generating and mass based. Herein lies the test for the nation nerves. Indeed India's future depends upon the rational choices made today and those to be made from now onward. History is full of examples of countries, which got crushed under their own follies just by ignoring the basic human values and cultural roots. Every economic gains or losses its credibility by its conduct and approach to human beings especially the have notes. The liberalisation and globalisation have to address themselves to the liberation of millions from the clutches of poverty and deprivation globally. Swami Ramakrishna Paramhansa once remarked. "While seeing goods in all persons and all things do look for the holes in the pot you purchase",[14] while embracing the new creed of globalisation we should not overlook the holes in the foreign pot and discard the time tested swadeshi pitcher.

NOTES

1. Verzola, Roberto, "Globlisation : Its Third Waves", *Nai Azadi Udghosh*, A Journal of Azadi Bachao Andolan, Allahabad, Vol. 10, No. 5-6, September-December, 2003, p. 4.
2. *Ibid.*, p. 5.
3. Chakravarthi, Raghvan, "South May be Trapped into New WTO Round", *Nai Azadi Udghosh, op. cit.*, Vol. 6, No. 3-4, May-April, 2001, p. 11.
4. Verzola, Roberto, *op. cit.*, p. 9.
5. Sethi, J.D., *International Economic Disorder*, Shimla, Indian Institute Advanced Study, 1996, p. 5.
6. Sharma, Jai Narain, *Alternative Economics: Economic of Mahatma Gandhi and Globalisation*, New Deep, Deep & Deep, 2003, p. XIII.
7. Hirst, Paul & Grahame Thompson, *Globalization in Question : The International Economy and the Possibility of Governance, Cambridge*, Polity Press, 1996, pp. 7-16.
8. Burnell, Peter J., *Economic Nationalism in the Third World*, Brighton, Wheatsheaf Books, 1986, Ch. 1.

9. Nayar, Baldev Raj, *Globlisation and Nationalism*, London, Sage Publication, 2001, p. 14.
10. Jai Narain Sharma, "The New Economic Policy: Myth and Reality" in Radhakrishnan, N &N. Vasudevan (eds.) *A Nation in Transition, India at 50*, New Delhi, Gandhi Media Centre, 1998, p. 211.
11. The Collected Works of Mahatma Gandhi, New Delhi Publications Division. The Ministry of Information and Broadcasting, Government of India, 1980, Vol. 13, p. 219.
12. Jai Narain Sharma, "Globlising Swadeshi", in Mishra, A.D. (ed.) *Challenges of 21st Century*, New Delhi, Mittal, 2003, p. 75.
13. Sharma, Rashmi, *Gandhian Economics: A Humane Approach*, New Delhi, Deep & Deep, 1997, p. 153.
14. Jai Narain Sharma, "Globlising Swadeshi", in Mishra, A.D. (ed) *Challenges of 21st Century, op. cit.*, pp. 77-78.

4

GANDHIAN ECONOMICS IN THE GLOBALIZED ERA

RAJ KUMAR AND KULBHUSHAN CHANDEL

Globalization is neither a new phenomenon nor a newly devised process, rather it has a long history as a political and cultural reality and as a religious and cultural movement. It is a process of social change in which geographical and cultural barriers are reduced. The first stage of globalization started when early Egyptian, Babylonian, Greek and Roman empires, united the world of their time. The second stage can be fraced to the later part of 15th century when European explorers voyaged out of Europe to "discover" new lands. Consequently the trade activities expanded between Europe and the new world. Gradually, the process of colonization started. The third stage of globalisation started in the nineteenth century along with the expansion of colonial empire and trade. The process of globalization intensified with the advent of industrial revolution in Europe as different countries in Europe demanded raw materials and sought the market for their products.[1] The industrial revolution has transformed the domestic economy into industrial economy and consequently new social class named as capitalist has emerged. The globalization of present is the manifestation of industrial revolution of 19th century.

The globalization has its origin in the rise of capitalism in Europe and America. Though the agenda of globalization was at the top of the economic programme of industrial countries, yet it could not be implemented due to certain complications. The period of First and Second World War has marked the deterioration in the global economic relations. An attempt has been made to go back to normal economic relations but this attempt failed due to world wide depression in 1929-30. After the Second World War, the war victorious countries especially Britain and America started to plan for New International Economic Order (NIEO). To establish the new world order a conference was held at Bretonwood. This conference recommended to establish three international organizations i.e. World Bank, International Monetary Fund and International Trade Organization.

The first two organizations were setup in 1945 but there was serious reservations about the third. Consequently, the interim organization for trade named as General Agreement on Tariffs and Trade (GATT), was setup in 1947. The developed countries made constant efforts through GATT to globalize the international trade but due to existence of cold war it became difficult for developed countries to fulfil their dreams. The disintegration of Soviet Union and its satellites into so many republics, collapse of East-European Block, end of cold war, rise of South Asian economies and development in the area of information technology made the way of globalization possible and easy. Hence, the Uruguay round of multilateral trade negotiations which was launched at Punta del Este in September 1986 was concluded successfully in Geneva on December 15, 1993 which made possible the way to establish the long awaited World Trade Organisation on 1st January 1995. With this it starts the new era of globalization in the history of international relations.[2]

Keeping in view the significance of Gandhian values and economics in the current globalized era, this study has been divided into three parts:

1. The 1st part deals with the conceptual framework of the term globalization.
2. The 2nd part of the study highlights the multiple dimensions of globalization with special reference to its impact on Indian economy.
3. In the 3rd section an attempt has been made to study the significance and relevance of Gandhian economics in a globalized world.

Globalization : A Conceptual Framework

"Globalization means free movement of capital, goods, technology, ideas and people. Any globalization that omits the last one is impartial and not sustainable"

– Branko Milanoric (Economist at the Carnegie Endowment for International Peace)

The term globalization has been defined differently in different contexts. In the broader sense it includes two things—integration of the world and interdependence of the sovereign nation-states. The term is all–encompassing and is defined and understood in both economic and non-economic contexts that broadly include socio-cultural, historical and political contexts.

Economic Contexts

Economic globalization constitutes the process of integration of national economies into international economy through trade, direct investments by corporations and multinationals, short-term capital flows, international flow of workers and technology. Globalization is the process of integrating various economies of the world without creating any hindrances in the free flow of goods and services, technology, capital and human capital. Hence, the term globalization has four parameters but the developed states would limit the same to three i.e. unrestricted trade flows, capital flows and technology flows. They insist on developing states to accept their definition of globalization. However, several economists in the developing world believe that this definition is incomplete and if the world has to become a global village then the fourth component, unrestricted movement of labour cannot be leftout.[3]

Non-Economic Context

In the non-economic context the term globalization refers to social, cultural and political changes taking place at global level. Hence, globalization encompasses the process of the intensification of economic, political, social and cultural relations across international boundaries. It is principally aimed at the universal homogenization of ideas, cultures, values, and even lifestyles as well as at the de-territorialization and villagization of the world. Globalization in sum means connecting people, connecting places, connecting cultures and connecting values.[4]

Therefore, globalization is not only a process of economic integration but it is a process of social, cultural, political and technological integration. Its aim is to enhance connectivity, closeness, togetherness, and interdependency. It is a phenomenon of unification. Its essence is integrated world with single order. Though globalization is not a new phenomenon, yet the present era has three distinctive features i.e. shrinking space, shrinking time and disappearing national boundaries. This helps not only in free flow of trade, capital, technology and labour but also free flow of ideas, norms, cultures and values. People around the globe are linked more deeply, more intensely and more immediately than ever.

Globalization has two important aspects integration and interdependence. The process of economic integration and interdependence has accelerated since 1990s due to break down of ideological barriers and development in the field of information technology. Consequently, today global integration is taking place at a very fast speed due to increased flow of trade, capital, money, technology, people information and idea across national boundaries. Similarly, interdependence has increased primarily due to increase in volume of trade. The process of globalization has been discussed in terms of "universalisation of particularism and particularization of universalism", that is, what is local is global and what is global is local. This two fold process has many aspects i.e. it is political, social and cultural process, but it is foremost an economic process. Hence, the globalization is the process of "critical transformation" that is bringing about end of geography, distance and boundaries, which is transforming the entire globe into "global village" and people into "global citizen".

The role of multi-national corporations (MNCs) cannot be underestimated in the pursuit of globalization. Since 1970 the global economic power broadly concentrated in three centres of the world - the USA, European Union and Japan. This triad had 37,000 multi-national corporations that controlled over 200,000 affiliates throughout the world. These multi-national corporations needed market for their products and globalization of economies was their prime requirement. The US, Japan and European union had a remote control over the economic, political and technological changes taking place all over the world. The major policies of IMF, WB and WTO are to a great extent guided by these states. The triad superpowers are exerting their influence on the triadic international economic institutions such as IMF, WB and WTO for accelerating the pace of globalization, liberalization and privatization. Consequently, the benefits of the liberalization of economies are siphoned away by these powerful conglomerates. The concept of globalization can also be examined in terms of triad of techniques, institutions and states. This triad relation is explained with the help of a diagram as follows:[5]

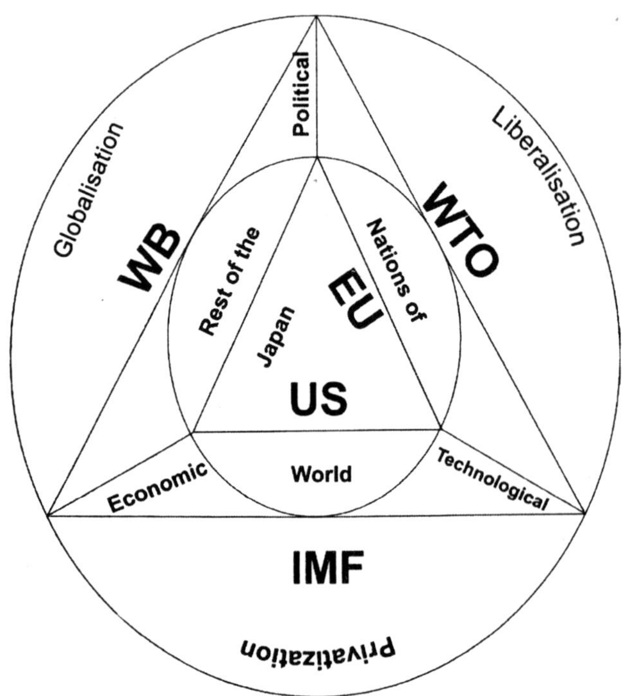

The Triad of Techniques, Institutions and Countries

Implications of Globalization

"Our primary concerns are that globalization should benefit all countries and should raise the welfare of all people throughout the world. This implies that it should raise the rate of economic growth in poor countries and reduce world poverty, and that it should not increase inequalities or undermine socio-economic security within countries"

– World Commission on the Social Dimension of Globalization (2004).

Globalization is an economic process of social change attempting to merge the national economies with mega international economies. The opening up of economy unleashed a new economic regime where market and private players recognized as significant constituents of globalization. This mega process of integration has a larger economic, political, socio-cultural and environmental implications. The academia is divided on the implication of globalization. Those who are in favour talk about its inevitability and economic opportunities, whereas critics talk about its skewness and distribution. According to critics globalization is nothing but a new form of western domination and imperialism or in words we can say that globalization is old wine in a new bottle.[6]

In the present era the concept of globalization has become panacea to solve all human problems. It is believed that the success of globalization will make the people happy, prosperous and contented and there would be no conflict, no poverty, no inequality, no unemployment, no tension, no violation of human rights, no malnutrition, no illiteracy and no disease etc. In the globalized era each individual and community will be so integrated with the world economy that the benefit would flow so gently that no individual would remain untouched by the prosperity of globalization. The integration of global economy would open many opportunities for millions of people around the world. The increased trade, new technologies, foreign investments, expanding media and internet connections are fuelling economic growth and human development. All these instruments offer enormous potential to eradicate poverty in the twenty-first century. So we have more wealth and technology and more commitment to a global community than ever before.[7]

Regarding globalization the reality is totally different. There has been increasing illusion among the policy makers in several parts of the world. The role of multinational corporations has been one of the dominating factors in the pursuit of globalization. These multinational corporations manage the global trade. Hence, it is corporate managed trade rather than free trade. The trade liberalization has failed and the poor are being marginalized because the way the trading system is working is not favourable to all. The globalization leaves the poorer countries behind the global competition, as the clear objective of capital mobility is attaining profit, prestige, and power. In the process of amassing wealth capitalists have exploited the people and natural resources and often left behind pollution, poverty, inequality, injustice, crime, corruption and general degradation of environment.[8]

The globalization has seriously challenged the identity and economic sovereignty as well as the working of nation-states. The de-territorialisation of nation-states has questioned their very existence. The economic decisions and the policies of states are not taken by their national governments rather by the powerful international financial and economic institutions such as International Monetary Fund, World Bank and World Trade Organization. This has created a serious threat to economic sovereignty of states as the role of states is being squeezed.

Globalization with the ultimate objective of profit maximization has also done great harm to the environmental balance. The environmental problems are more common and serious than the economic problems. The advocates of globalization maintain that trade helps the natural environment, as rich countries can better afford to protect their unspoiled area. Whereas, the environmentalists claim that the pursuit of national wealth drives global environment degradation and the globalization accelerates this process. The economic and environmental colonialism should give way to ecological modernization. For this a green philosophy of development, green policies, green technology, green products, green markets, green benches in courts and after all green education can contribute a lot in protecting the environment while promoting economic development. The economic and political globalization should be accompanied by globalization of the concerns for environment.[9]

The employment situation in India has worsened in the post globalization era. The rate of growth of employment was 2.04 per cent during the year 1983-84 which declined to a low level of 0.98 per cent during the period 1994-2000. The organized sector which was considered as the engine of growth failed to generate enough employment. During 1994-2000 employment growth in organized sector was merely 0.53 per cent. The growth of employment in public sector was negative (-0.03 per cent) and that of private sector was 1.87 per cent. Hence, the enlargement of private sector employment failed effectively to offset the deceleration in public sector. Globalization has increased the process of proletarianization of labour. The problem of unemployment, casualisation, lower wages, part time jobs and less or no security in jobs have further increased to a greater degree. It has also reduced the bargaining power of trade unions.[10]

There is no doubt that poverty has declined from 36.02 per cent in 1993-94 to 28.27 per cent in 2004-05, though at relatively decreasing rate in the post liberalized era. Further, the decline in poverty in scheduled castes and scheduled tribes has been considerably slow than in other categories. In the period 1999-2000, the proportion of population below poverty line among scheduled castes and scheduled tribes was 36 per cent and 44 per cent as against 16 per cent in case of other categories. It may be noted that the growth of gross domestic product has been 9 to 10 per cent during current year where the rate of poverty reduction is low. This exhibited the unequal distribution of income and wealth between the rich and poor.[11]

Stiglitz exposes the hypocrisy of western world. In the name of globalization the western countries have forced the poor countries to eliminate their trade barriers but kept up their own barriers and prevent developing countries from exporting their agricultural products. To protect their domestic industry, they impose various types of protectionist measures such as social clause, child labour clause, anti- dumping duties, environmental issues and other measures. The number of suicides committed by farmers in India was direct result of double standards adopted by the developed countries to sell their agricultural product like cotton in world market at relatively low prices, thereby eliminating Indian cotton growers from competition. The W.T.O. agreement on agriculture stipulates that developed countries would reduce their subsidies by 20 per cent in six years and developing countries by 13 per cent in ten years. But as per the fact developed countries tried to circumvent their agreement by providing green box and blue box subsidies support to agriculture.[12]

The cheap imports from developed countries lead to the closure of a large number of vulnerable small scale enterprises. The WTO agreement do not discriminates on the basis of industries or enterprises. Thus small scale industries have to compete not only with large units within country but also with the multinational corporations and their cheap products. Consequently, the small scale industries are losing their market and are becoming sick or have to close down. The small scale sector in India contributes 40 per cent of manufacturing output, 50 per cent of employment and 33 per cent of exports. Hence, in the name of globalization and consumer interests, multinational corporations continue to swallow the small scale industries and will eventually eliminate them from the market.[13]

Gandhian Economic Model—An Alternate to Globalization

The Gandhian economic thought is relevant at all times and for all the countries of the world. Though Gandhi was not economist like Adam Smith, Ricardo and Keynes, yet his economic thought is more significant in many dimensions. Morality, spiritualism and non-violence was the soul of Gandhian economic thought. The fundamental of his thought was minimum needs, respect and love for humanity, truth, non-violence, simple living, trusteeship and decentralization of both political and economic powers. The basic objective of Gandhian economic model was spiritual as well as the welfare of masses. He rejects the every economic law that is based upon the narrow idea of profit earning instead of welfare of society. *Sarvodaya, Swadeshi* and development of small scale industries, cottage and khadi Udyog were essential aspects of his economic thought.

Gandhi was misunderstood by many as he was primarily against industrialization and mechanization. As per his opinion, if industrialization is able to solve the problems of poverty, starvation, unemployment, exploitation and economic inequality then it is a welcome step. But on the contrary, Gandhi believed that instead of solving these economic problems, capitalism not only aggravates the intensity of these problems but also violates the fundamental principle of non-violence and exploitation. The primary aim of Gandhian economics was to attain maximum self-sufficiency at the village or community level. He laid emphasis on the idea of 'village swaraj' in which village is a complete and independent republic.

The study of globalization and its impacts makes it clear that instead of solving the problems like poverty, starvation, economic inequality, unemployment and exploitation, it has further enhanced the gravity of these problems. Globalization primarily seems to be an imperialist camouflage of developed world and imperialism has no place in the scheme of Gandhian economics.

Gandhi was not against globalization or internationalism rather he said that the structure of any kind of world federation should be based on the principle of non-violence, cooperation, and truth. Exploitation and violence should be abdicated in world affairs. The imperialist principles are inconsistent with the principle of cooperation, non-violence, truth, and partnership. The present form of globalization is imperialist designed globalization based on exploitation of masses and natural resources of third world states. This form of globalization is inconsistent with nature and man both as it violates the basic fundamental of non-violence. Those who are advocating the thesis of globalization are the champions of exploitation and oppression, and the root cause of global terrorism.

In this chapter an attempt has been made to study the main aspect of Gandhian economic thought, which are discussed as follows :

Economics and Ethics

Gandhian makes no distinction between economics and ethics. Economics that hurt the moral well being of an individual or a nation is immoral and hence, sinful. The economics which disregards the moral values is untrue. The extension of law of non-violence in the domain of economics means the introduction of moral values as a factor to be considered in regulating international commerce. An economics that inculcates mammon worship and enable the strong to amass wealth at the expense of weak, is false and dismal science. It spells death. The true economics, on the other hand stands for social justice and it promotes the good of all equally including the weakest section of society, hence it is indispensable for decent life.[14] If we analyse the present era of globalization in the light of these ethical standards then we will find that this form of globalization is highly immoral as it takes into consideration only market, profits, prestige and power. Gandhi rejects the economic thought of Adam Smith as it lacks "human element".

Full Employment—Supremacy of Man

Gandhi advocates the concept of full employment because man is of a supreme consideration in his economic order. He endorsed the idea of Khadi, cottage and small-scale industries at village level to attain the situation of full employment. He was against all those economic plans that not only exploit the raw materials of a country but also neglect the manpower. According to him the economic constitution of India and that of world should provide food, clothing and work to every one. He also recommended that the means of production of elementary necessities of life should remain in the control of masses and any effort to monopolize these means of production by any country, nation, or a group of person would be unjust. America is an industrialized country in the world and yet it has not banished poverty and inequality. This is because it neglects the manpower and helps to concentrate power in the hands of the few who amass wealth at the expense of the many.[15] Though the advocates of globalisation make high promises to create ample employment opportunities, yet in reality the position is entirely reverse. Instead of providing employment to the masses, the process of globalization has reduced the employment opportunities.

Dignity of Labour

Gandhian economic philosophy accords the all respect to the dignity of labour as he says, "who eat without work are thieves". Bodily sustenance should come from bodily labour and intellectual labour is necessary for the culture of mind. He was in the favour of division of labour, but the division of labour should not be in such a manner as the intellectual labour is confined to one class and bodily labour to another class. If everyone lives by the sweat of brow, then this earth would become paradise. Though the intellectual labour is superior to bodily labour but it can never be substitute for bodily labour. Gandhi was strictly against the tendencies of begging and advocates the rule "no labour, no meal". He analysed that people living in village are semi-starved as they lack willing obedience to labour, where as the compulsory obedience of labour breeds poverty disease and discontentment.[16]

Simple Living High Thinking

Simple living occupies the special place in Gandhian

economic thought. We should stop our unlimited wants, if we want to live the happy and contented life. Gandhi believe in the philosophy that the less we possess, the less we want, and the better we are. In the world there is no slavery equal to that of desires. Those who are discontented, however, much he possesses become the slave of his desires. To lead a contented and self-sufficient life lies in our own hands. In the present global scenario we are becoming the prey of consumerism which is dangerous not only for village economy but also for the nation. Gandhi was of the opinion that high thinking is inconsistent with the complicated material life. Western states are today groaning under the heel of the monster god of globalization. The shadow of materialism under the umbrella of globalization has also polluted the thinking process of our country man. Gandhi felt that it is not necessary to return to old absolute simplicity. But it will have to be a reorganization in which village life will dominate, and in which brute and material forces will be subordinated to the spiritual forces. All the graces of life are possible only when we learn the art of living nobly.[17]

Swadeshi

The purpose of the *Swadeshi* doctrine in Gandhian economic ideas is to make village economy strong, self-supporting, and self-reliant and exchange only such necessary commodities with other villages as are not locally producible. *Swadeshi* as defined by Gandhi is a spiritual discipline and a swadeshist should learn to live without hundreds of things which today he considers necessary. The ruinous departure from swadeshi in the economic and industrial life is responsible for deep poverty of the masses. The doctrine of *Swadeshi* is consistent with law of humanity and love. To reject the foreign manufacturers merely because they are foreigner, would be criminal act and a negation of swadeshi spirit. A true votary of *Swadeshi* will never harbour ill will and hate towards the foreigner. It is not a cult of hatred and exploitation, rather it is a doctrine of selfless service that has its roots in the purest *Ahimsa* i.e. love.[18] The basic spirit of globalization is against the doctrine of swadeshi as the mass production by mega multinational corporation and free trade is going to destroy the fabric of swadeshi and making the village economy dependent on foreign goods. Gandhi was also in the favour of globalization whereas every village is self-sufficient and one country is not going to exploit the resources and market of other country.

Economic Equality

Gandhi believed that all must have equal opportunities to grow and develop in the life. He does not believe in dead uniformity as it is not nature's law that all men born are equal and free. All men are not born with equal intellect. Even in the most prefect world we shall fail to avoid inequalities, but we can only avoid strife and bitterness. Economic equality in Gandhi's conception does not mean that everyone would literally have the same amount of worldly goods. It simply means that everybody must have enough for his needs. Hence, the real meaning of economic equality is "to each according to his needs", which includes, balanced diet, decent house, better educational facilities and adequate medical facilities to everyone. Therefore, the cruel inequality that exist today will be removed by purely non-violent means only.[19] The process of globalization has created a glaring inequalities and it can only be countered with the Gandhian way.

Decentralization

Gandhi laid emphasis on decentralization. It will help us to achieve human happiness and mental and material growth. Centralisation as a system is inconsistent with a non-violent structure of society. Gandhi wants decentralization not only at economic level but at political level also. The real spirit of democracy can only be attained with the help of democratic decentralization i.e. through the Panchayati Raj System. He stressed that the villages should be independent republics and the role of government should be limited to those spheres of activities, which cannot be held by village panchayats. He affirms that without decentralization it is impossible to ensure individual liberty and spiritual growth. Gandhi does not accept only the decentralization of political power, rather he pleads for decentralization of both economic and political power. The success of political decentralization depends on economic decentralization. His views on economic decentralization stem from his concept of *swadeshi*, economic equality, self-contained village economy, and non-violence. The objective of economic decentralization cannot be achieved in an industrial civilization rather it can be achieved in self-sufficient village economy. The exploitation is the essence of violence and only the rural economy can eschews exploitation altogether. The effective political and economic decentralization will help to counter the evil effect of globalization on political and economic sovereignty of nations.[20]

Village Communities

Gandhi was convinced that if India is to attain true freedom and through India the world also, then sooner or later the fact must be recognized that people will have to live in villages not in towns and in huts not in palaces. In his economic thought the village *swaraj* means a complete village republic and independence of its neighbour for its vital wants. Village community is such a society in which the role of state becomes undesirable as every individual is self-disciplined in such a way that he is never a problem to his neighbours. The ideal village will contain intelligent human being living in clean conditions and environment, where there is full freedom, no disease, where voluntary co-operation is essential condition for dignified and peaceful existence. It is a society free from exploitation, inequality, class domination, class conflict, communal disturbance, strike and any kind of violence. The essentials of village republic are: self-regulation, self reliance, and self-republic.[21] Hence, if our villages republics are enough strong from economic and political point of view then no external force including the western dominated globalization can make us weak and slave.

Self-Sufficiency

Gandhi stressed that the unit of society should be a village or call it a manageable small group of people. This small group of people should be self-sufficient and this self sufficiency should be based on mutual cooperation and interdependence. Self-sufficiency here means that village must be self reliant in regard to food, cloth and other basic necessities of life. Self-sufficiency does not mean that we should not get from outside the village rather we should produce more what we can, in order to obtain in exchange what we are unable to produce. Hence, self-sufficiency is a kind of service to society. If all villages are self-sufficient then no one will be in trouble including the nation. National economy is the reflection of village economy. Strong village economy means the strong national economy.[22] The evil effects of globalization can only be countered by a nation if its village economy is strong and sufficient.

Khadi and Village Industry

In the Gandhian economic thought villages should be the nerve centre of independent India, and India should not be known by her cities like Bombay and Calcutta but by millions of people inhabiting in seven lakh villages. *Khadi* is the only tool that will make our village economy strong and self-sufficient. *Khadi* is the sun of the solar system and the planets are various cottage and small-scale industries, which can support *Khadi* in return. *Khadi* is not only the beginning of economic freedom and equality but also the symbol of unity of humanity, simplicity and domesticity. *Khadi* means wholesale *swadeshi* mentality which includes the decentralization of the necessities of the life. The revival of village industries with the help of Khadi will help to make every village of India industrious. Hence, in this way the *Khadi* will provide employment opportunities to the masses on one side and help to remove the poverty on other side.[23]

The Place of Machinery

Gandhi believes that mechanization is good when the hands are too few whereas it is an evil when there are more hands than required for the accomplishment of work. Gandhi was not absolutely against the installation of big industries but he wants that the big industries should be either nationalized or be under the state control. Simultaneously, he was in the favour of improvement in the small scale and cottage industry. According to him any act that displace the hand labour is criminal act, if it fails to provide the alternative employment opportunities to the masses. In his economic thought the supreme consideration is man. Hence, he was not against the industrialization but he was totally opposed to its craze and indiscriminate multiplication because industrial civilization is unable to solve the problems of poverty and unemployment. Therefore, Gandhi was in favour of natural economy in which villages are self-sufficient. Gandhi made clear mention in his economic thought that he has no share in spoliation of nation in the name of industrialization. He did not want to industrialize only some pockets of country rather he was in favour of such a system of industrialization in which every village is industrialized. In his view the strong nation is inhabited by the strong village economy.

The Evil of Industrialization

Gandhi was well aware about the evil effects of industrialization. He believes that the industrialization on a mass scale will necessarily lead to passive and active exploitation of villages, labour, consumer and resources as the problems of competition and marketing are inherent in industrial civilization. Gandhi was concerned with the insufferable plight of countrymen. Therefore, he wants that the pauperism must go but industrialization is not a remedy for it. He was against the exploitation of one nation by the other as he was totally convinced that industrialization depends entirely on the exploitation of market, labour and resources. The Gandhian economic model aims at developing the agriculture and industry side by side and to integrate both of them for societal good. He was in the favour of production by masses rather the mass production and he was also against the large-scale industries producing the consumer goods.[25] In the name of globalization the giant multinational corporations are entering in consumer goods, in agricultural sector and forcing the national governments to liberalize and privatize the public sector. In addition to it the multinational corporations are not investing in key and basic industries but are investing only in profitable and consumer projects. Hence, instead of reducing the evil effect of industrialization in globalized era, these evil effects have further increased which are against the spirit of Gandhian economic order.

Trusteeship

Gandhi was absolutely convinced that the dead uniformity is not possible in any society and present society is divided into two classes i.e. landlord and proletariat, capitalist and labour and ruler and ruled etc. Thus there is bitterness between these two classes which will give rise to violent class war. He was not in favour of accumulation of wealth in the hands of few people because the violence and exploitation is a root cause for the accumulation of wealth. He offered the unique non-violent tool of trusteeship which will help for the transformation of capitalist order of society into egalitarian one. He was aware that any kind of transformation of society that is based on non-violent means will fail to develop non-violent culture in the society. He was in favour of concept of trusteeship instead of class war as recommended by Karl Marx. The philosophy of trusteeship is based on the principle of *'Aparigrah'* (non-possession) and *'Sambhava'* (equability), referred to in the holy *Gita*. These principles will help in the change of heart and attitude of the ruling class. The philosophy of trusteeship does not mean forced transformation rather it means transformation by choice. But if the capitalists fail to follow the principle of trusteeship then the weapon of non-violence and non-cooperation should be used. In this direction the establishment of a strong Panchayati Raj System will help to form strong public opinion in the favour of trusteeship, when the people will understand its implications. As the trustee has no heir except the society.[26] Therefore, under the Gandhian economic order the character of production is determined by social necessity not by personal greed, whereas in the era of globalization there is a fierce competition among the few multinational corporations to capture the market of foreign hand. This will create the perpetual economic crisis, unemployment and discontentment among the human beings across the globe.

The study thus reveals that globalization is not a panacea for the world economic crisis, rather globalization is deepening this economic crisis. It is not only threat to the economic sovereignty of a country but also a challenge to the political and cultural sovereignty of people. The agenda of globalization is designed by the shrewd multinational corporations of United States, Europe and Japan, which is implemented by World Bank, International Monetary Fund and World Trade Organisation. The entire process of globalization is based on exploitation and violence which is against the basic principle of Gandhian economic order. The remedy lies in the deglobalisation of the dehumanized trade, investment, information technology and aid schemes. The globalization is pushing the world into dangerous direction which breeds the violence, exploitation, poverty, inequality, corruption, unemployment, injustice, crime and discontentment in the society. Hence, the Gandhian economic model is the only worthwhile alternative for man's peaceful, purposeful, successful and happy existence. In fact we want culture of peace and harmony, therefore, we must have the technology of peaceful co-existence. The rehumanisation of science, technology and industry is the ardent requirement of twenty first century. The globalization is widening the gap between individual and society, rich and poor, city and village, local and global whereas the only solution to bridge this gap lies in the Gandhian Economic order.

NOTES

1. Sinha, Manoj. "Globalization and Consumerism: A Study of its impact". In A.D. Mishra, *Globalization Myth and Reality*, (New Delhi: Concept Publishing Company), pp. 188.
2. Aswathappa K., *Business Environment for Strategic Management.* (Delhi: Himalayan Publishing House), pp. 39-40.
3. Dutt, Ruddar, Sundharam, K.P.M., *Indian Economy*, (Delhi: Sultan Chand and Co.), pp. 248-249.
4. Singh, Arun Kumar, "Globalisation, Sovereignty and Human Rights: A Perspective", in A.D. Mishra, *op.cit.* pp. 134-136.
5. Muralivalla Bhan, T.V. "Economic Prospects and Environmental Problems of Globalisation", in *Ibid.*, pp. 163-164.
6. Dynamics of Globalisation. *The Tribune*, pp. 4 (Spectrum). 20.4.2008.
7. Mishra, *op.cit.*, p. 4.
8. *Ibid.*, pp. 8, 10.
9. Muralivalla Bhan, *op.cit.*, pp. 155 - 165.
10. Dutt Ruddar, Sundharam, K.P.M., *op.cit.*, pp. 249-251.
11. *Ibid.*, pp. 256-257.
12. *Ibid.*, pp. 806.
13. *Ibid.*, pp. 805.
14. *The Selected Works of Mahatma Gandhi – The Voice of Truth*, Vol. VI, (Ahemdabad, Narayanan Publishing House), pp. 321-323.
15. *Ibid.*, pp. 323-326.
16. *Ibid.*, pp. 330-335.
17. *Ibid.*, pp. 326-330.
18. *Ibid.*, pp. 336-339.
19. *Ibid.*, pp. 339-342.

20. *Ibid.*, pp. 343-344.
21. *Ibid.*, pp. 344-347.
22. *Ibid.*, pp. 348-351.
23. *Ibid.*, pp. 385-395.
24. *Ibid.*, pp. 379-384.
25. *Ibid.*, pp. 376-379.
26. *Ibid.*, pp. 364-375.

5

GLOBALIZATION AND ENVIRONMENTAL CRISIS

Gandhian Perspective

AMIT K. SINGH

Globalization has become a buzzword[1] and it is a dominant discourse in post cold-war era. Globalization has become a catchword, so much abused in popular discourse that one is no longer sure of its real meaning. It connotes different things to different people.

In General, Globalization is the emergence of a complex web of interconnectedness that means that our lives are increasingly shaped by events that occur and decisions that are made, at a great distance from us.[2] It also implies that the local, regional, national, international and global events constantly interact with each other. Anthony Giddens, Director of the London School of Economics, defines globalization as the intensification of worldwide social relations which link distant localities in such a way that local happenings are shaped by events occurring many miles and vice versa.[3]

The enthusiasts and supporters of globalization (Bhagwati, 2004; Wolf, 2004) regard it as a wholly benign process, heralding the long awaited deliverance of humanity from economic backwardness, under-development and misery. On the other hand, the critics of globalization (Falk, 1999; Petras and Veltmeyer, 2001; Chomsky, 2002; Klein, 2002; Monbiot, 2003; Singh, 2005) while varying considerably in their views—have mounted a powerful attack against holding it to be a benign force.[4]

The critics of Globalization insist that it has created new problems for humanity in following ways :

(a) It enhances the hiatus between and within nations.[5]
(b) It advocates about global culture but in the name of global culture, American culture is being forced and imposed by market forces through Multinational Companies.
(c) The process of Globalization discards village and villagers. It is urban-centric development process.
(d) In present consumer culture, [6] the relationship between man and environment is at stake.

The current study focuses on the aforementioned statements forwarded by these critics. We would also like to come out with the Gandhian solutions to them. Thus the analysis of Globalization and environmental crisis with Gandhian perspective is the main object of present study.

Economic Inequality and Gandhian Insight

Among intellectuals, one often hears the claim that global economic integration is leading to rising global inequality—that it benefits the rich more than the poor.

"Globalization has dramatically increased inequality between and within nations". (Jay Mazur, Foreign Affairs) Inequality is soaring through the globalization period within countries and across countries and that's expected to continue. (Noam Chomsky)[7]

Globalization shows that it had induced inequality. "The bi-model distribution of income across the globe is becoming even more distinct. The rich are getting much richer while the poor are growing in number and many are staying poor.[8] Today the rich countries account for about 60 per cent of the world GDP but only for about 15 per cent of the world population. According to Yurlov, in 1960 about 20 per cent of the population in the richest countries had 30 times more the income of the poor and in 1997 it was 74 times. The gap between the richest and the poorest country was about 3 to 1 in 1820 and 11 to 1 in 1913. It rose to 35 to 1 in 1950 and 72 to 1 in 1992.[9]

Even, in the richest country, the economic inequality exists. For instance, in America, the wealthiest 10 per cent of American families own 84 per cent of the stock and 90 per cent of the bonds, as well as 92 per cent of business assets.[10]

This economic inequality is almost similar in developed countries as well as developing countries. For instance, Norway (HDI 1) . Australia (HDI 2) Canada (HDI 3) have the ratio of richest 10 per cent to poorest 10 per cent at 5.3 per cent, 12.5 per cent and 8.5 per cent respectively. Similarly, India (HDI 115) and Burundi (HDI 160) has ratio of richest 10 per cent to poorest 10 per cent at 9.5 per cent and 7.8 per cent respectively. The ratio of richest 20 per cent to poorest 20 per cent in Canada (developed country) India (developing country) and Burundi (least developed state of Africa) is almost similar. This ratio is 5.2 per cent, 5.7 per cent and 5.2 per cent respectively (See Table 5.1)

This shows the economic inequality at global level. Globalization is supposed to be one of the major reasons behind the economic inequality. Gandhian perspective may help in making globalization process more egalitarian.

Gandhi has great vision for equality, which is more relevant in the present era of Globalization. Gandhi favours for such pattern of economy in India as well as world where no one should be deprived from basic facility of food and cloth.[11] Gandhi was never supporter of accumulation of wealth in few hands. In the context of India he urges, the distribution of wealth should be equal for common mass of the India which mainly consists of seven lakh villages.[12]

Table 5.1: Economic Inequality

Human Dev. Index	Survey year	Share of Income or Consumption				Inequality Measures	
		Poorest 10%	Poor-est 20%	Rich-est 20%	Richest 10%	Rich-est 10% to poorest 10%	Riche-st 20% poore-st 20%
Norway	1995	4.1	9.7	35.8	21.8	5.3	3.7
Australia	1994	2.0	5.9	41.3	25.4	12.5	7.0
Canada	1994	2.8	7.5	39.3	23.8	8.5	5.2
Sweeden	1992	3.7	9.6	34.5	20.1	5.4	3.6
Belgium	1992	3.7	9.5	34.5	20.2	5.5	3.6
U.S.A.	1997	1.8	5.2	46.4	30.5	10.6	9.0
India	1997	3.5	8.1	46.1	33.5	9.5	5.7
Burundi	1992	3.4	7.9	41.6	26.6	7.8	5.2
Niger	1995	0.8	2.9	53.3	35.4	46.0	20.7

Source : Human Development Report, 2001.

Thus, the economic inequality should be handled and tackled by the Gandhian insight which will be beneficial for further developments of Globalization process.

Myth of Global Culture

The ongoing Globalization, based on the Washington Consensus, is aimed at bringing cultural uniformity throughout the world. It does not want to leave any space for cultural diversity. In other words, it wants to impose American culture and American way of life on everyone everywhere. It seems that the world had no alternative but to accept American ideas, values and way of life. This intention also reflects in the writing of different scholars.

Thomas L. Friedman declares, "We Americans are apostles of the fast world, the prophets of the free market and high priests of high tech. We want "enlargement " of both our values and pizza huts. We want the world to follow our lead and become democratic and capitalistic, with a web site in every Computer and with everyone, everywhere pumping its own gas. [13]

D. Mcouil too equates "Globalization to Westernization in general" and "Americanization in particular".[14] Gandhi was against this tendency of global homogeneous culture.[15] Gandhi says, "What is good for one nation seated in one condition is not necessarily good enough for another differently suited. One man's food is after another man's poison. Physical geography of a country has a predominant share in determining its culture. A fur coat may be necessity for the dweller in the polar region but it will smother those living in the equatorial regime".[16]

Contrary to Gandhian vision of *swadeshi* and indigenous culture, the process of globalization is trying to transform the local culture.[17] While globalization may be the prevailing force, this does not mean that localization is without significance. The particularity of place and culture can never be absolutely transcended. Even, now the concept of Globalisation[18] is becoming more popular. In this concept of Globalization it is believed that localization is complementary to the Globalization. This concept of Globalization establishes the importance of Gandhi's vision in a new intellectual fashion.

Need for Village Centric Development

Where are villages in the process of globalization, the capitalist mode of development is the main engine of the development, industrialization and urbanization are mainly preferred and villagers are left behind for instance, only 10 per cent of the world population was urban at the start of the 20th century. A figure which has gone up to almost 50.1 at the beginning of the 21st century.[19]

It is expected that even in countries like India, there would be migration of more than 140 million people to urban areas over the next 5 to 10 years. This process of development is creating a new problem in India. In metros and big cities, services sector is booming but agriculture sector is at stake in villages. This is a paradox that Call Centres are providing a new way of life to middle urban class with handsome amount of salaries on the one hand while farmers are regularly committing suicides on the other. After the sixty years of independence, more than 70 per cent of our people live in villages and 80 per cent of our poor live in rural areas.[20] However, Gandhi was aware of the soul of India. In his words, India primarily resides in villages but they are not receiving the due attention of the government. The new economic policy that Indian Government adopted in 1991 also hoodwinks this fact. This is not only a case with India but also with most of the developing states. In developing countries more than two third of the population resides in villages but they fail to be the prime focus of globalization process. Here again Gandhi sounds relevant when he remarks : "To develop India is to develop its villages. India is to found not in its cities rather in 7,00,000 villages".[21]

He continues, "I would say that if the village perishes India will perish too. India will be no more India. Her own mission in the world will get lost and it can exist in the simplicity and prosperity of the villages only. For the strategy of development along with peace, one has to achieve real freedom."[22] The words of Gandhi are simple and one can hardly afford to ignore them.

In this context the two builders of modern India, Gandhi and Nehru have serious ideological disagreement.

Gandhi wrote to J.L. Nehru on Oct. 5, 1945 "I believe that if India, and through India the world, is to achieve real freedom, than sooner or later we shall have to go and live in the villages—in huts, not in palaces. Millions of people can never live in cities and palaces in comfort and peace. Nor can they do so by killing one another, that is by retorting to violence and untruth. I have not the slightest doubt that, but for the pair of truth and non-violence, mankind will be doomed. We can have the vision of that truth and non-violence only in the simplicity of the villages.[23]

Thus, for Gandhi, the development of villages is also concerned with well being of humanity. Gandhi also offers us the solution of the present problem of Environmental crisis.

Gandhi and Environmental Challenge

Never has there been a clearer case of Nero fiddling while Rome burnt. Present environmental pollution has created danger for humanity. Today the environment is degraded, waterways assaulted and the atmosphere corrupted. [24] In present crisis, Gandhian thought and practice has become relevant once again. Much before the environmental consciousness began to expand in modern times. Gandhi has brought out a manifesto of counter-culture in *Hind Swaraj* in 1909[25]

Human civilization is at stake due to environmental crisis. It has different dimensions. Global warming is one of the greatest challenge of twenty first century. Global terrorism has been declared one of the Global Agenda at UN Millennium Summit 2006[26], but scientific advisors of British Prime Minister believe that Global warming is more dangerous problem than Global terrorism.[27] The 2007 report of International Panel on climate change also justifies this argument. It bodes ill for Global warming and the disastrous implication for the planet. The recently released summary by the Inter-Governmental Panel on Climate Change (IPCC) says that there has been a sharp increase in carbon emissions just in recent times. It has rose from 6.4 billion tonnes per annum in the 1990s to about 7.2 billion tonnes per annum in the year 2000-2005.[28] This is an increase of 12.5 per cent in just a few years. It has resulted in carbon emissions increasing to 26.4 billion tonnes each year.[29] As a result of these green house gases hampering the earth's heat from escaping, the average temperature over the earth has increased by 0.76 degrees celsius from what it was at the time of the industrial revolution.[30] Going by the estimates for warning, a rise in global temperature of 1.1 degrees celsius by 2099 appears inevitable while the increase could soar to a dangerous and possibly unmanageable maximum of 6.4°C with less effective intervention[31]. George Monbiot in his remarkable work, *Heat : How to Stop the Planet Burning* makes clear that, "at 1.5 degrees or less, an extra stress of 5 million people for hunger, chance of getting about 18 per cent of the world's species and green land lost is there". It also holds that by 2100 AD, sea level will rise by 7 to 23 inches.[32] Scientists also warn that equatorial lands, home of hundreds of millions will become uninhabitable, as food and water will run out due to climate changes.[33] IPCC report also holds that about 40 animal and plant species face extinction as rising temperature is working on ecosystem. It further points out that 29 billion tonnes of carbon dioxide poured into the atmosphere each year is acidifying the oceans – threatening to destroy coral reaps and many commercial fish species. By the middle of the century, the report warns, more than 200 million people would be displaced from their lands by rising sea levels, floods and droughts and many more facing early deaths due to malnutrition and heat stress. Polar bears are already on the extinction. A new threat of the quick melting of ice around polar bears, has overshadowed the traditional ones—dumping of toxic wastes and off shore drillings.[34] The effects of climate change are economic also. For example, the pressure group friends of Earth say, failure to take action to combat climate change will cost the global economy $20 trillion a year by the mid of the century [35]. It also says that allowing global warming to continue unchecked will mean a temperature rise of 4 degrees C by 2100 AD causing economic damage worth up to 8 per cent of global G.D.P. A recent study establishes that there have been agricultural losses worth $ 5 billion annually from 1981-2002. It can well be co-related with temperature rise over that period.[36] The *Environmental Research Letters* also show that almost 30 per cent of the variation has been registered in the global agricultural yields due to rise in temperature.[37] Thus the environmental hazard is on the threshold.

India, The Homeland of Gandhi Makes no Exception

India is also facing the problem of environmental pollution in different forms. The result of the melting of most of the Himalayan glaciers by 2030, as predicted by the UN panel on climate change could be truly catastrophic for India and its neighbors.[38] The Himalayan glaciers are largest store of water outside the polar ice caps and feed seven great Asian rivers - Ganges, Indus, Brahamputra, Mekong, Salween, Yangtze and Huang Ho. The glaciers are believed to be retreating at a rate of about 10-15 meters a year. The first danger of the melting down could be widespread flooding. It could be followed by irreversible droughts, threatening the livelihood of millions of people. This would create a massive water crisis. The Gangetic basin alone is home to more than 500 million people.[39] According to glaciologist Syed Iqbal Hussain, the loss of glacier melt down would reduce July–September flows by two–thirds, causing water shortage for 37 per cent of Indian irrigated land.[40]

Agriculture in India will be also hit for multiplicity of reasons. For instance,

(a) Rising sea levels due to warming will mean flooding in costal areas - which are often the most fertile area[41].
(b) Monsoons will become more intense and heavy rains will form a great proportions of rainfall in a season.
(c) Dryland farmers will be badly hit. A rise of two degrees will result in falling rice yield according to study at the Indian Agriculture Research Institute.

Along with these problems, India is also facing air pollution and water pollution. India has one of the highest levels of Indoor air pollution in the world with more than 75 per cent of households using solid fuel for cooking.[42]

Groundwater is poisonous in several states. A study conducted by UNICEF states that groundwater is poisonous in U.P. It further states that Arsenic contamination is quite high in 49 districts of the state.[43] Thus environmental crisis prevails in India at alarming stage today.

Gandhian Perspective:

Gandhi says : "*If you are to satisfy your need, the earth will supply everything four you. If it is for greed the world can never satisfy that. It will destroy the whole of nature.*"[44] Exactly this is happening all over the world. The Stockhome Conference in 1971 had proclaimed that "The protection of the environment is a major issue which affects the well being of people and economic development throughout the world". Gandhi's *Hind Swaraj* is a manifesto to warming against mad race after civilization or modernization characterized by materialism and wrong model of development[45]. Western pattern of industrialization encourages ever - growing material standard of life. And for this purpose they adopt ruthless exploitation of natural resourses minerals and fossil fuels. For instance U.S.A. consumes 30 to 50 per cent of worlds annual production[46] although it has only 6 per cent of worlds total population. Therefore, unlimited technical progress is thus favoured in order to maximize output because more is always better. (*Ye dil mange more*). The WWF conservative said that humans are stripping nature at an unprecedented rate and will need two planets worth of natural resources every year by 2050 on current trends.[47] It also creates inequality. Over the past four years the worlds 200 richest people have doubled their wealth to more than one trillion US dollars, while 1.3 billion people are living on less than a dollar per day. This leads to social tensions and conflicts.

India may be the best example of this model of development. India has been a great civilization but surprisingly became a consumer society. Different Market Surveys show that consumerism is window to new India and shopping has become our national sport[48]. India is supposed to be a spiritual global leader but now a days the market culture is greatly affecting our cultural values and ethos. Consumption is an important form of self expression and a major way of demonstrating one's identity[49].

Conclusion

As solution of this problem Gandhi suggests: *Do not go to greed, live at the level of need only. The nature will supply everything for you*[50]. The Humanity that has already suffered and lost its credibility, pines its hope in Gandhian Mārg. The simple solution of this complex universal problem is, *simple living and high thinking* as Gandhi suggests. Let us conclude with the lines of Arnold Toynbee :" *It is becoming clear that a chapter which had western beginning will have an Indian ending if it is not end in the self destruction of the human race*" [51].

NOTES

1. Jagdish Bhagwati, *In Defense of Globalization,* (New Delhi: Oxford University Press, 2004), p. 13
2. Andrew Heywood, *Key Concepts in Politics,* (London: Macmillan Press Ltd, 2000), pp. 243-243.
3. Manfred B. Steger *Globalization A Very Short Introduction,* (London: Oxford University Press, 2003) p. 10.
4. Baldev Raj Nayar, *India's Globalization Evaluating the Economic Consequences,* (New Delhi : Vistar Publications, 2007), p. 02.
5. Joseph Stuglitze, *Globalization and its Discontent,* (New Delhi : Penguin Books India, 1998), p. 24.
6. See, S. Crook., J. Pukulski and M. Waters, *Postmodernism,* (London: Sage 1992).
7. Quoted from, Michael M Weinstern, *Globalization What's New,* (New York : Columbia University Press, 2005), p. 96.
8. Murphy Craig N., "Political Consequences of New Inequality", *International Studies Quarterly,* 2001, 45 348
9. Yurlov Felir N., "Globalization, Inequality and Threats to Sustainability Development", *World Affairs,* 5(1), Jan-Mar, 2001, pp. 36-53.
10. Richard Higgott, *Globalization and Regionalization, New Trends in World Politics,* (The UAE : Emirates Centre for Strategic studies and Research, 1998), pp. 33-54.

11. Mahatma Gandhi, *Young India,* 15-11-1927.
12. Mahatma Gandhi, *Young India,* 23-3-1921.
13. Thomas L. Friedman, "A Manifesto for the Fast World", *The New York Times Magazine,* March 28, 1999.
14. D. Mcquail, Mcqualis, *Mass Communication Theory,* (London : 2000), p. 221.
15. F.J. Lechner and J. Boli (eds.), *The Globalization Reader,* (London : Blackwell, 2001).
16. M.K. Gandhi : *Young India,* 25-7-1929.
17. For Localization, See Colin Hines, *Localization A Global Manifesto,* (London: Earthhscan, 2000).
18. B. Ramesh Babu, "Globalization and the Indian Nation-State" in *Interpreting Globalization,* (New Delhi : Rawat Publication 2004), pp. 168-189.
19. Urban Legends, *Business and Economy,* March 23 - April 4, 2007, p. 13.
20. Somanath Chatterjee, "The Developmental Challenge in Rural India", *The Hindu,* 4 April, 2007, p. 10.
21. M.K. Gandhi, *India of My Dream,* p. 91.
22. *Ibid,* p. 104.
23. Gandhi to J.L. Nehru, October 5, 1945.
24. Ronald J. Terchek, *Gandhi Struggling For Autonomy,* (New Delhi : Vistar Publications, 2000), p. 235
25. *The Collected Works of Mahatma Gandhi,* (New Delhi : 1963), Vol. 10, p. 145.
26. www. bbc.hindi.com
    www.hindustandainik.com
27. Nagraj Adve, "Implications of Climate Panel Report", *Economic and Political Weekly,* March 24, 2007, p. 1001.
28. IPCC Report, pp. 2-3.
29. Nagraj Adve, *op. cit.*
30. "A Climate Change Warming", *The Hindu,* February 10, 2007, p 10.
31. Ramesh Thakur and Collin Bradford, "Climate Change and Global Leadership", *The Hindu,* February 10, 2007, p. 10.
32. Jonathan Leake, Warming Sparks Extinction Fears, *The Times of India,* April 2, 2007, p . 1.
33. Simon Garfield, "Polar Bears on Climate Change", *The Hindu,* 6 March, 2007, p. 11.
34. Larry Elliott, "Warming Will Cost Trillions", *The Hindu,* October 14, 2006, p. 11.
35. Nitin Sethi, "$5 Billion Worth Crops Destroyed Annually", *The Times of India,* 4 April, 2007, p. 15.
36. *Ibid.*
37. "Himalayan Melt Down Catastrophic for India", *The Times of India,* April 14, 2007, p. 9.

38. *Ibid*
39. *Ibid*
40. Nagraj Adve. *op.cit.*, p. 1002.
41. India High on Indoor Air Pollution: WHO Report, *The Hindu*, March 24, 2007, p. 7.
42. Akhilesh Kumar Singh, Groundwater is Poison in U.P, *The Times of India*, October 24, 2006, p. 5.
43. Ramjee Singh (ed). *Gandhi and theFfuture of Humanity*, (Varanasi : Manak Publication, 2004), pp. 181-82.
44. Ramjee Singh (ed), *Gandhi and the Twenty First Century*, (New Delhi: Peace Publishers, 2005), p. 156.
45. *The New York Times*, 11 March,1985.
46. Only 2 Earths can Sustain Us, *The Times of India*, 25 October, 6, p. 1.
47. Shiv Visvanathan, Shop Till you Drop, *The Times of India*, 25 Oct, 6, p. 10.
48. Girish Mishra, Globalization and Culture: Some Aspects, *Mainstream*, August, 16, 2003, p. 15.
49. Ramjee Singh, *op.cit.*, pp. 181-82.
50. *Ibid.*

6

GLOBALIZATION AND GANDHI

ANIL ARORA

Globalization is not a trend, it is not an affair, it is not an intended game, but it is actually the international system that replaced the cold war system and like the cold war system globalization has its own rules, logics, pressures, incentives, gears and moving parts that will and do attract everyone's country, everyone's company and everyone's community, either directly or indirectly.

—**Thomas Friedman**

Now globalization, not colonization, has become the defining moment in history. It has consequences ranging from our philosophical understanding of ourselves to more mundane, material circumstances governing our lives. The era of globalization may be seen to commence with the end of the Cold War, the fall of the Berlin Wall, and the establishment of the "Washington Consensus" of the Bretton Woods institutions affirming the merits of markets.

Today, Tomorrow and Everyday underlines that Gandhi has a timeless relevance. He predicted in the second quarter of the twentieth century that industrial capitalism governing the world would leave humanity in a soulless mess. By the end of the century his prediction had been realised. We had suffered two World Wars and were, until very recently, trapped in the Cold War between capitalism and communism, waged by the two superpowers in Africa, South East Asia, the Middle East and the Caribbean, destroying the life sources of these regions—roads, bridges, soil, fields, forests, etc., and killing millions of people.

Even as colonialism lost its functionality the money holders of the world had plotted an even more destructive economic system. The old capitalism had masqueraded as liberalism; the new masquerades as neo-liberalism and globalization.

Globalization is the restructuring of colonisation with far more dire consequences. It is the conversion of the vast sector of the human race, living mostly in the so-called Third World, into a global market for exploitation by the neo-capitalists, in the main, the G-8 Nations. The decolonised has been re-colonised, this time round, not by "mother countries", but by "mother industries", a few multi-nationals whose sole interest is profit which it pursues licentiously with practically no restraints. After all, the earliest colonisers were trading companies, the Dutch East India and the British East India, not nation- states and we are reverting to that situation.

Whereas the first capitalism, or "liberalism", was constrained by governments, neo-liberalism or globalisation subsumes governments and indeed the whole of society. It exploits freely, without any restraints, neither of governments nor of any moral order. The International Monetary Fund and World Bank invented at the end of Second World War to rescue and revive European and Japanese Economies, today prey on "Third World" governments in particular and bend them to their economic policies that are anti-democracy, anti-poor, anti-humanity, focussed on securing giant corporations their monopolistic profits.

The capitalism and political freedom do not necessarily go hand in hand. Capitalism is very successful in creating wealth but it does not assure freedom, social justice and the rule of law, it is not designed to safeguard universal principles and concludes. While we can speak of the triumph of capitalism we cannot yet speak of the triumph of democracy. If we care about universal values such as freedom and democracy, we cannot leave them to the care of market forces.

George Soros, from within the capitalist rank, confirms this when he states; "The protection of the common interest used to be the task of the nation state. But the powers of the state have shrunk as global capital markets have expanded. When capital is free to move around it will avoid any state that seeks to impose taxes and regulations. Since capital is essential to the creation of social goals, governments must cater to its demands often to the detriments of social goals. This holds true for all governments, even the United States."

So capital governs, and the global capitalists lay down the policy to exploit and plunder the world regardless of the destruction to nature or humanity. Any government desiring foreign capital has to submit to this policy, which, like colonialism, is a one way traffic of resources plundered and transferred from the poor to the rich; from the south, from Africa, Asia and South America, to the North–Europe, the UK, the USA, Japan and Canada. It is, in turn, the sale of manufactured goods and machinery to the former colonies, the "Third World", at exorbitant prices, made more exorbitant by the devaluation of indigenous currencies.

Globalization is reduced to a single component, trade, with its global media that fashions the tastes of the world and manipulates the market. The main orchestrator and beneficiary of this process is the USA which enjoys 50 per cent of the world market in many industries; controls more than half of the world business activity, and two-thirds of advertising and marketing services. Globalization is essentially Americanisation.

Soros informs us that "capitalism is very successful in creating wealth" and Felix Yurlov expands on this when he reports that the world's per capita income tripled in the last 50 years, that the world GDP grew ten fold-from $30 million to $30 billion. That revenue from the entertainment and book business grew "from $67 billion in 1970, to $200 billion in 1991, (the USA being the chief beneficiary and the biggest exporter, with fifty per cent of the revenue of Hollywood coming from overseas). Cultural products move in a one-way stream, from the rich to the poor."

The peoples of the world have never been as divided in their standards of living in the entire history of the human race as today. Globalization has produced more inequality than ever before. The assets of the three richest countries in the world today are greater than the combined GNP of the 48 least-developed countries.

The rich countries enjoy 60 per cent of the world's GNP but have only 15 per cent of the world population. In 1960, 20 per cent of the world's richest countries had 30 times the incomes of the poorest 20 per cent; in 1997, 74 times.

The gap between the world's richest and poorest countries has doubled in the last 50 years. It was 3:1 in 1820, 11:1 in 1913, 35:1 in 1950 and 72:1 in the nineties.

"Mahatma Gandhi regarded economics as a moral science and laid tremendous emphasis on the ethical aspect of the problem. Economics that hurts the moral well-being of an individual or a nation and does not cater to the needs of the poor and down trodden is immoral and, therefore, sinful. Its goal is not pure material benefits but advancement of humanity on its road to progress. No one's gain should be anybody's loss, financial, physical, moral or spiritual. The Mahatma denounced the concept of 'Economic Man' because the mind of this industrialized robot suffers an almost complete black out when it comes to freedom and responsibilities of a human person.

"That is why Gandhi formulated his economic principles in the context of his design of an ideal social order : a non-violent non-exploitative, humanistic and egalitarian society. Satisfaction of needs and moral elevation of individual were not anti-thetical for him.

"I do not want my house to be walled in on all sides and my windows to be stuffed. I want the cultures of all lands to be blown about my house as freely as possible. But I refuse to be blown off my feet by any.

"Trusteeship provides a means of transforming the present capitalist order of society into an egalitarian one. It gives no quarter to capitalism, but gives the present owning class a chance of reforming itself; It is based on the faith that human nature is never beyond redemption. It does not recognise any right of private ownership except so far as it may be permitted by society for its own welfare."

He saw the capitalist as dispensable but the worker was the core of society. This is in sharp contrast to globalisation which weakens the worker and makes him dispensable and replaceable with technological innovations and which strives to eliminate his bargaining power by getting rid of trade unions if possible. For Gandhi, machinery and technology have no right to exist if they invade the rights of workers.

Our problem today is not a question of insufficient resources–we have enough resources. The problem is that these are appropriated by a few multi-national companies and their shareholders. Almost a century ago Gandhi said "there is enough for everyone's need, but not enough for everyone's greed." But Gandhi said, "A certain degree of physical comfort is necessary but above a certain level it becomes a hindrance instead of a help; therefore the ideal of creating an unlimited number of wants and satisfying them, seems to be a delusion and a trap. The satisfaction of one's physical needs must come at a certain point to a dead stop before it degenerates into physical decadence.

Europeans will have to remodel their outlook if they are not to perish under the weight of the comforts to which they are becoming slaves." In order to protect their economic interests, countries go to war - military war as well as economic war. Gandhi said, "People have to live in villages communities and simple homes rather than desire to live in palaces." Millions of people will never be able to live at peace with each other if they are constantly fighting for a higher living standard. We cannot have real peace in the world if we look at each other's countries as sources for raw materials or as markets for finished industrial goods. The seeds of war are sown with economic greed. If we analyze the causes of war throughout history, we find that the pursuit of economic expansion consistently leads to military adventures. There are far more resources today than ever before in human history and despite the fact that there are far more people dependant on them than ever before, our capacity to produce more than out-strips our population growth. Our problem is not resources; our problem is distribution of resources equitably, to service need and not greed. Unfortunately, the focus is on greed, and greed is insatiable.

Since the Russian revolution, the world has been broadly divided into the socialist and capitalist sphere. However, with the demise of the USSR, the communist ideology has been thrown in the 'dustbin of history' by many theorists - Francis Fukayama being the most prominent. However, evils of liberal hegemony are also coming to the forefront - increasing inequality in countries embracing capitalism, huge balance of trade deficits tying up developing countries to western corporations and WTO/IMF norms leading to crisis and bankruptcy in many countries. In such a scenario, Gandhi and his ideas on the economy are being hailed by many as the 'Third Way'-a suitable compromise between the leftists and free marketeers that ought to suit all classes. However, if we scrutinise Gandhian attitudes towards economics, we find a lot of similarities with both liberalism and communism. For instance, through the Swadeshi Movement, From his early days in South Africa, Gandhi distrusted governments as inevitably soul-less machines concerned with perpetuating their power and patronage. Gandhi hoped that India's future would be in the hands of decentralized panchayats at the village level. He said:

> "My idea of village *Swaraj* is that it is a complete republic independent of its neighbours for its own vital wants and yet interdependent for many other in which dependence is a necessity."

Those who have experienced *Swaraj*, Gandhi believed, will not cower before-brute force, and nor will they desire to use brute-force. Gandhi advocated rejection of western textile and home spinning of cotton for Indians - this amounts to very much left wing protectionism which Nehruvian India adopted for over 35 years until under Dr. Manmohan Singh, India began its journey to free market economics. On the other hand, Gandhi backed small and decentralized form of government which sided very much with Liberal views. This, however, was rejected by India ever since independence and a huge bureaucracy was established under Nehru, the brunt of which is still borne by India. Thus, Gandhi held a very idealist view of economic globalization where states would be self-sufficient on most accounts but mutually dependent on some. His view negated the cornerstone of the principle of succeeding in modern economics - rapid industrialization. Self-sufficiency can only be maintained by maintaining a competitive edge in today's world of free market. Without unique selling points, domestic industries are bound to be overrun by a foreign competitor. Gandhi's views rested on the principles of co-operation and understanding - today it's more about competition and profit making. However, Gandhi's desire to safeguard peasants' rights seems valid even today, where one of the most heated debates on the WTO is between the

US, EU and G-20 led by India and Brazil about agricultural subsidies.

Gandhi is probably the first serious critique of industrialism, his critique being based on both moral and economic grounds. Gandhi's reaction against industrialisation, was basically on account of the inequalities it bred, and the unemployment it created. He was anti-machine to the extent that it did not benefit all alike but rather resulted in a few exploiting the many and creating unemployment. Mechanical power, in his view, deprived man of his God-given means to livelihood. Mechanical power he emphasised is justified only if it does not result in unemployment. Gandhian economics demands full employment, contending that man lives by his labour and when his labour is taken away from him he does not live at all, materiality or spirituality.

For Gandhi, the Supreme consideration is man-machine should not have ascendancy over him. It is beneath human dignity to lose ones individuality and become a mere cog in the machine. Once he remarked, "I want every individual to become a full-blooded, full developed member of society." Full employment, he believed, could only be achieved if "the means of production of elementary necessities of life remain in the control of the masses. The disease of the masses, he said, "Is not want of money so much as it is want of work."

"Machinery has its place," he conceded, "but it must not be allowed to displace the necessary human labour. Men go on saving labour till thousands are without work and thrown on the open streets to die of starvation. I want to save time and labour, not for a fraction of mankind but, for all, I want the concentration of wealth, not in the hands of a few but in the hands of all."

"Machinery, he held, "merely helps a few to ride on the backs of millions." Central to Gandhi's economics is self-sufficiency. He opposed industrialisation because he foresaw the excesses it would lead to, nibbling away at the soul of man and eventually leaving him soulless, without conscience or fellow feeding. He drew a parallel between urbanisation and where the city exploited the village, and colonisation, where the country lived on the resources of another. His remedy in both instances is self-sufficiency, not dependancy on foreign trade, or foreign investments. He saw real planning as the best utilisation of the whole manpower of India and the distribution of raw products of India in her numerous villages instead of sending them outside and re-buying finished articles at fabulous prices.

He would thus be totally opposed to globalisation for it deprives people of self-sufficiency and independence and converts them into clients of the multi-nationals.

Industrialisation was expected to enrich the world. The reverse has happened. Pre-industrial humanity enjoyed a greater sense of well-being than post industrial. It is this fact that led Gandhi to view the rural area the village as the preserver of human values and thus the fulcrum of his society. He saw the village as the place of the Truth he sought.

The problem of industrialism was its centralisation, of machines in factories, of power in the boss. He supported decentralisation and small communities where relations were personal, and values kept alive by interpersonal contact and guidance. Gandhi saw India destroyed through industrialisation. His sarvodaya was thus a confederation of small interdependent communities, each self-sufficient in itself and thus not beholden to the other.

He saw the village as the anchor of democracy and the villager the ideal man. "Take away his chronic poverty and his illiteracy you have the finest specimen of what a cultured, cultivated free citizen should be."

While this hankering after the rural is impractical, what Gandhism is promoting here is the small group, personalised living, so that the human can be rescued from the anonymity of mass society and be more in control of himself. His emphasis should be seen generally on the small manageable group rater than specifically on the villages.

Gandhi is against the centralisation of power and saw that as resulting in domination and elimination of small collectives, small societies, small countries. Where western philosophers divide, Gandhi unites both on social and personal levels. He returns us to ourselves and to God. Where capitalism focuses on the material exploitable body, Gandhi focuses on the soul, the source of personal power. Where neo-liberals pursue unlimited profits, unrestrained by any rules (their definition of the freedom of the market and a free society), Gandhi places us securely in the embrace of God and therein lies our unity as a human race.

We are born equal, children of the one and only God, equally entitled to all His resources. Gandhi's equality does not trespass on individuality. He states: "While we are born equal, meaning we have a right to equal opportunity, all have not the same capacity. It is in the nature of things impossible. Some will have ability to earn more, others less... I would allow a man of intellect to earn more, I would not cramp his talent, but the bulk of his greater earnings must be used for the good of the state. They would have their earnings only as trustees."

The society he offers, Sarvodaya, is also rooted in divinity. He defines man (and woman) as "a special creation of God. Man is not a brute. His distinguishing characteristic is self-restraint. Man has reason, discrimination and free will. He uses his reason to worship God", which, in the Gandhian concept, "is to live in terms of the moral order, God's order."

Gandhi states: "The Divine powers within us are infinite. The aim of life is to serve God. The soul's natural progress is towards selflessness and purity. Man's ultimate aim is the realisation of God and all his activities, social, political, religious have to be guided by the ultimate vision of God. Serving others is part of this endeavour. The only way to find God, is to serve others. Man is not at peace with himself until he has become like unto God."

A major part of Gandhi's criticisms towards industrialisation was geared towards preserving India's rich natural resources. As globalisation has progressed, so has the tendency to try and exploit every possible resource in the country to increase the GDP. Rapid deforestation has occurred throughout the developing world and serious environmental hazards are faced by most developing countries today. Moreover, corporate power has undermined governmental efforts at curbing environmental loss, as the American withdrawal from the Kyoto Protocol vividly depicted. However, conservation processes led by the UN and also at the national and even local level, are gradually gathering speed in the second phase of globalisation, i.e., whereby most of the evils of globalisation are now being questioned and checked

Thus, the crucial question facing us surely is–Are the notions of Gandhi and Globalization contradictory? Not necessarily, it seems. Some of his ideas may seem utopian and unrealistic in the global society today, while others may seem in direct opposition to everything globalisation and liberalisation stands for. However, many of his principles remain valid even today and applied worldwide, the most notable being the principle of *satyagraha*. He brought forward practical issues facing the globalisation process today–that of environmental concerns, equality of rights for all, rural development and evils of violence. However, to sum up Gandhian attitudes towards globalisation as it stands today, it seems apt to conclude by quoting Gurudev Rabindranath Tagore :

"We have for over a century been dragged by the prosperous West behind its chariot, choked by the dust, deafened by the noise, humbled by our own helplessness and overwhelmed by the speed. We agreed to acknowledge that this chariot-drive was progress, and the progress was civilisation. If we ever ventured to ask, `progress towards what, and progress for whom', it was considered to be peculiarly and ridiculously oriental to entertain such ideas about the absoluteness of progress. Of late, a voice (Gandhi) has come to us to take count not only of the scientific perfection of the chariot but of the depth of the ditches lying in its path."

7

GANDHI IN THE GLOBALIZED WORLD

HARISH K. THAKUR

Gandhi seems to be the one among few people today who would be remaining at the mainstream of political thought for centuries to come. His ideas and philosophy have been studied quite profusely in India and worldwide and he works as an institution of guidance for the thinkers, statesmen, and policy-makers alike. In today's globalized world the ideas of Gandhi still bear the gloss and have the potential of guiding the people towards the establishment of a more humane and just society.

The time Gandhi emerged on the global scene as the steward of Indian nationalism and a voice against apartheid, several forces were at work. It was a transitional phase when many states were in the process of making and many nationalities awakening against the colonial monster. Indian nationalism, that in the later stages had turned out to be the handiwork of Gandhi alone and which had become the torch of rising for the many has become an event to be analyzed and scrutinized time and again, obviously because of the crucial experimentation and staunch belief of Gandhi that righteous means would bring the success in the end.

The introduction of machines in industry, agriculture and press with the advancement of technology which had ushered in the era of industrialization far back were the events of global interconnection and interdependence for Gandhi. He himself was the product of this global phenomenon as he had his education at Britain and early engagements at South Africa. His wide experience abroad and the knowledge of the global happenings prepared him mentally against the pros and cons of the forthcoming events.

His ideas over globalization, initially understood in the terms of westernization were not far from the existing direly felt needs of the hour. He opined that globalization was not an evil but to believe that everything western was superior was not the correct stand to take. He did not perceive any threat to our culture due to globalization but he did believe that it would lead to environmental hazards and consumerism - both of which have proved correct. Today world over NGOs are working along Gandhian principles to save and improve the environment and to spread peace through his works.[1]

Gandhi further remarked when he felt the need to have full flow of benefits emanating from the stream of western advancement, which for him was the result of industrialization. He held "I do not want my house to be walled in on all sides and my windows to be stuffed. I want the cultures of all lands to be blown about my house as freely as possible. But I refuse to be blown off my feet by any.[2]

One can see the urge to stand on one's own and respect for the idea of self-dependence in these words of Gandhi. It was under the guidance of this impulse that he talked of simple and dignified life which could be realized only in the simple ways of living such as agriculture, cottage industry, and self-sufficient small economic units etc.

At one stage there was an open declaration from the west over the ultimate extinction of Gandhian, Marxist and such other political alternatives which had commanded the political thinking of the last two centuries. This sense of fear and self-imposed skeptic is visible from the "contemporary political thinking epitomized in Francis Fukuyama's famous chauvinistic reformulation of Hegel's the '*End of History*' that the West had achieved the final decisive political victory. Gandhian and the other political alternative have been defeated and rendered obsolete. Those who attempt to adopt a Gandhian political orientation at odds with the dominant features of contemporary political thinking will create dysfunctional political structures, will be smashed by modern political forces, and will be shown to be historically irrelevant".[3]

His widely acclaimed idea of non-violence also receives non-chalance in today's world. For many people, his approach, although, looks good but technically sounds impractical as the states are today well equipped in arms and weaponry. His non-violent rebellion that drove the British colonial rulers out from the subcontinent in 1947 seems to have done its work.

To quote Pasrichia, "as a hero and symbol of India's freedom movement, Gandhi leaves something to be desired. Gandhi's policy of just showing the other cheek or non-violence seems to be challenged today. Now Indians are more aware that we should have fought for our freedom. The India of today is a changed one and has lesser regards to the idea of non-violence and even lesser to the idea of turning the other cheek to the enemy. Subhas Bose, a Cambridge University-educated aristocrat who launched his political career in Calcutta, was against the pacifist ways of Gandhi in favour of violent revolution, forming a rebel army and joining forces with the Axis powers.[4] The famous Indian National Army charms the Indians more of late. No matter the current phase of hot blood shows and violence in Bollywood movies is not over, but one can't overlook the success of Sanjay Dutt's role in ***Lage Raho Munna Bhai***, a trend setter in tinsel world. The movie that portrayed the hero working on the advice of Gandhi and getting all the problems solved was such a big success that even Indian government passed an anti-corruption bill after getting inspiration from the movie. The people went into the streets to check routine irregularities by resorting to ***Gadhigiri.***

It seems ironic that the worldwide anti-globalization movements often portray Gandhi as someone who shared the same side of the ideological spectrum, when Gandhiji himself was clearly a product of globalization. He was educated in London, started his political activities in South Africa before he even joined the political arena in India and greatly influenced by western figures such as Jesus, Tolstoy, Thoreau and Ruskin. Friedman's distinction of the current version and the historical dimension of globalization[5] is not new as "Gandhi himself identifies globalization as an ancient phenomenon, whereby he claimed that it was not a bigger threat to India as various races starting from the Greeks and Huns to the British had invaded India but ended up being a part of the nation".[6]

He believed that the mingling of cultures in India would not be a threat to India's own customs and culture. However, he did identify that the establishment of a global society would carry certain dangers for the sovereign nations such as colonialism, both cultural and political, industrialization, and commercialization of the economy leading to class antagonism and environmental hazards. Today, we see many of those problems emerge clearly in our lives and hence, Gandhi's relationship with globalization remains extremely important and his ideas valid even today.

The ideas of Gandhi over the social construction and economic planning have been evaluated time and again and his posture against the industrial society needs to be dissected again as the world moves towards a more decentralized order. "In contradiction to the altruistic philosophy of *Sarvodaya,* the conventional economies are based on the concept of economic man, which means that an individual is motivated by economic considerations, and in real life, he tends to serve his self interests mainly in terms of economic gains".[7] Theoretically, Gandhi was not a student of economics. However, his economic ideas bear the impression of his views about man and society. Spirituality runs in every idea of Gandhi and his views about economy and planning are solely guided by this element.

About socialism Gandhi observes "socialism is a beautiful word, so far as I am aware, in socialism all the members of the society are equal—none low, none high. In the individual body head is not high because it is at the top of the body, nor are the soles of the feet low because they touch the earth. Even as the members of the body are equal, so are the members of the society. This is socialism. Socialism begins with the first convert. In order to reach such state, we may not look on things philosophically and say that we need not make a move until all are converted to socialism".[8] His socialism was the outcome of his broader approach towards human life and relations in society. His idea was the one of equal wages based on his doctrine of bread and labour. It was different from the one of communists for whom the distribution of wages was to be based on work, its quality, and quantity and on the principle 'to each according to his work'.[9]

Gandhi himself was a great believer in the preservation of the ancient Indian culture and norms of society. However, with India's integration in the world community, especially during the last decade of the 20th century, it could be argued that western cultural hegemony has affected India and most other developing countries. Urban India today seems very much in an age of 'diet Coke, flat screen televisions and super express highways'. It is not this that Gandhi would have been against, but it is the automatic assumption of the superiority of anything originating from the west that Gandhi would be dissatisfied with. These problems are very much real in today's India - crashdiet courses and anti-wrinkle treatment creams have been a fad in urban India, yet Gandhi would argue that the Indian alternatives are in no way, inferior. Consumerism is another western attitude that Gandhi would be against, a phenomenon which is rapidly engulfing urban India's middle class. However, this is not to say that cultural globalisation is something which we should vehemently oppose. In the latter half of the 1990s and in the early years of the new millennium, we clearly notice a reversal of trends in some ways. It is increasingly seen that Indian culture, along with ones like Chinese, have influenced the west in many ways. Oriental restaurants are on every major street of most of the famous western cities, there is a considerable Oriental diaspora among the top professionals and academics in the west, Indian music, films, Oriental clothes are getting a global fame. This is something Gandhi would have highly appreciated–a true global culture without a hegemonistic impact which was witnessed in the first phase of globalisation and undisputed western dominance.[10]

Ever since the emergence of two blocs at global level and the consequent warfare the relevance of Gandhi remains as powerful as it was before. Although, the world was relegated to the battleground of capitalist-communist maneuvers yet the third voice remained prominent and the ideas of non-alignment and neutrality derived strength from the ideas of peace and non-violence of Gandhi.

In the post-independent India the trend of decentralization earmarked in the constitution itself was largely due to views opined by Gandhi. The Panchayati Raj Institutions (enshrined in Article 40 of the Indian Constitution and new amendments that laid a permanent foundation of the concept) and the delegation of more powers to the rural and urban local governments was one of the dreams of Mahatma. Though, his views over industrialization and large scale investments did not follow the suit, yet opening up of economy for more competitors and rescue it from the shackles of accredited few was also an outcome of his ideas.

Although, the nationalization of banks and large industries in India and other protectionist measures, aimed at achieving an inner stability and dependency among the policy makers but it did not provide the real clue for the emancipation of the ordinary poor. It was this necessity that Gandhi kept in mind and talked of decentralization of powers to the poor and development of local cottage industries. Cons apart, the parity that Gandhi achieves with his ideal is unparalleled and we land somewhere near the more globalized world of the day.

The rapid development and progress attained via large scale industries and the modernization process has met its necessary end. Where on the one hand the communist regimes failed to solve the questions of labour and employment the western liberal states are quarreling with the idea of international barriers to sell their goods. The process of integration of states on communication, capital and currency level is on and it is not far to see the further consolidation of states purely guided by the national economic interests. The transformation of the border tight states into a global village reaches somewhere near the Gandhian society of self-sufficient economy where the role of the state gets minimized and the role of individual receives more attention.

However, the more alarming thing is the developing of the minuscule trade groups into the huge one across the borders having great resources and potential. They are forcing the smaller and marginal one into the peripheral areas and this was the concern Gandhi did show decades back. He had the eye to see the inherent dangers of large-scale production. One way out he saw for this was the idea of swadeshi.

In the words of Gandhi :

"Swadeshi is that spirit in us which requires us to serve our immediate neighbours before others, and to use things produced in our neighbourhood in preference to those more remote. So doing, we serve humanity to the best of our capacity. We cannot serve humanity by neglecting our neighbours."[11] Except the idea of *swadeshi* the tool of communication and transportation also doesn't go neglected. In the words of Wood, "Local, short-distance transportation should receive every encouragement but long hauls should be discouraged because they would promote urbanisation, specialisation beyond the point of human integrity, the growth of a rootless proletariat, – in short, a most undesirable and uneconomic way of life.[12]

What we can come out from the views of Gandhi today is to opt for a shift from the current disequilibrium in economics and go for a more fragmented, decentralized, and autonomous way of life. Schumacher had rightly pointed out decades back that we are moving ever more rapidly into a world dominated by the large-scale complexity; high capital intensity which eliminates the human factor; and violence. In order to ensure survival, he recommended new guidelines which point towards smallness rather than giantism, simplification rather than complexity, capital saving rather than labour saving - and towards non-violence. The profit motive throws humanity and the planet out of equilibrium. The emphasis has to be shifted back to the person rather than the product. Costs have to be measured in human terms by taking cognizance of happiness, beauty, health and the protection of the planet.[13]

Thus this is the time to ponder over the other alternatives and check the unhindered flow of developments into a more socialist and Gandhian mould of planning where the centre of the development will be welfare of man, of course one and all, and the capital saving for the good of more, labour increase to generate employment and economic concentration to eliminate poverty and economic disparities.

NOTES

1. Aruni Mukherjee, University of Warwick, www.mkgandhi.org/articles/globalisation/htm.
2. *Ibid.*
3. Douglas Allen, "Gandhi, Contemporary Political Thinking, and Self - Other Relations", in B.N. Ray, (Ed.), *Contemporary Political Thinking*, (New Delhi: Kanishka Publishers, 2000), pp.132-33, See also Francis Fukuyama, *The End of History and the Last Man*, (New York: The Free Press, 1992).
4. A.Pasrichia, Boston.com/news/world/asia/articles/mahatma_legacy/p.1
5. Thomas Friedman, *The World is Flat: A Short History of the Globalized World in the 21st Century*, (Allen Lane, 2005).
6. Mukherjee, *op.cit.*
7. Parmeshwary Dayal, *Gandhian Theory of Social Reconstruction*, (New Delhi: Atlantic Publishers, 2006), p. 201
8. M.K. Gandhi, *Socialism of My Conception*, Delhi, pp. 1-2
9. Benudhar Pradhan, *The Socialist Thought of Mahatma Gandhi*, Vol-II, (Delhi: GDK Publications, 1980),pp. 347 to 450.
10. For a detailed discussion see Mukerjee, *op.cit.*
11. *Young India*, August 20, 1919.
12. Wood, 1987, p. 247
13. Schumaker, qtd. by Weber, Gandhi and Buddhist Economics,www.mkgandhi.org/budhist.htm

8

HUMAN RIGHTS IN THE GLOBALIZING WORLD

ASHU PASRICHA

Human rights are a set of universal claims to safeguard human dignity from illegitimate coercion, typically enacted by state agents. These norms are codified in a widely endorsed set of international undertakings: the "International Bill of Human Rights" (Universal Declaration of Human Rights, International Covenant on Civil and Political Rights, and International Covenant on Social and Economic Rights); phenomenon-specific treaties on war crimes (Geneva Conventions), genocide, and torture; and protections for vulnerable groups such as the UN Convention on the Rights of the Child and the Convention on the Elimination of Discrimination against Women. International dialogue on human rights has produced a distinction between three "generations" of human rights, labelled for their historical emergence. Security rights encompass life, bodily integrity, liberty, and sometimes associated rights of political participation and democratic governance. Social and economic rights, highlighted in the eponymous International Covenant, comprise both negative and positive freedoms, enacted by states and others: prominently, rights to food, health care, education, and free labour. More recently discussed collective rights may include rights such as membership in a cultural community and access to a healthy environment. These "generations" of rights often involve different sets of actors and different levels of state accountability.

The term human rights, as it is most commonly used, describes those rights which every individual is entitled to enjoy. The contemporary international statement of these rights is the Universal Declaration of Human Rights (the UDHR), which, we can say, recognises two broad sets of rights. These would be:

- *Civil and Political Rights* which deal with the protection of life, liberty, and security of the people. Under this heading, all governments should guarantee that no one is enslaved or subjected to arbitrary arrest, or detention, or to torture. In other words, in terms of this category, everyone is entitled *inter alia* to fair justice and the right to freedom of thought, conscience and religion, and freedom of expression.
- The second category of rights deals with *Economic, Social and Cultural Rights,* whereby governments are expected to try, progressively, to improve the living conditions of their citizens. For example, the state must guarantee the right to fundamental necessities such as the right to food, clothing, housing and medical care, the protection of the family, and the right to social security, education and employment.

However, in practice, many countries of the north, as well as the media, have come to use the term human rights in a rather restrictive sense. In referring to human rights, the stress has been on civil and political rights to the exclusion from consideration as a matter of rights the fundamental issues contained under the second category.

We cannot talk of human rights and globalization as some omnipotence in the sky or golden colours at dawn. Not abstractions but actualizations are our focus. The right to life, the foremost of human rights, is more than mere breath or tactile sense of touch. Field J., in Murm *vs.* Illinois[1] observed "... By the term 'life' something more is meant than mere animal existence. The inhibition against its deprivation extends to all those limbs and faculties by which life is enjoyed. The provision equally prohibits the mutilation of the body by the amputation of an arm or leg, or the cutting out of an eye, or the destruction of any other organ of the body through which the soul communicates with the outer world. The deprivation not only of life, but of whatever God has given to everyone with life, for its growth and enjoyment, is prohibited by the provision in question, if its efficacy be not frittered away by judicial decision". The Supreme Court of India has adopted this definition.

In Francis Coralic Mullin[2], Bhagwati J. observed: "The fundamental right to life ... is the most precious human right and ... forms the arc of all other rights". The learned Judge added: "... The question which arises is whether the right to life is limited only to protection of limb or faculty, or does it go further and embrace something more. We think that the right to life includes the right to live with human dignity and all that goes along with it, namely, the bare necessaries of life such as adequate nutrition, clothing and shelter over the head and facilities for reading, writing and expressing oneself in diverse forms, freely moving about and mixing and co-mingling with fellow human beings".

The finer graces of civilization which make life meaningful must be defended by the New World Human Order. A few more judicial dicta are apt to grasp the noble amplitude of the human right to life.

Pathak, C.J., stated as below in this regard in paragraph 5 of Vikram Deo Singh *vs.* State of Bihar[3]:

"We live in an age when this Court has demonstrated, while interpreting Article 21 of the Constitution, that every person is entitled to a quality of life consistent with his human personality. The right to live with human dignity is the fundamental right of every Indian citizen, and so ... the State recognizes the need for maintaining establishments.

for the care of those unfortunates, both women and children, who are the castaways of an imperfect social order for whom, therefore, of necessity, provision must be made for their protection and welfare".

Sabyasachi Mukherjee, J. as he then was, expressed himself thus in Ramsharan *vs.* Union of India[4]: "It is true that life in its expanded horizons today includes all that give meaning to a man's life including his tradition, culture and heritage, and protection of that heritage in its full measure would certainly come within the encompass of an expanded concept of Article 21 of the Constitution".

The importance of life and liberty was recognized in the following words by Pathak, C.J., in paragraph 7 of Kehar Singh *vs.* Union of India [5]

"To any civilized society, there can be no attributes more important than the life and personal liberty of its members. That is evident from the paramount position given by the courts to Art. 21 of the Constitution. These twin attributes enjoy a fundamental ascendancy over all other attributes of the political and social order, and consequently, the Legislature, the Executive and the Judiciary are more sensitive to them than to the other attributes of daily existence".

Kuldip Singh J. in Mohini Jain[6] added a new dimension: "Right to life is the compendious expression for all those rights which the courts must enforce because they are basic to the dignified enjoyment of life. It extends to the full range of conduct which the individual is free to pursue. The right to education flows directly from the right to life. The right to life under Article 21 and the dignity of an individual cannot be assured unless it is accompanied by the right to education . . .

"Basic needs of man have traditionally been accepted to be three - food, clothing, and shelter. The right to life is guaranteed in any civilized society. That would take within its sweep the right to food, the right to clothing, the right to decent environment and a reasonable accommodation to live in. The difference between the need of an animal and a human being for shelter has to be kept in view. For the animal it is the bare protection of the body; for a human being it has to be a suitable accommodation which would allow him to grow in every aspect - physical, mental and intellectual.

Article 25 (1) of the Universal Declaration of Human Rights, 1948, specifically recognizes "housing" as one of the rights relating to living. Article 11.1 of the International Covenant on Economic, Social and Cultural Rights, 1966, also recognizes "housing" as a part of the right to adequate standard of living. Reference has been made to these documents because they do provide some guide to understand the width of our fundamental rights.

Shakespeare, in *The Merchant of Venice,* says what is sound jurisprudence of human rights. 'You take my life when you take the means whereby I live'.

"Social and economic rights, in short, are as vital as political and civil rights. Indeed, basic human rights are integral and "we murder to dissect". The Third World, wallowing in want and victimized by exploitation, may even regard economic survival as too important to be neglected. There is a point of confluence where materialism, as primary human needs and elimination of suffering, meets spirituality as mate".

The concept of human rights first appeared in a national context, in the French and United States Constitutions, and subsequently in most national constitutions. Regional and international progress in human rights was made first in Europe. International standards were formulated and made legally binding through treaties and global institutions which protected the individual outside the structure of the nation state. Recently, there had been a further breakthrough in the development of human rights. The Geneva decision marked a global acceptance of responsibility for human rights.

Some commentators accused human rights activists of an "overproduction" of human rights. Although human rights activists insisted on the indivisibility of rights, that rights were all of a piece, this was not so. For this there were human rights of many different kinds: the concept was complex and heterogeneous. Historically, different kinds of rights had emerged at different times. In the eighteenth and nineteenth centuries civil and political rights had dominated the discourse. By the end of the nineteenth century and into the twentieth, welfare rights began to emerge. And more recently rights to a clean environment, to peace, and similar concepts had come to the forefront.

Unfortunately, there was now some trend to detach current discourse about human rights from its earlier philosophical roots and use it simply as a basis for claims. This blurred the legal basis for human rights. It is arguable that it would be better to arrive at a narrower set of human rights with a stronger philosophical and political foundation.

Globalization exposed the weaknesses of human rights under the United Nations system. Human rights had been developed in the context of states, and the institutions that protected human rights were national institutions. Human rights had been conceived in terms of protection against national political forces, but now power was shifting from states to globalised economic forces. And there were plenty of abuses from multinational companies, in terms of their employment practices, but the power of these companies was so great that the local national institutions could not do much.

There was a need to rethink the framework of rights. It was often not right to blame the government of a country for lack of rights: it might not be within that government's control. This was to attribute responsibility where no authority existed. To protect human rights in a global context one needed global institutions, but effective institutions were not yet present. Within a national context, central authorities had emerged before rights, and were therefore available to protect rights when these emerged subsequently. Yet in the international context, rights had emerged before the corresponding institutions. One needed a global authority to make human rights universal.

Linking human rights with ethics and globalization represents a connection whose time has come. And yet the task is daunting. Every day brings further evidence of the unacceptable divide in our world; the harsh statistics of millions living in extreme poverty and enduring conflict. The increasing frustration and disillusionment with market-led globalization is evidenced by the protests at the G-8, the World Trade Organization, the European Union and other summits.

We are at the edge of a big idea – the shaping of ethical globalization But how? What are the components, the linkages, and the energies that need to be harnessed? Nearly 14 years have passed since the adoption of two important international declarations, one by the world's governments (the final Declaration and Programme of Action from the World Conference on Human Rights, adopted in Vienna in June 1993), the other by the world's religious leaders (the Declaration of the Religions for a Global Ethic adopted in Chicago just five months later).

These documents were, in many ways, ahead of their time in addressing what world leaders at the UN Millennium Summit identified as the central challenge we face today: ensuring that globalization becomes a positive force for all the world's people.

It is a measure of the rapid pace of social change that neither document refers specifically to the term globalization which has today become so central to our attempt at describing our times. However, both offer the vision and proposals for how I believe we should go about responding to the growing "backlash against globalization".

Building an ethical and sustainable form of globalization is not exclusively a human rights matter, but it must include the recognition of shared responsibility for the universal protection of human rights. That responsibility is shared by all of us, individuals, the religions, corporations, states, international financial institutions and the United Nations - all of us.

Over 50 years ago, the drafters of the Universal Declaration of Human Rights stressed the link between respect for human rights and freedom, justice and peace in the world and called for a just international and social order. That Declaration also affirmed that the true meaning of human rights is one that embraces duties and community as well.

What is emerging is the need for globalization as an economic process to be subject to moral and ethical considerations and to respect international legal standards and principles.

The 144 members of the World Trade Organization have all ratified at least one human rights instrument. All but one have ratified the Convention on the Rights of the Child, and 112 have ratified the International Covenant on Economic, Social and Cultural Rights. When negotiating and implementing international rules on trade liberalization, these governments should bear in mind their concurrent obligations to promote and protect human rights mindful of the declaration made in Vienna Declaration 1993, that "human rights are the first responsibility of governments".

While the WTO agreements provide a legal framework for the economic aspects of the liberalization of trade, the norms and standards of human rights balance this by offering a legal framework for trade liberalization's social and ethical dimensions.

What does that mean in practice? It means answering questions such as:

- Is trade truly free and fair? The developing countries have heard many promises over the years but have too often found that, in practice, access to markets where developing countries hold competitive advantages has been denied.

- Do intellectual property rules consider the cultural rights of indigenous and local communities?
- Are intellectual property rules conducive to ensuring access to drugs under the World Health Organization essential drug list?

On this last question let us consider the issue of AIDS. For all the virus's own neutrality as between nationality, class and gender it is now dominantly infecting and affecting the poorer classes and countries in the developing world, with women increasingly the more vulnerable.

A lack of respect for human rights is linked to virtually every aspect of the AIDS epidemic, from the factors that cause or increase vulnerability to HIV infection, to discrimination based on stigma attached to people living with HIV/AIDS, to the factors that limit the ability of individuals and communities to respond effectively to the epidemic. Our work and that of others has shown that emphasis on the human rights of victims can make a great difference.

Human tragedies of this kind, although not normally on this scale, are often the first disturbers of moral conscience and the first prompters of moral response. Given the global range of the pandemic, only a global response will be effective.

These dimensions of the pandemic would uncover the deeper roots in cultural practices and in the multiple economic, social and health privations. As these are only in part locally or nationally generated, and particularly in the economic sphere are of international origin in even the most remote Zambian village, one is rapidly entangled in the inequities of world trade and the failure of international aid.

Lack of adequate nutrition, of basic medicines, of clean water, of elementary education, of suitable employment, of equality for women, among a multitude of other privations, increase the vulnerability of these poor people to HIV and AIDS. The poverty deprives them in turn of the means of treatment and care which are available to the wealthy.

And just as poverty makes them more vulnerable to HIV so infection and disease in turn increase their poverty through extra medical costs, loss of income, funeral costs and so on. If one were to trace on the globe the lines of the privations contained in the UN Development Programme Human Development annual reports they would coincide almost exactly with the line of infection by HIV.

The insights of the poor, deprived and suffering are essential to our enterprise of developing a globalizing ethic with a human rights component. People living with HIV/ AIDS and their associates could be one matchless source.

A key characteristic of economic globalization is that the actors involved are not only states but private power in the form of multinational or transnational corporations. It is now the case that more than half of the top economies in the world are corporations not states, and international investment is increasingly private.

Thus a new challenge is to ensure that such powerful actors in the globalized economy are accountable for the impact of their policies on human rights.

It is worth noting that it involves the encouragement of self-regulation or ethics to uphold human rights and environmental standards rather than legally binding regulation. However, we should also note that there is considerable debate over whether such ethical codes can be fully effective. There is a trend towards holding companies accountable through legal rules for the human rights and environmental impact of their policies. The Compact calls on business leaders, trade unions and NGOs to join forces behind a set of core values in the areas of human rights, labour standards and the environment.

If globalization is conceived as turning the whole world into one global village in which all peoples are increasingly interconnected and all the fences or barriers are removed, so that the world witnesses a new state of fast and free flow of people, capital, goods and ideas then the world would be witnessing unprecedented enjoyment of human rights every where because globalization is bringing prosperity to all the corners of the globe together with the spread of the highly cherished values of democracy, freedom and justice.[7]

On the other hand if globalization is conceived as turning the world into a global market for goods and services dominated and steered by the powerful gigantic transnational corporations and governed by the rule of profit then all the human rights of the people in the world, particularly in the south would be seriously threatened.[8]

Literature on globalization in general, by both the so called advocates and opponents of globalization is abundant. However, the critics of globalization lay much more emphasis on its impact on human rights, particularly of the poor people and of the developing countries. Their analysis and conclusions are usually supported by facts and figures drawn from international reports and statistics to prove that human rights have been adversely affected by globalization. They usually relate one or the other aspect of human rights to one or the other aspect of globalization, such as relating poverty in developing countries to debt or relating unemployment to privatization, or relating health deterioration to the monopoly of medicine patents. Or they enumerate the aspects of deteriorations in human rights, such as impoverishment and lowering standards of living, increasing inequality discrimination, deprivation of satisfaction of basic needs such as food clean water and housing, illiteracy.... etc. and explain these facts by globalization in general through making comparisons between the state before globalization (usually before the 1990s) and after it, such as stating that "progress in reducing infant mortality was considerably slower during the period of globalization (1990-1998) than over the previous two decades.

The advocates of globalization do not deny the fact that in some regions basic human rights are not respected during the past decade but they explain this by the resistance of some countries and peoples to globalization and they claim that globalization must have winners and losers. The loser's resistance to globalization is attributed to their state of stagnation and rigidity or to their traditional culture or even to the nature of their religions which is anti-democratic and anti-modernization.[9]

Human Rights Violations

Violations of human rights agreements, particularly those of economic, social and cultural rights are not met by practical punishments or deterrence measures the reactions of both international organizations and local human rights groups do not exceed criticism, condemnation or demonstrations at most. On the contrary violations of economic rules of globalization and agreements are met with very severe practical measures such as economic boycotting and cutting of aids.

Many authors provide evidence on the adverse effects of governments adoption of globalization economic agreements on basic human rights due to the reduced overall government spending on services and satisfaction of basic human needs and the increasing tendencies towards privatization of these services.

Vandana Shiva states that "during 1979-81 and 1992-93, calorie intake declined by three per cent in Mexico, 4.1 per cent in Argentina, 10.9 per cent in Kenya, 10.0 per cent in Tanzania, 9.9 per cent in Ethiopia. In India, the per capita cereal consumption declined by 12.2 for rural areas and 5.4 per cent in urban areas. "She explains these figures by saying that countries cannot ensure that the hungry are fed because this involves laws, policies and financial commitments which are protectionist".[10]

She also offers evidence on the impact of globalization agreements on the right to health: "Under the trade Related Intellectual Property agreement of the World Trade Organization, countries have to implement patent laws granting exclusive, monopolistic rights to the pharmaceutical and biotech industry. This prevents countries from producing low cost generic drugs. Patented HIV/AIDS medicine costs $15,000, while generic drugs made by India and Brazil cost $250-300 for one years treatment. Patents are, therefore robbing AIDS victims of their rights."

Diana Smith shows how the policies associated with globalization affected primary health care services. She states that: "introducing the market mechanism into the provision of health care obviously makes services less available to the poor. The privatization of health and hospital services also makes the poor suffer as services become more oriented towards those who can pay. In addition, essential drug policies, which aim to make necessary pharmaceuticals available to all at an affordable price, are threatened by increasingly liberal policies towards pharmaceutical companies. Finally, increasing unemployment and poverty add to the nations health problems by creating extra demands on reduced government services."[11]

The authors of Global Issues state that "the lives of 1.7 million children will be needlessly lost this year (2002) because world governments have failed to reduce poverty levels "and "Progress in life expectancy was also reduced for 4 out of 5 groups of countries, with the exception of the highest group (life expectancy 69-76 years), also "progress in reducing infant mortality was also considerably slower during the last two decades than over the previous decades".[12]

Consequences of Violations of Human Rights

Globalization has brought in its train, great inequities, mass impoverishment and despair. It has fractured society along the existing fault lines of class, gender and community while, almost irreversibly, widening the gap internationally between the rich and the poor nations. While it has enriched a small minority of persons and corporations within nations and within the international system, it has marginalized and violated the basic human rights of millions.

Globalization has resulted in gross human rights violations for millions of workers (particularly women workers), peasants and farmers, and indigenous communities. It has also resulted in serious impairment of the Right to Development of countries and peoples of the South.

No doubt that the widespread violations of human rights is related to the widening gap between the rich and the poor, both on the global and on the local levels. International Statistics prove this fact. It shows that:

- Half the world - nearly three billion people - live on less than two dollars a day.
- The wealthiest nation on earth has the widest gap between rich and poor of any industrialized nation.
- The top fifth of the world's people in the richest countries enjoy 82 per cent of the expanding export trade and 68 per cent of foreign direct investment — while the bottom fifth, barely more than 1 per cent
- A few hundred millionaires now own as much wealth as the world's poorest 2.5 billon people.

(a) (i) So far as workers are concerned, globalization has resulted in the violation of the fundamental right to work. In their drive for profits, companies, in particular TNCs, have been restructuring their operations on a global scale. The result has been massive unemployment. In 1995, the ILO announced that one-third of the world's willing-to-work population was either underemployed or unemployed, the worst situation since the 1930s. In its latest available report (2006-07), the ILO notes that the world unemployment situation still remains "grim". It is only fair to add that the ILO Report does not attribute this "grim" unemployment situation solely or even mainly to globalization, arguing that "economic liberalization" will bring far greater gains as compared to the alternative of protectionism. While conceding that there is "some basis" for concerns about "the negative social effects of globalization", it contends that it is "not true that globalization is an overwhelming supra-national force that has largely usurped national policy autonomy ..." It asserts that "national policies can, and should, give priority to mitigating negative effects on globalization" of financial markets), and the desperate and helpless attempts by the national regimes to come to grips with the soaring unemployment situation in the face of the continuing onslaught of the "supra-national" financial markets, the above bland assertion about "national policies" has an air of unreality about it. The goal of full employment, which was one of the pillars of the social consensus that prevailed after the Second World War, has been jettisoned by nearly all governments.

(ii) Globalization has also engendered or accentuated the process of the casualization of labour and the informalization of labour. Employers are increasingly resorting to employing workers on part-time, short-term, contracts. They are also resorting to the informal economy by farming out or sub-contracting work, e.g. in textiles and electronics. More ominously, many factories which were previously part of the formal economy have moved their operations entirely to non-unionized workforces in new locations and/or sub-contracted units. Here, not only are the wages low, but the legal protection of workers is minimal.

To obtain some idea of the size and scale involved in this process of informalization, we need only turn to India. A mere 8 per cent of the labour force is in the formal economy while over 90 per cent work in the informal economy. The latter are not unionized, have little or no legal protection or security and are subject to ruthless exploitation. Significantly, more than 50 per cent of the workers in this sector are women.

When the Indian Government adopted a policy of economic liberalization in 1991, many companies (including TNCs) with factories in the high-wage city of Mumbai (formerly Bombay), got rid of their unionized labour force (mostly male workers) by a variety of insidious means and moved their operations to low-wage and depressed areas to avail themselves of the large supply of unorganized and unprotected, mainly female, labour.

This trend is not peculiar to Bombay but is a fact of life under globalization in all the major industrial areas in India. Amrita Chhachhi, an activist, describes the problems of women workers in the electronics industry in Delhi thus: "As a result of the current economic policy, even well known TV firms [are] sub-contracting industrial work. This has resulted in a large number of small ancillary units where women are employed at below minimum wages. These units are so flexible that they can close down operations and relocate them at short notice. As a result, all attempts at organizing women labourers have been failures. It has become extremely difficult to even trace the movement of these units from location to location. Unionization is impossible in this scenario."[13]

(iii) Globalization, with its demand for "flexible" labour, has resulted in the "feminization of labour". The point is that the overwhelming majority of female labour in the South is concentrated in low-wage industries such as textile, clothing and footwear production. Workers in such industries are not only inadequately protected as regards health and safety, but they also do not enjoy security of employment in view of the tendency of such investors to move offshore to cut costs. Thus, textile workers in South Korea have been retrenched as a result of the relocation of their factories to countries such as Bangladesh and Vietnam.

(iv) Mention must also be made here of the fact that the impact of globalization on traditional cottage industries has also adversely affected women workers. Thus, cheap imports have resulted in the closure of a number of such industries in India and Pakistan and the retrenchment of their largely women workers.

(v) Finally, globalization has, by intensifying the tendencies towards uneven development within countries and within regions, intensified the development of the phenomenon of migrant workers. Such workers (especially those who cross national frontiers) are subject to a whole range of human rights violations – discrimination, absence of labour protection, low wages, and physical and (in the case of women) sexual abuse.

(b) Globalization poses a serious threat to the right of livelihood of millions of traditional farmers in the South. As the hitherto protected agricultural sector of the South is, in compliance with the requirements of the GATT Final Act, opened up to imports (mainly from the North) and as land laws are revised to facilitate corporate farming, there will inevitably be large-scale displacement of such communities. Fears have also been expressed that the patenting of seeds by multinationals such as Cargill will result in traditional farmers being displaced. This concern has given rise to massive demonstrations by farmers, particularly in India.

All these developments, and in particular the drive under the WTO regime to make access to food mainly dependent upon market mechanisms, are a threat to food security – the most fundamental of all human rights.

(c) Globalization has provided a new impetus to the destruction of the habitat and livelihood of indigenous communities in many countries of the South. The continuing displacement of such communities as a consequence of the intensification of such economic activities as mining and logging is a grim reminder of such violations of human rights.

(d) Where the mechanism for promoting globalization has been the IMP/World Bank, SAP, it has resulted in a massive violation of human rights. Analyzing the impact of such programmes on the realization and enjoyment of selected economic, social and cultural rights. Danilo Turk, a Special Rapporteur for the Commission on Human Rights, in a report prepared for the UN, pointed out that these programmes had resulted in a violation of the right to work, the right to food, the right to adequate housing, the right to health, the right to education and the right to development.[14] The combined effect of the violation of the right to food and the right to health has had devastating consequences. According to Davison Budhoo, an economist who had worked with both the World Bank and the IMP before he quit the latter in protest against its policies, on the basis of the figures released by UNICEF, it is estimated that those policies led directly to the death of 70 million children under 5 years in the Third World between the years 1982-1990 and indirectly to the destitution and impoverishment of several hundred millions more.[15]

As for the violation of the Declaration on the Right to Development, which was adopted at the UN General Assembly in 1986, the Report of the UN Global Consultation on the Realization of the Right to Development as a Human Right observes:

Failure to take into account the principles of the right to development in agreements between states and the World

Bank, IMP and commercial banks with regard to external debt repayment and structural adjustment frustrates the realization of the right to development and of all human rights. The prevailing terms of trade, monetary policy, and certain conditions tied to bilateral and multilateral aid, which are all perpetuated by the non-democratic decision-making processes of international economic, financial and trade institutions, also frustrate the full realization of the right to development.[16]

If the proposal by the EU for an MIA within the framework of the WTO or the proposal for an MAI by the OECD is adopted, then the Right to Development, so far as countries of the South are concerned, will be further whittled away.

The Right to Development "implies the full realization of the right of peoples to self-determination", which includes "the exercise of their inalienable right to full sovereignty over all their natural wealth and resources". The same right also includes the right of peoples and nations "to freely pursue their economic, social and cultural development." As the adoption of the MIA or the MAI will result in the loss of countries' right to regulate the entry, behaviour and operations of foreign investment in the interests of their own people, it is not difficult to appreciate why it is bound to result in an impairment of the Right to Development.

Conclusion

It is clear that, more than ever, the cards are stacked against the South. When these countries attained political independence in the 1950s and 1960s, the whole question of the path of development open to them came into question. After some fitful starts, it became evident that it was not possible for the countries of the South to embark on the path of industrialization (which was perceived as the only way to escape from the blight of underdevelopment) by integrating themselves into the international capitalist system. The only alternative open to them was to opt for the path of independent self-sustained development, with the state taking the leading role.

Consequences of violation of human rights leads to an increasing feelings of deprivation and injustice among the populations of the different countries of the world which is enhanced by the rapid and unprecedented advance in communication and information technologies, which really turned the world in this respect into a global village, the deprived are exposed daily, if not every minute to images and evidences of the huge gap in standards of living between the rich and the poor.

Some consequences of this deprivations of human rights are social and political unrest and even violence and counter violence. It also leads to an increasing resort to suppression and to chaos. Paradoxically the expenditure on suppressing protest and violence may be equal to or even exceeds the ought to be expenditure on implementing economic, social and cultural human rights for all the peoples of the world. What matters more is the loss of human lives and the loss of constructive contributions which all the deprived could have offered to the economic, social, scientific and cultural advancement of humanity if they were granted their basic human rights. Racism, prejudices, and discrimination are negatively associated with justice and implementation of human rights.

There is enough evidence that the world wealth is in general, rapidly increasing due to the advance in science and technology and that it is more than enough to satisfy the needs of all the dwellers of the globe. What is needed is the globalization of human rights and prosperity, but how?

This whole thesis was, however, challenged by the recent phase of globalization when a small number of countries in East Asia began to display dramatic economic results by opening up and deregulating their economies and integrating them with the international capitalist system.

The North paraded these countries as models which the rest of the countries of the South should emulate. As a result, country after country began to queue up in the quest for "Tigerhood".

With the onset of the financial crisis in Asia, the illusion that globalization is the way out for the countries of the South is now being laid to rest. Clearly, the whole question of the path of development which nations of the South should opt for is as open as ever. It is hoped that this crisis will provide an opportunity for some re-thinking, debate and hard decisions.

NOTES

1. Field J., in Murm *vs.* Illinois, 94 U.S. 113.
2. Francis Coralic Mullin, 1981 S. C. 746.
3. Vikram Deo Singh *vs.* State of Bihar, AIR 1988 S.C. 1782
4. Ramsharan *vs.* Union of India, AIR 1989 S.C. 549, paragraph 13
5. Kehar Singh *vs.* Union of India, AIR 1989 S.C. 6531 paragraph 7
6. Kuldip Singh J. in Mohini Jain, 1992 (3) S.C.C. 666
7. Friedman, Thomas L., *The Lexus and the Olive Tree : Understanding Globalization,* Cairo: International Publishers, 1999.
8. Paul L. S.J., Education for Globalization, America : America Press, 2002.
9. Hufbaur, Gray C., *Globalization Facts and Consequences,* Institute for International Economics, 2001.
10. Vandana Shiva, "Violence of Globalization", *The Hindu* (New Delhi, India) March 25, 2001.
11. Diana Smith, What Does Globalization Mean for Health?, Third World Network, 1999.
12. Global Issues, Causes of Poverty, http://www.globalizationissues.org/Traderelated/Facts.asp
13. Hensman, R., "Minimum Labour Standards and Trade Agreements: An Overview of the Debate", *Economic and Political Weekly,* 20-27 April, 1996.
14. Danilo Turk, "How World Bank — IMF Policies Adversely Affect Human Rights", *Third World Resurgence,* May 1993, p. 23.
15. Budhoo, D., "IMF—World Bank Wreak Havoc on Third World", *Third World Resurgence,* July 1992, p. 17.
16. Danilo Turk, "How World Bank — IMF Policies Adversely Affect Human Rights", *op. cit.*

9

GLOBALIZATION

Myth or Reality

MANOJ RAJAN

People around the world are more connected to each other today than ever before. Information and money flow more quickly than ever and leaves its impact on every sphere of human activity. Goods and services produced in one part of the world are increasingly available in all parts of the world within the blink of eyes. International travel is more frequent and international communication is commonplace.

We live in an intensely interdependent world in which all the peoples on the earth with their immense differences of culture and historical experience are compressed together in instant communication. We face today a world of almost infinite promise, which is also a world of terminal danger. This phenomenon has been titled "Globalization."

The word 'globalization' is now used widely to sum up today's world order. It means they increasingly integrate the world into one capitalist political economy operating under a neo-liberal free market ideology. Economic globalization as witnessed in the world today is not a new phenomenon. It has been evolving for the past several years and gaining momentum day by day. The trend, at present, is a shift from a world economy based on national market economies to a borderless global market economy increasingly governed by one set of rules. In this context, globalization means global economic liberalization, developing a global financial system and a transnational production system which is based on a homogenized worldwide law of value. The demise of the Cold War helped the emergence of a new aggressive competitive global economic order. This was possible mainly due to the integration of the newly industrialized countries and much of the developing nations. Although globalization and market liberalization have made some progress in terms of economic growth in certain countries, it has also had many negative impacts in developing societies.

The so called Era of Globalization is fast becoming the preferred term for describing the current times. Just as the Depression, the Cold War Era, the Space Age, and the Roaring 20's are used to describe particular periods of history; Globalization describes the political, economic, and cultural atmosphere of today which we can feel in every aspects of our life. While some people think of Globalization as primarily a synonym for global business, it is much more than that. The same forces that allow businesses to operate as if national borders did not exist also allow social activists, labour organizers, journalists, academics, international terrorists and many others to work on a global stage.

Globalization, although often described as the cause of much turbulence and change, is in fact the umbrella term for the collective effect, the change itself. Globalization (i.e. the aggregate change we observe in our factories, storefronts, indeed generally across our economies and lifestyles) is caused by four fundamental forms of capital movement throughout the global economy. The main four important capital flows includes: Human Capital which includes Immigration, Migration, Emigration and Deportation etc. Financial Capital which includes Aid, Equity, Debt, Credit and Lending etc. Resource Capital which includes Energy, Metals, Minerals and Lumber, etc. Power Capital which includes Security Forces, Alliances, and Armed Forces etc.[1]

Most of the stresses and complexities confronted in the general macro affairs of countries, communities, and the interactions between them, can be traced to these four main flows. Connectivity available via cheaper telecommunications and modes of travel— made more accessible to more people facilitates these interactions at a rate unprecedented in history. Cultural and political frictions at all levels can thus be explained as arising from the difference in opinion between two or more parties about the origination, treatment, timing, ownership or value of one.

The International Monetary Fund (IMF) defines globalization as the growing economic interdependence of countries worldwide through increasing volume and variety of cross-border transactions in goods and services, free international capital flows, and more rapid and widespread diffusion of technology. Meanwhile, The International Forum on Globalization defines it as the present worldwide drive toward a globalized economic system dominated by supranational corporate trade and banking institutions that are not accountable to democratic processes or national governments. While notable critical theorists, such as Immanuel Wallerstein, emphasize that globalization cannot be understood separately from the historical development of the capitalist world-system.[2] The different definitions highlight the ensuing debate of the roles and relationships of government, corporations, and the individual in maximizing social welfare within the globalization paradigms. Nonetheless, it is clear that globalization has economic, political, cultural, and technological aspects that may be closely intertwined.

"Globalization" has different means and we can summarizes it in following way:

- Globalism, if the concept is reduced to its economic aspects, can be said to contrast with economic nationalism and protectionism. It is related to laissez-faire capitalism and neo-liberalism.

- It shares a number of characteristics with internationalization and is often used interchangeably, although some prefer to use globalization to emphasize the erosion of the nation-state or national boundaries.
- In its cultural form, globalization has been a label used to identify attempts to erode the national cultures of Europe, and subsume them into a global culture whose members will be much easier to manipulate through mass media and controlled governments. In this context, massive legal or illegal immigration has been allowed, mainly in European countries.
- The formation of a global village closer contact between different parts of the world, with increasing possibilities of personal exchange, mutual understanding and friendship between "world citizens", and creation of a global civilization.
- Economic globalization there are four aspects to economic globalization, referring to four different flows across boundaries, namely flows of goods/services, i.e. 'free trade', flows of people, of capital, and of technology. A consequence of economic globalization is increasing relations among members of an industry in different parts of the world, with a corresponding erosion of national sovereignty in the economic sphere. The IMF defines globalization as the growing economic interdependence of countries worldwide through increasing volume and variety of cross-border transactions in goods and services, freer international capital flows, and more rapid and widespread diffusion of technology. [3]
- In the field of management, globalization is a marketing or strategy term that refers to the emergence of international markets for consumer goods characterized by similar customer needs and tastes enabling, for example, selling the same cars or soaps or foods with similar ad campaigns to people in

different cultures. This usage is contrasted with internationalization which describes the activities of multinational companies dealing across borders in financial instruments, commodities, or products that are extensively tailored to local markets. Globalization also means cross-border management activities or development processes to adapt to the emergence of a globalized market or to seek and realize benefit from economies of scale or scope or from cross-border learning among different country-based organizations.

- In the field of software, globalization is a technical term that combines the development processes of internationalization and localization.
- Many, such as participants in the World Social Forum, use the term "corporate globalization" or "global corporatization" to highlight the impact of multinational corporations and the use of legal and financial means to circumvent local laws and standards, in order to leverage the labour and services of unequally-developed regions against each other.

There is much academic discussion about whether globalization is a real phenomenon or only an analytical artifact (a myth). Although the term is widespread, many authors argue that the characteristics attributed to globalization have already been seen at other moments in history. Also, many note that such features, including the increase in international trade and the greater role of multinational corporations. Some authors prefer the term internationalization rather than globalization while they mean business. In internationalization, the role of the state and the importance of nations are greater, while in globalization, we found missing the term nation states most of the occasion. So, they argue that the frontiers of countries, in a broad sense, are far from being dissolved, and therefore this globalization process is not happening, and probably will not happen, considering that in world history, internationalization never turned into globalization (the European Union and NAFTA are yet to prove their case). Some maintain that globalization is an imagined geography;[4] that is, a political tool of ruling neo-liberalists, who are attempting to use certain images and discourses of world politics to justify their political agendas.

Critics of the economic aspects of globalization contend that it is not, as its proponents tend to imply, an inexorable process that flows naturally from the economic needs of everyone. The critics typically emphasize that globalization is a process that is mediated according to elite imperatives, and typically raise the possibility of alternative global institutions and policies, which they believe address the moral claims of poor and working classes throughout the globe, as well as environmental concerns in a more equitable way. In terms of the controversial global migration issue, disputes revolve around both its causes, whether and to what extent it is voluntary or involuntary, necessary or unnecessary increase in international flow of capital including foreign direct investment.

In terms of the controversial global migration issue, disputes revolve around its causes, whether and to what extent it is voluntary or involuntary, necessary or unnecessary; and its effects, whether beneficial, or socially and environmentally costly. Proponents tend to see migration simply as a process whereby white and blue collar workers may go from one country to another to provide their services, while critics tend to emphasize negative causes such as economic, political, and environmental insecurity, and cite as one notable effect, the link between migration and the enormous growth of urban slums in developing countries. According to "The Challenge of Slums," a 2003 UN-Habitat report, "the cyclical nature of capitalism, increased demand for skilled *versus* unskilled labour, and the negative effects of globalization "in particular, global economic booms and busts that ratchet up inequality and distribute new wealth unevenly"[5] contribute to the enormous growth of slums.

Various aspects of globalization are seen as harmful by public-interest activists as well as strong state nationalists. This movement has no unified name. "Anti-globalization" is the media's preferred term; it can lead to some confusion, as activists typically oppose certain aspects or forms of globalization, not globalization per se. Activists themselves, for example Noam Chomsky, have said that this name is meaningless as the aim of the movement is to globalize justice. Indeed, the global justice movement is a common name. Many activists also unite under the slogan "another world is possible", which has given rise to names such as *altermondialisme* in French.

Economic arguments by fair trade theorists claim that unrestricted free trade benefits those with more financial leverage (i.e. the rich) at the expense of the poor. Many "anti-globalization" activists see globalization as the promotion of a corporatist agenda, which is intent on constricting the freedoms of individuals in the name of profit. Some "anti-globalization" groups argue that globalization is necessarily imperialistic, is one of the driving reasons behind the Iraq war and is forcing savings to flow into the United States rather than developing nations; it can therefore be said that "globalization" is another term for a form of Northernization, as it is believed by some observers that the Northern countries are truly beneficiaries of globalization.

Some argue that globalization imposes credit-based economics, resulting in unsustainable growth of debt and debt crises. The financial crises in Southeast Asia, that began in the relatively small, debt-ridden economy of Thailand but quickly spread to Malaysia, Indonesia, South Korea and eventually was felt all around the world, demonstrated the new risks and volatility in rapidly changing globalized markets. The IMF's subsequent 'bailout' money came with conditions of political change (i.e. government spending limits) attached and came to be viewed by critics as undermining national sovereignty in *neo-colonialist* fashion. Anti-Globalization activists pointed to the meltdowns as proof of the high human cost of the indiscriminate global economy.

The main opposition is to *unfettered* globalization[6] (Neoliberal; laissez-faire capitalism), guided by governments and what are claimed to be quasi-governments (such as the International Monetary Fund and the World Bank) that are supposedly not held responsible to the populations that they govern and instead respond mostly to the interests of corporations. Many conferences between trade and finance ministers of the core globalizing nations have been met with large, and occasionally violent, protests from opponents of "corporate globalism".

Some "anti-globalization" activists object to the fact that the current "globalization" globalizes money and corporations, but not people and unions. This can be seen in the strict immigration controls in nearly all countries, and the lack of labour rights in many countries in the developing world.

Another more conservative camp opposed to globalization is state-centric nationalists who fear globalization is displacing the role of nations in global politics and point to NGOs as encroaching upon the power of individual nations. Some advocates of this warrant for anti-globalization are Pat Buchanan and Jean-Marie Le Pen.

Supporters of democratic globalization can be labelled pro-globalists. They consider that the first phase of globalization, which was market-oriented, should be completed by a phase of building global political institutions representing the will of world citizens. The difference with other globalists is that they do not define in advance any ideology to orient this will, which should be left to the free choice of those citizens via a democratic process.

Supporters of free trade point out that economic theories of comparative advantage suggest that free trade leads to a more efficient allocation of resources, with all countries involved in the trade benefiting. In general, this leads to lower prices, more employment and higher output.

Libertarians and other proponents of laissez-faire capitalism say higher degrees of political and economic freedom in the form of democracy and capitalism in the developed world are both ends in themselves and also produce higher levels of material wealth. They see globalization as the beneficial spread of liberty and capitalism.

Critics argue that the anti-globalization movement uses anecdotal evidence to support their view and that worldwide statistics instead strongly support globalization:

- The percentage of people in developing countries living below US$1 per day has halved in only twenty years, although some critics argue that more detailed variables measuring poverty should instead be studied.
- Life expectancy has almost doubled in the developing world since Second World War II and is starting to close the gap to the developed world where the improvement has been smaller. Child mortality has decreased in every developing region of the world. Income inequality for the world as a whole is diminishing.
- Democracy has increased dramatically from almost no nation with universal suffrage in 1900 to 62.5 per cent of all nations in 2000.
- The proportion of the world's population living in countries where per-capita food supplies are less than 2,200 calories (9,200 kilo joules) per day decreased from 56 per cent in the mid-1960s to below 10 per cent by the 1990s.

- Between 1950 and 1999, global literacy increased from 52 to 81 per cent of the world. Women made up much of the gap: Female literacy as a percentage of male literacy has increased from 59 per cent in 1970 to 80 per cent in 2000.
- The percentage of children in the labour force has fallen from 24 per cent in 1960 to 10 per cent in 2000.
- There are similar trends for electric power, cars, radios, and telephones per capita, as well as the proportion of the population with access to clean water.

However, some of these improvements may not be due to globalization, or may be possible without the current form of globalization or its negative consequences, to which the global justice movement objects.

Some pro-capitalists are also critical of the World Bank and the IMF, arguing that they are corrupt bureaucracies controlled and financed by states, not corporations. Many loans have been given to dictators who never carried out promised reforms, instead leaving the common people to pay the debts later. They thus see too little capitalism, not too much. They also note that some of the resistance to globalization comes from special interest groups with conflicting interests, like Western world unions. However, there are also many anti-capitalists who are against the World Bank and the IMF because they believe they are too capitalist and only in interests for profit.

Others, such as Senator Douglas Roche, O.C., simply view globalization as inevitable and advocate creating institutions such as a directly-elected United Nations Parliamentary Assembly to exercise oversight over unelected international bodies.[7]

Richard Barnet of the Institute of Policy Studies describes globalization in terms of four increasing webs of global commercial activity: *global cultural bazaar, the global shopping mall; the global financial network; the global work-place.*[8] The global cultural bazaar promotes the notion of uniform cultural values and products across the world. This idea influenced billions of people, shaping their goals and homogenizing their tastes and attitudes towards a desired fantasy lifestyle. The unprecedented increase in global trade – the buying and selling of goods and services among countries – has created a planetary supermarket. The cultural bazaar and shopping mall intersect through the vehicle of advertising. Media has become a powerful player in the globalization process.

In fact, globalization of economies has also led to the globalization of media. Media is used to impose the culture and power of the wealthy nations from the global North. The global financial market has created a new atmosphere to search for quick profits. The foreign exchange market is mainly dealing with currency speculation, bet for or against foreign currencies. The increasing mobility of jobs has created global workplaces and this has boosted international labour migration.

In other words, the globalization and market-oriented economic reforms helped transnational companies shift their manufacturing units to developing countries. Because of this more people are crossing borders in search of jobs and in most conditions people are forced to work in inhuman conditions for lower wages. All these proved the fact that globalization is not a simple but a very complex set of process that operates at multiple levels – political, economic and cultural. Nicaraguan scholar Xabier Gorostiaga argues that in "this era of globalization humanity is perceived as fundamentally one, with a common destiny that is the result of a technological revolution in information and communication and the awareness of the unsustainability of the current way of life".[9]

In an article titled "The Human Rights Debate in an Era of Globalization: Hegemony of Discourse"[10], Nikhil Aziz describes two kinds of globalization based on Richard Falks theory on the making of Global Citizenship. He argues that we can see globalization in different perspectives: Globalization from Above (GA) and Globalization from Below (GB). At the political level, GA manifests itself in its action of the Western countries, particularly the United States of America, and global financial institutions in pressuring countries of the South to democratize. This translates as the adoption of a Western-style liberal democratic system of governance. They closely tie economic Globalization from above to the political aspect in that (1) the source of pressure for change is the same, and (2) close links are alleged between the ideologies of free markets and free societies. Economic Globalization from above entails countries of the South to accept—within the parameters of the dominant World capitalist system—the imposition of Structural Adjustment Programmes (SAP), neo-liberal economic policies, including the wholesale liberalization of domestic economies, to allow unrestricted entry to transnational capital. On a cultural level, GA arises from the control of the global information and communication networks by Western media corporations; and the spread of modern technologies of a consumerist culture, and Western cultural expressions as the global culture.

Globalization has substantially contributed to the intensification of debt, poverty and economic crisis in the developing world. The Structural Adjustment Programmes (SAP) designed and imposed by the global creditor institutions is a typical instrument to create a favourable atmosphere for globalization, which ultimately affects developing countries. In order to meet the mandates set by the SAP, a country spends less by cutting back government expenditures, social services, and economic investments so that resources can be placed elsewhere. More money is being spent on export orientation, which results in local economies becoming dependent on the integration with the world economy. The international lenders demand poor economies to divert substantial resources away from sectors serving domestic needs: withdraw all subsidies for poor people, privatize the state sector, deregulate the market, and decrease wages. In effect, this process opens up countries to globalization. Thus structural adjustment programs and import-export-led strategies of industrialization were becoming the part of a political and economic restructuring process, a prelude to globalization.

The advocates of globalization give philosophical justifications to accept export-led growth, lower wages and living standards for workers, shrinking government budgets, and extremely high interest rates. They say "There Is No Alternative"—TINA, the phrase coined by British Prime Minister Margaret Thatcher in 1980s. Powerful institutions like the International Monetary Fund, the World Bank and the World Trade Organization raise the TINA, argument to persuade the developing nations to qualify themselves to borrow money. The developing countries are left into no option but to accept the liberalization and market-oriented reforms. Under this liberalization policy production tends to be export-oriented. Meeting the basic needs of the people becomes less important. State-run factories or enterprises are often privatized to suit the needs of foreign investors. Free trade and liberalization lead to competition and local producers, like farmers, have to suffer the consequences.

Globalization has created a situation where the role and importance of nation-state is becoming irrelevant. Kenichi Ohmae, widely recognized as one of today's top business gurus, asks, in a world where economic borders are disappearing and money flows around the globe beyond the reach of governments, 'who, indeed needs the nation-state?" He argues that 4 Is-Investment (sic), Industry, Information technology and Individual consumers[11] — make the traditional middleman function of nation-states, and of their governments, largely unnecessary. Because, the global markets for all the is work just fine on their own, nation-states no longer have to play a market-making role. In this situation multi-national corporations are becoming the actors even in international politics. A growing trend to promote the idea of recapturing the capitalist frontier and its lost values is more visible through the globalization and market liberalization in the developing countries.

It is true that a few rich or middle class people have emerged in societies where transition to market system has been introduced. China and Vietnam are typical examples. In these countries a newly rich class has emerged as a result of globalization and market reforms. Several other Asian countries are also witnessing the emergence of a few—rich and middle class people at the expenses of many poor. These new rich and middle class are really the products of globalization and they provide the market for imported products and further strengthening the economy of the developed countries.

While analyzing the economic development, social status and political consciousness of the new rich in Asia, Richard Robinson and David S. G. Goodman observe that it is as consumers that the new rich of Asia have attracted an interest of almost cargo-cult proportions in the West. They constitute the new markets for Western products: processed foods, computer software, educational services and films and television soaps. They are the new tourists, bringing foreign exchange in hard times. What has helped such an enthusiastic embrace of the Asian new rich is that they are emerging at a time when prolonged recession and low growth rates have depressed home markets in the West.[12]

The emergence of the new middle class and their wealth manifest themselves in the society in several ways. This is more visible through a new emerging culture, which Robinson and Goodman describe as Mobile phones, McDonalds and middle-class revolution. It is estimated that 55,000 people a day regularly pass through the McDonalds restaurant in central Beijing (China's first, opened in 1992)

– to pay for a hamburger much more than the most Chinese will earn in a fortnight.[13] This McDonald and Mobile phone culture has already spread among the new-rich in many developing countries because of the globalization of markets. Even Cambodia and Bangladesh the world's most poverty stricken countries, are affected. A globalization of taste has occurred in every field of the developing world.

Consumer goods like Levis Jeans, Nike athletic shoes, and Hermes scarves are visible all over the world now. A decade ago Kenichi Ohmae described this process[14], driven by global exposure to the same information, the same cultural icons, and the same advertisements, as the "Californiazation" of taste. He now argues that, today, however, the process of convergence goes faster and deeper. It reaches well beyond taste to much more fundamental dimensions of world-view, mind-set.

There are now, for example, tens of millions of teenagers around the world who, having been raised in a multimedia-rich environment, have a lot more in common with each other than they do with members of older generations in their own cultures.[15] Well, one group is considering this an achievement of globalization. On the other hand, the reality is that, "globalization requires the humiliation of hundreds of millions of people keeping them in constant insecurity, pitting them against one another in a competitive struggle for survival".[16] The Human Development Report of 1997 says; Globalization can also shift patterns of consumption. Luxury cars and soft drinks can rapidly become a part of daily life, heightening relative deprivation. The pattern can increase absolute poverty by undermining the production of goods on which poor people rely. A flood of imported wheat can shift consumption away from sorghum or cassava, making them scarcer in loyal markets.

Globalization has brought in its train, great inequities, mass impoverishment and despair. It has fractured society along the existing fault lines of class, gender and community while, almost irreversibly, widening the gap internationally between the rich and the poor nations. While it has enriched a small minority of persons and corporations within nations and within the international system, it has marginalized and violated the basic human rights of millions.

Globalization has resulted in gross human rights violations for millions of workers (particularly women workers), peasants and farmers, and indigenous communities. It has also resulted in serious impairment of the Right to Development of countries and peoples of the South.

(i) So far as workers are concerned, globalization has resulted in the violation of the fundamental right to work. In their drive for profits, companies, in particular TNCs, have been restructuring their operations on a global scale. The result has been massive unemployment. In 1995, the ILO announced that one-third of the world's willing-to-work population was underemployed or unemployed, the worst situation since the 1930s. In its latest available report (1996-97), the ILO notes that the world unemployment situation still remains "grim".[17] The goal of full employment, which was one of the pillars of the social consensus that prevailed after the Second World War, has been jettisoned by nearly all governments.

(ii) Globalization has also engendered or accentuated the process of the casualization of labour and the informalization of labour. Employers are increasingly resorting to employing workers on part-time, short-term, contracts. They are also resorting to the informal economy by farming out or sub-contracting work, e.g. in textiles and electronics. More ominously, many factories, which were previously part of the formal economy, have moved their operations entirely to non-unionized workforces in new locations and/or sub-contracted units. Here, not only are the wages low, but also the legal protection of workers is minimal.

There are also various debates about the mutual impact of terrorism and globalization show the multifaceted relationship between the two phenomena going on. Summarizing briefly the arguments exposed so far it could be said that globalization provides means for the global terrorism by its technological advances; it also gives causes for such terrorism primarily by creating great discrepancies in the economic conditions in various countries of the world. While analyzing the relationship between globalization and causes of terrorism, it is also perceived as a resistance to the domination of the United States in the world. The world itself, in words of Baudrillard, resists domination. These arguments lead are connected with the idea that terrorism became truly a global actor, which is confirmed by the fact that such organizations as Al Qaeda achieve truly global dimensions. It uses global networks and advances causes that are deeply connected with the way the politics of the world function.

On the other hand, the analysts who promote the idea that because of the threat of terrorism the process of globalization will be just advanced also have important arguments. The process of globalization does not seem to have stopped and the form of it is not much different from the one experienced before the September 11th attacks either. To the contrary, the assertion of hegemony by United States has recently reached rather impressive dimensions. The world is gathered around the United States in its fight against terrorism, which also means the affirmation of its dominant position in the world.

Globalization has its winners and losers. With the expansion of trade, market, foreign investment, developing countries have seen the gaps among themselves widen. The imperative to liberalize has demanded a shrinking of state involvement in national life, producing a wave of privatization, cutting jobs, slashing health, education and food subsidies, etc. affecting the poor people in society. In many cases, liberalization has been accompanied by greater inequality and people are left trapped in utter poverty. Meanwhile, in many industrialized countries unemployment has soared to levels not seen for many years and income disparity to levels not recorded since last century. The collapses of the economies of the Asian Tigers are examples of this. The Human Development Report of 1997 revealed that poor countries and poor people too often find their interests neglected as a result of globalization. Although globalization of the economy has been characterized as a locomotive for productivity, opportunity, technological progress, and uniting the world, it ultimately causes increased impoverishment, social disparities and violations of human rights. That is what we see today.

NOTES

1. "Confronting Globalization", Shelly Walia, *The Hindu*, September 9, 2007.
2. *Ibid.*
3. IMF, *World Economic Outlook*, May, 1997.
4. Walia, *op.cit.*
5. "The Challenge of Slums", *UN- Habitat Report, 2003.*
6. Walia, *op.cit.*
7. *Ibid.*
8. Cited in Carole, Collins, "A World in Mutation", *WSCF Journal*, December 1995.
9. Xabier, Gorostiga, Jeremy Brecher, (ed.), *Latin America in the New World Order in Global Visions: Beyond the New World Order,)* (Bostan, MA: South End Press, 1993), p. 67
10. Nikhil Aziz, "The Human Rights Debate in an Era of Globalisation: Hegemony of Discourse". *Bulletin of Concerned Asian Scholars*, Vol. 27, No 4, Oct-Dec., 1995.
11. Kenichi Ohmae: *The End of the Nation State*, (New York: The Press, 1995), pp. 2-5.

12. Robinson Richard and Goodman David S.G.(eds). "The New Rich in Asia: Economic Development, Social Status and Political Consciousness", *The New Rich is Asia,* London: Routledge, 1996, p. 1.
13. *Ibid.* p. 226
14. Ohame, *Op.cit,* p. 15.
15. *Ibid.*
16. Seabrooke Jermey, "Internationalism *versus* Globalisation", *Asia-APEC Internet message,* September 11, 1996.
17. International Labour Resources and Information Group, "Getting to Grips with Globalisation", *Workers World,* No 3-4, January-February, 1996.

PART - II

10

NEHRU AND GLOBALIZATION

MOHAMMED KHALID

Global vision of India has been deeply indebted to Jawaharlal Nehru, the architect of modern India. This vision started to develop during the freedom movement in the form of various resolutions passed by the Indian National Congress.[1] Throughout the national struggle for freedom Nehru remained the chief statesman of Congress on foreign policy and India's world view. As head of Foreign Department of the All India Congress Committee, Jawaharlal Nehru consistently explained the Congress position on various issues facing the world and the fundamentals of India's foreign policy well before 1947. The opposition to imperialism, liberal internationalism, neutralism, neo-Marxism and Gandhian internationalism were made by him as the leading ideological currents in India's foreign policy after its independence.[2]

As the clutches of European colonial powers weakened and the freedom dawned over the countries of Asia, Africa and Latin America, Nehru pronounced anti-imperialist stance and projected neo-Marxist and liberal understanding of India's world view. The Constitution of India, which too has a strong stamp of Nehru, embedded the liberal internationalism in its Article 51, which enjoins upon India, "...to promote international peace and security, maintain just and honourable relations between nations; foster respect in international law and treaty obligations in the dealing of organized peoples with one another; and encourage settlement of international disputes by arbitration."[3]

As the Cold War set in, Nehru advocated and promoted the idea of neutralism in India's foreign policy. This, neutrality was named as non-alignment and turned to be the credo, posture and vehicle of India's foreign policy.[4] The neutrality of Nehru did not mean the shirking away from the world politics. In a speech in Washington in 1949 he said, "Where freedom is menaced and justice threatened or where aggression takes place, we can not be and shall not be neutral."[5] In the Cold war context, Nehru looked at the world from a rational and pragmatic prism. Strongly favouring an independent foreign policy he rejected the idea of being with anybody. His global vision reflected in his first official broadcast on September 7, 1946 as Vice-President of Executive Council of Viceroy of India. He termed non-alignment an active foreign policy of full participation in world affairs, anti-colonialism, and opposition to racist policies, international cooperation to create one world. As a great apostle of the Non-Alignment, in March 1947 Nehru said, "for too long, we of Asia have been petitioners in western courts and chancelleries. That story must now belong to the past. We propose to stand on our own feet... We do not intend to be a plaything of others..."[6]

Speaking in Parliament on 28 March 1951, he said, "By aligning ourselves with any one power, you surrender your opinion, give up the policy you would normally pursue because some body else wants you to pursue another policy. I do not think that it would be a right policy for us to adopt. If we did align ourselves we would only fall between two stools.[7] His tryst with destiny address to the nation on 15 August 1947 also was laced with concern for entire humanity when he said, "...It is fitting that at this solemn moment we take the pledge of dedication to the service of India and her people and to the still larger cause of humanity".[8]

Nehru had consistently been anti-Nazi and anti-Fascist and fiercely loved freedom. In the early years of India's independence, while Soviets openly scoffed at the very idea that India was genuinely independent, Nehru's statements and actions dispelled those fears of entire Eastern bloc.[9] It was his global vision and corresponding actions which brought self-respect and enhanced India's international standing. Not only did Nehru declare India to be non-aligned, but he also advised all the Afro-Asian nations, which had attained independence, to keep themselves away from the two warring camps. Nehru ridiculed the suggestion that non-alignment was a sign of weakness. He was of the firm conviction that the non-aligned countries could play a positive role as mediator and keep the two power blocs away from a clash.

Nehru was a product of anti-imperial nationalism and foreign policy under him was that of self-respect that required distancing from both the blocs into which world was divided at that time.[10] Till 1962, the Sino-Indian conflict, Nehru had unchallenged sway on India's foreign policy and Parliament did not play much of a role in shaping it. He favoured an "area of peace" in Asia where nations will regulate their relations according to five paramount principles of peaceful community living called Panchsheel.[11] Once he said in Parliament that, "The normal ideas is that security is protected by the armies. That is only partly true; it is equally true that security is protected by policies. A deliberate policy of friendship with other countries goes farther in gaining security than almost anything else."[12]

A true internationalist, Nehru persistently showed his involvement in international affairs. For example, on the Palestine issue, India was among 13 nations who voted against the UN General Assembly resolution 181 for the partition of Palestine in 1947.[13] In the same year, as a member of the UN Special Committee on Palestine (UNSCOP), India proposed a minority plan which called for the establishment of a federal Palestine with internal autonomy for the Jewish illegal immigrants. Similarly, during the Korean crises, when Prime Minister Attlee called a Commonwealth Prime Ministers' Conference in London, Nehru proposed that there should be a cease-fire in Korea. He urged that diplomatic recognition should be withdrawn from Chiang Kai-shek regime of Taiwan. He continuously stood for the restoration of China's membership of the United Nations including permanent membership of the Security Council and the veto power.[14]

He espoused African freedom during India's own struggle for independence. Hardly had he become head of the Interim Government on September 1, 1946, that he began to exhort Asia and the world to help Africa. He told the Asian Relations Conference in New Delhi in March 1947: "We of Asia have a special responsibility to the people of Africa. We must help them to take their rightful place in the human family."[15] At the conclusion of the Asian-African Conference in Bandung in 1955, he felt compelled to point out:

"Everything else pales into insignificance when I think of the infinite tragedy of Africa ever since the days when millions of Africans were carried away as galley slaves to America and elsewhere, half of them dying in the galleys. We must accept responsibility for it, all of us, even though we ourselves were not directly involved."

"Even now," he continued, "the tragedy of Africa is greater than that of any other continent, whether it is racial or political. It is up to Asia to help Africa to the best of her ability because we are sister continents."[16]

He saw to it that India did its utmost to promote African freedom and play a leading role on behalf of Africa in the

United Nations and other fora until newly-independent African nations could take over. He rejoiced at the march of freedom in Africa by the early 1960's and the formation of the Organization of African Unity. He said on August 12, 1963: "... perhaps the most exciting thing that is happening in the twentieth century is the awakening of Africa.... It is, I think, a major event in history and, what is more, it is going to play an ever-growing part in the coming years. We in India have naturally welcomed it."[17]

He advocated for a "peace zone" shielded from the Cold War, and build a concert of non-aligned nations to secure the total abolition of colonialism and promote a world without arms and war. The decision of the African States in 1963, to join the Non-aligned countries en bloc, made Africa the one continent that was totally non-aligned, and was seen as the best tribute to the labours of Jawaharlal Nehru.

Globalisation: Causes and Consequences

Globalization is a process by which events, decisions and activities in one part of the world have significant consequences on other part of the globe. It extends beyond economic interdependence to include dilution of time and space dimensions as a result of spread of information technology. The rapid growth in international financial transactions, fast growth in trade and commerce, rise in foreign direct investment (FDI), the emergence of global markets, and sharing of technologies and ideas through rapid expansion of a globalised transportation and communication system are the important characteristics of globalisation. It has occurred due to the role of unfettered market forces, technological innovations and deregulation of economies. Technological innovation has contributed to globalization by supplying infrastructure for trans-world connections. Developments in the transportation and communication systems and data processing have enabled the global links to become denser, faster, more reliable, and cheaper. In other words, global relations have developed with the help of new technologies that have in turn affected the cross-planetary contacts. The establishment of these links have been further facilitated by various rules, procedures, norms, and institutions. New tax laws, labour legislations, and environmental codes have encouraged global investment and supported new regulatory frameworks.[18]

As Karl Marx had said that capital by its nature drives beyond every spatial barrier to conquer the whole Earth for its market,[19] the global markets offer prospects of high profits through mass production and sales which feed the global markets. The developed countries have pursued globalization and have shifted their production facilities wherever costs were low and earnings high throughout the world. The telecommunication facilities have made electronic finances possible whereby the world-wide financial network could be monitored and controlled with ease from a single location.

The ever spreading globalization process has changed the contours of social geography and has the potential of wider economic, political, and cultural implications. Economically, it has substantially altered the organization of production, exchange, and consumption. Many firms have initiated global operations by setting up affiliates across the world and form trans-world alliances with other companies. Mergers and acquisitions between and among various companies are found to occur as business adjusts to global markets. Many multinational corporations have relocated their production facilities as globalization reduces transport and communications costs. All this economic restructuring has raised vital issues of human security related to employment, labour conditions, poverty, and social cohesion.[20]

Politically, globalization has significantly influenced the governance, conduct and authority of the state.[21] Territorially based laws and institutions are not proving sufficient by themselves to regulate contacts and networks that operate in trans-world spaces. Globalization, therefore, has stimulated greater multilateral collaboration between states as well as the growth of regional cooperation like the European Union, ASEAN, and EPEC etc. The resultant situation of multi-layered and diffuse governance raises far-reaching questions about the nature of sovereignty and democracy in a globalizing world.

Culturally, globalization is disrupting traditional relationships between territory and collective identity. The growth of trans-world connections has encouraged the rise of non-territorial cultures. As a result, identity is becoming less fixed on territory, in the form of nation-states and ethnic bonds. As much the multiple cultures become densely intertwined in supraterritorial flows, as much more encouragement to hybridity where individuals develop and express a mix of identities.[22]

It will not be out of place to mention that the development strategy adopted by India, prior to the liberalisation of 1991, laid much emphasis on self-reliance and rapid industrialisation. This strategy did not meet the expected levels and subsequent political instability greatly hampered India's economic growth. With an acute shortage of foreign economic reserves, India reached on the verge of bankruptcy. Under the circumstances, the country had to leave the Nehruvian path of economic development in a bid to integrate into global economy. It opened its economy to foreign investment, reduced import terrifs significantly, removed quantitative restrictions, reformed its financial sector, adjusted government monetary policies to stabilise its dwindling economy. Thus the process of globalisation engulfed India which had to submit before the rising world-wide market forces and the domestic financial compulsions.

Nehru and Globalization

Globalization as we know it today being a recent phenomenon did not exist in the times of Jawaharlal Nehru when he was Prime Minister of India. He was an internationalist but this kind of global economic integration was somewhat alien to his worldview.[23] His formative years as a student in Britain and later as a leader of the Indian National Movement were marked by the inter-War period when major industrialized countries of the West were resorting to protectionism to maintain domestic employment and international trade was shrinking. He had seen the Great Depression of 1930s causing considerable disruption in relations between the countries. Agriculture and industry demanded government protections to the domestic market from the threat of cheap imports which had given rise to the protection of trade. Britain retreated into this protectionism in the autumn of 1931 ending its age old free trade policy. Nehru had seen the world divided into competing trade blocks, which had dangerous implications for the international peace. As Prime Minister of India, Nehru was deeply aware of the implications of depending on grants and aid from the wealthy Euro-America and the International Monetary Fund (IMF) and International Fund for Reconstruction and Development (World Bank). It was during his times that Soviet Union appeared to be gaining ground while the market economies of the 'Democratic West' were struggling to manage their economic problems. All these and many more events shaped Nehru's economic vision for the independent India.

Nehru inherited India which was economically poor, technologically undeveloped and educationally almost illiterate. There was no financial sector, agriculture was self-sustaining and industry was abysmally limited in its diversity. It was a Herculean task for him to start economic development of the country of 360 million, a majority of whom was far away from scientific temper. Realizing the inbuilt inadequacies of its economy, he did not consider India to be ready yet for the challenges of international competition. His focus was on export promotion and import substitution in self-regulated phases so that whatever efforts India made should be from a position of self-assurance and self-reliance. In other words, he preferred not to compromise the independence of country's economic policies in the name of economic liberalism. To be part of the dynamics of the free market did not lure him. His policies suffered and even collapsed during his life-time though, but his commitment and efforts to build a new economically self-reliant India can not be doubted. The failure of his economic policies must be equally shared by the bureaucratic and administrative structure of his time.

Nehru was a democratic socialist committed to secularism, science and technology, economic self-reliance and a democratic culture. He did not have a parochial vision; on the contrary, he recognised that future would pose new challenges to India which would need a fresh approach. Aware of the future challenges and needs, he emphasizes on the spread of education among the people and setup a large number of schools, colleges and universities. He setup world class institutions such as the Indian Institutes of Technology and the Indian Institutes of Management, which are a very important part of Nehruvian legacy. Establishment of the Indian Council of Medical Research (ICMR), Indian Council of Agricultural Research (ICAR), Council for Scientific and Industrial Research (CSIR), University Grants Commission (UGC) etc. are just a few examples of his broad and global vision of India's future. Retention and promotion of English as a link and official language has proved to be an important advantage for the country, especially in some of the new growth areas created by recent globalization such as IT enabled services.

Nehru was an incorrigible believer in democracy with a human face. It was Nehru's firm conviction that socialism, tempered by humanism, was capable of creating a new man committed to the means as noble as the ends. The economic policies of India especially after liberalization are nowhere near Nehru's economic thinking. The economic reforms and policies resolutely and ruthlessly adopted by the country might have been because of the grim realities of ongoing globalization and little scope for any other option, but the fact is that these policies are professedly far away from Nehru's vision and perceptions. For example, Nehru encouraged flow of foreign capital into India only under strict scrutiny and on certain conditions so that unrestricted foreign investment did not cripple indigenous enterprise and destroy the entrepreneur's spirit of self-reliance which was the main thrust of Nehru's policies. He was against massive doses of foreign aid which, in his view, would only lead the country permanently into a 'debt trap'. He favoured the use of imported science and technology only in the context of the modernisation and rationalisation of key industries —particularly those manufacturing capital goods and other items essential to rapid industrialisation. Also, he believed in and advocated for the restructuring of agriculture sector and setup 'agro-based' industries so that India, the land of farmers, could achieve a higher standard of living and better quality of life.

The economic values Nehru so cherished have rendered obsolete and redundant. The forces of liberalisation and globalisation have become so strong that India had to dilute its socialistic pattern of development and mixed economy. Due to the conditions imposed by the World Bank and the International Monetary Fund for the resuscitation of the fragile and week Indian economy. Nehru's economic policy, based on controls, quotas and licenses, was designed not only to protect Indian industry from threats, internal as well as external, but to discipline it so that it became socially accountable. These policies also failed because his well-intentioned policies were misused by the Indian public sector industry which under the protection and patronage of the State became flabby, lethargic and unresponsive to the challenges of international competition and the expectations of the captive domestic market. Bureaucracy in the country became the ultimate authority hampering innovativeness and halting progress. Most of the public sector undertakings became over-staffed and suffered from under performance, sluggishness and substandard quality. Many of such industries had to be liquidated or put under private partnership or even had to be declared as sick units. After transfer into private hands the same enterprises started showing profits and became efficient in their working. Nehru's policies thus were termed only the dreams of a visionary because of their intellectual and ideological nuances which had no relevance in the wake of globalization. Indeed, it is not easy to relate his-day economic policies to the present-day brutal and ruthless economics of globalization.

Nehru's Economic Policies and Globalization

On becoming the Prime Minister of India in 1947, Nehru launched a number of economic reforms. Being a firm believer in state control over the economic sectors, and his socialist ideals compelled him to introduce laws for land redistribution in order to curtail the economic disparity in India among the landed and the landless classes. He introduced Five Year Plans in 1951 to determine the mode of government expenditure and grants in important development sectors like agriculture, industries and education. The economists of globalization accuse all these policies today as responsible for slow and sluggish growth of Indian economy all these years. In the age of globalization the role of the state has significantly altered. State authority even sovereignty is seriously under threat which Nehru would never have allowed to happen. Globalization has weakened the state control over investment, and trends of development. The World Trade Organisation, the International Monetary Fund and the World Bank, which are US-dominated institutions are shaping the course of development in various countries and designing the shape of global economy. While European Union is vying to become effective competitor in the world market NATO is standing guard to secure the Western capital. Nehru would never have agreed to render the state a hostage to the forces of globalization.

Nehru stood for international economic cooperation and development which should benefit all the sections of the society. However, the present day globalization in creating an elite club of new haves and have-not in every country and creating a sharp division between the countries on both sides of the digital divide. As a result dissensions are being fuelled with different connotations in the countries of both the categories. The process of Globalization aims at creating entire world as a single economic entity, a unified market within which capital and economic activity moves and flows without restraints. The underlying theory is that markets, if left to them, are supremely efficient in allocating resources. If this is true, then as artificial restrictions (such as tariffs or exchange controls) are removed, any economic activity from finance to consumption will settle in the location where it can be performed most efficiently. Only the rich and mighty stand to be benefited from this situation.

Nehru's Economic Ideology and Globalisation

Socialism did play an important role in Nehru's ideological make-up, but he himself denied any kind of overt Socialist tendencies in the economic policies adopted by him. Nehru advocated a kind of mixed economy. He believed that any kind of unquestioned ideological adherence to any form of economic tenet, or 'ism' would not be in the interest of India's growth. On the one hand, as a devoted Gandhian, he had strong belief in the betterment of rural economy and on the other, he had a strong belief that development of heavy industry would be the best way to serve India's economic interests. However, the globalization has polarized India as never before. One India is highly rich, highly educated, highly scientific but highly insensitive to the other India which is dismally poor, unbelievably unaware and illiterate, and abysmally hide-bound and traditional. Nehru intended to create a balance between the rural and the urban sectors through his economic policies and that both could go hand in hand. He denied to carry forward the age old city versus village controversy and hoped that in India, both could develop together. He wanted the development to reach the last man in the millions of villages. In the present globalization context, where the capacity of governments to conduct domestic policies is seriously under threat and national governments are becoming powerless in the face of increasingly mobile capital, labour and production, no one will spare time to think of the well-being of the last man in the village contrary to the Nehru's vision.

Nehru inspired the industrialists to provide a fillip to India's economy. However, he had strict reservations on the question of foreign investment. Wary of foreign investment, Nehru's nationalist ideals confirmed in him the belief that India was self-sufficient to bolster her own growth. Although he did not officially decry the possibility of foreign investment in direct terms, he did stress that the sectors of foreign investment would be regularized, and the terms and conditions of investment and employment would be strictly controlled by government rules in case there were possibilities of a foreign investment. Moreover, Nehru emphasized that the key sectors will always be in government hand.

As opposed to the Nehru's vision, present day globalization can not be imagined without the foreign direct investments. In fact the developing countries including India crave for it. After India adopted economic reforms in 1991, all its Prime Ministers and many of the Chief Ministers of the States have bee-lined to the developed countries to attract investments from Multinational Corporations. There is a race to outsmart each other in alluring FDI by offering various subsidies, facilities, land at cheaper rates etc. In this process ideology has taken a back seat and consideration of integration into the global economic dynamics has come to the forefront. As is well known that the developed countries are home to most of the Multinational Corporations, of the largest 600 MNCs in the world about 45 per cent belong to the United States. Japan with almost 16 per cent, and Great Britain with over 10 per cent come next. Largest share of FDI by MNCs originating from the developed countries end up in the developing countries of Asia and Africa and does not come without strings. India too has made as many compromises on the economic front to attract FDI, which is absolutely contrary and opposed to the Nehruvian economic ideology and approach.

Nehru's policy towards the rural economy was strongly for the rural self-development of India. He tried to boost India's cottage industries. Much on the lines of Gandhi, Nehru believed that the rural and cottage industries of India played a major role in the economic fabric of the country. He was also of the belief that small scale industries and cottage industries were effective solutions to the massive employment problems that remained a perpetual issue of concern throughout his life time. Contrary to his efforts for rural development the lowering of tariff barriers under the WTO pressure has glutted Indian market with goods from outside especially China forcing a large number of small scale industries to shut down. Small scale producer has become trader of the foreign goods under the circumstances.

Globalization and Dilution of State Sovereignty

Nehru envisioned India as a Sovereign Democratic Republic. He wished to build the country as a modern democracy. He built the political and administrative institutions to give a decisive and important role to the state. The present Globalization has effectively taken away the choice of decision-making from the preview of the state. The dictates of the IMF and World Bank along with the directions of WTO has left little space for the state to exercise its sovereign will on its domain. Be it economic, political cultural or social. Most of the international financial institutions are working under the influence of United

States, and most of the MNCs belong to her. Therefore it is incumbent upon the US administration to promote and protect the interests of these big companies who bring hefty revenues and profits back home. United States blatantly interferes in the economic policies in the host developing countries directly or through its Ambassadors.

Traditionally, Indian ministers would keep American Ambassador at a distance. Bureaucrats rarely socialized with foreign diplomats. Though governments yielded ground on certain international issues to the big powers yet, they always kept their dignity claiming that there was no external interference in country's internal affairs. After India took to economic reforms things began to change. The respective US Ambassadors became more and more assertive and audacious. They offered policy advice that too in public. The US Ambassadors David C. Mulford, or his recent predecessors such as Frank Wisner or Robert Blackwill have been meddling into various internal matters of India. Even when Indira Gandhi, Rajiv Gandhi and V.P. Singh were the Prime Ministers, envoys restrained themselves from interfering or commenting on the internal matters of the country. Under the National Democratic Alliance rule, the U.S. Ambassador's visibility rose considerably, as well as the pitch of his demands—for instance, on compensating Enron with $2 billion to $3 billion for shutting down the plant, or on WTO negotiations. Lal Krishna Advani the Home Minister of the time developed a special relationship with Blackwill and both used to meet on fixed days. Similarly, the U.S. influence has considerably increased since Manmohan Singh became the Prime Minister. It is only recently that the US Ambassador David C Mulford remarked that time is of the essence for operationalising the nuclear deal. This statement was highly criticized. While C P Bardhan of the Communist Party of India said, "We should have our own time table", and the CPI(M) politburo member, Sitram Yechury, attacked

Mulford for his remarks, saying "he need not interfere in India`s internal affairs."

Under Nehru, no Foreign Ambassador would have dared to make public pronouncements. Ambassador J.K. Galbraith, himself a distinguished economist, had a close intellectual, professional and personal friendship with Nehru. But Nehru never let that interfere with his policy on critical issues of the day, such as the Sino-Indian conflict, Berlin Blockade, or the Cuban missile crisis. He was respectful not just of India's fierce pride in her policy independence. The ever increasing institutional and governmental interference from outside has posed a serious threat to India's sovereignty.

Nehru was a humanist and respected rule of law. He declared in a speech to the American Congress in 1949, "We have placed in the forefront of our Constitution those fundamental human rights to which all men who love liberty, equality and progress aspire—the freedom of the individual, the equality of men and the rule of law."[24] The economic policies of Nehru are often blamed for the poor economy of India in the subsequent years. However, it cannot be denied that his decisions were necessitated by the needs of the times. India needed to effectively harness its domestic means as well as strengthen its governmental control to lay the base for future privatization. It is often speculated that Nehru would have embraced the economic reforms and economic liberalization of the late twentieth century.

India is grappling with the challenges posed by Globalization and trying to find solutions within the framework of her democratic polity. In the Post-Cold War period India is charting its course in a globalizing world. Political parties in India are fully aware that globalization is a reality. The Indian National Congress, which harps on Nehru as builder of modern India has left his economic ideology behind to grab the opportunity, the globalization offers.

In his lifetime, Jawaharlal Nehru enjoyed an iconic status in India and was widely admired across the world for his idealism and statesmanship. His birthday, November 14, is celebrated in India as Children's Day in recognition of his lifelong passion and work for the welfare, education and development of children and young people. Children across India are taught to remember him as *Chacha Nehru* (Uncle Nehru). He remains a popular symbol of the Congress party which frequently celebrates his memory. Congress leaders and activists often emulate his style of clothing, especially his mannerisms. Nehru's ideals and policies continue to shape the Congress party's manifesto and core political philosophy. However under the force of globalisation his economic policies had to be abandoned or at least diluted. It can thus be said that Nehru's economic policies are far away from structural reforms and post Cold-War globalisation. Like he created a middle path in the form of mixed economy and non-alignment, had he been there on the Indian political scene, he could have certainly devised a middle path.

NOTES

1. From 1885 till India's independence, Congress passed several resolutions, deprecating, objecting and rejecting various foreign policy moves taken by the British Indian Government. See, Palmer, Norman D, "*Foreign Policy of the Indian National Congress*", in Misra, K.P., *Foreign Policy of India*, New Delhi, Thomson Press, 1977, pp. 11-14; Also see, "Congress Develops a Foreign Policy", in Nehru, Jawaharlal, THE DISCOVERY OF INDIA, OUP, 1982, pp. 416-22.
2 Bhaskaran, R., "*The Philosophical Basis of India's Foreign Policy*", in Misra, *op.cit.*, p. 22.
3. Basu, D.D., *Introduction to the Constitution of India*, New Delhi, Prentice-Hall of India, 2002
4. For review of implications of Nehru's views on India's foreign policy, see, Power, P F, "Indian Foreign Policy: The Age of Nehru", *The Review of Politics*, Vol. 26, No. 2, April 1964, pp. 257-86.
5. See, Brecher, Michael : *India and World Politics* : Krishnamenon's View of the World, New York, 1968, p. 3.
6. See, "Prospects of the Non-Aligned Movement", *International Studies*, Vol. 20, 1981, pp. 67-79.

7. Quoted in, *Nehru's Thoughts, op. cit.*, p. 103.
8. Reprinted in, Brian, Mc Arthur, *Penguin Book of Twentieth Century Speeches*, London, Penguin Viking, 1992, pp. 234-37
9. For early days of Indo-USSR Relations, see, Arthur Lall, "Change and Continuity in India's Foreign Policy", Orbis, No.10, 1966-67, pp. 91-105.
10. See, Werner Levi, "India Debates Foreign Policy", *Far Eastern Survey*, Vol. 20, No. 5, March 1951, pp. 49-52.
11. See, Alan de Rusett, "*On Understanding Indian Foreign Policy*", in Misra, *op. cit.*, p. 107.
12. Nehru, Jawaharlal, *India's Foreign Policy*: Selected Speeches, September1946-April 1961, New Delhi, Publication Division, Government of India, 1961, pp. 1-3 and 79.
13. On 29 November 1947 the United Nations voted to terminate the British Mandate of Palestine by 1 August 1948. A resolution to that effect was passed by 33 for and 13 against votes. For details, see, Bregman, Ahron : *Israel's Wars* : A History Since 1947, London Routledge, 2002; Louis, W M : *The British Empire In Middle East* : *Arab Nationalism*, the United States and Post-War Imperialism, OUP, 1986.
14. *The Times*, 12 September 950; and 11 June, 1955; *The Hindu*, 3 January.
15. See, *Asian Relations*: Being Report of the Proceeding and Documentation..., New Delhi, Asian Relations Organisation, 1948.
16. Nehru's speech at the concluding session on April 24, 1955. Cited in, Shiela Dikshit, *Jawaharlal Nehru : Centenary Volume*, New Delhi, OUP, 1989.
17. See, *Nehru and Africa*, p. 37.
18. The discussion is based on, Kochler, Hans (Ed.): *Globility Versus Democracy? The Changing Nature of International Relations in the Era of Globalization*, Vienna, International Progress Organisation, 2000; Steger, Manford : *Globalization : A Very Short Introduction*, Oxford University Press, 2003; Stiglitz, Joseph E., *Making Globalization Work*, Oxford University Press, 2003; Wolf, Martin: *Why Globalization Works*, Yale University Press, 2004.
19. See, Marsden, Richard: *The Nature of Capital*, Marx after Foucault, Routledge Studies in Social and Political Thought 20, London, Routledge, 1999; Vladimir, Lenin : *Imperialism, The Highest Stage of Capitalism*, London, Lawrence and Wishart, 1948.
20. Walfens, Paul J.J. (*et. al*), *Globalization, Economic Growth and Innovation Dynamics*, Springer Publishers, 1999; also see, Badr Alam Iqbal, "Globalization and Multinational Corporations in South Asia", *SARID Journal*, Vol. 1, Issue 1, 2000.
21. See, "Political Globalization", at www.politicalglobalization.com; and Chris W Brooks, "Globalization—A Political Perspective", www.bi.ulaval.ca/Globalization-Universities.

22. See for details, Dieter Sanghaas, "Modernity and Anti Modernity – Facing Cultural Globalization", www.boell-meo.org/en/web/268.htm, David Rethkop, "In praise of Cultural Imperialism? Effects of Globalization on Culture", www.globalpolicy.org/globaliz/culture.
23. Montek S Ahluwalia,"India in a Globalising World", 27th Jawaharlal Nehru Memorial Lecture, London, 20 April 2005.
24 Jawaharlal Nehru, "Address to the US House of Representatives," Washington, DC, 13 October 1949. S. Gopal, ed., *Selected Works of Jawaharlal Nehru*, 2nd Ser., Vol. 13, New Delhi : Jawaharlal Nehru Memorial Fund, 1992, p. 303.

11

NEHRU, NAM AND GLOBALIZATION

A Decadal Reference Running into Centuries

RAJINDER S. CHAUHAN

In this cyber-age when the world has reached at the threshold of man the names that once mattered are fast becoming obsolete and insignificant. However, there are people who by their farsightedness, vision, and tremendous contribution in the social, economic, and political arena would keep on haunting the minds. The same is true of Nehru in India who is also known as 'global utopian idealist' because of his continuous pre-occupation with the ideas of One World, United Asia, and World federation. It is this dimension of Nehru's philosophy and vision that makes him as relevant as Gandhi and in certain respects even more. This paper is a study of the initial phase when the foreign policy of India got shape under Nehru in its contemporary global contextuality. Of late there has been a shift in India's foreign policy especially in the post-cold war era largely because of the emerging new equations but this doesn't mean that India has done away with the basics which stand as firm as ever. It deals with the role of Nehru in framing the Foreign Policy of India in conjunction with Non-Alignment as it courses into 21st century.

The obsession of Nehru in such high-pitched ideals were largely guided by the adversity of times and India's placement in a formidable situation where states were fast aligning themselves on military lines, a phenomenon worth alarming in the post-World War II era. It was necessarily because of these prevalent conditions that Nehru could devise a neo-mean in global relationship i.e. Non-Alignment with positive relationship with the global fraternity. This also earned him the title of an 'Idealist Internationalist'.

His non-aligned policy came under severe criticism for neglecting national security as India suffered humiliating defeat in 1962 war at the hands of China. Later India could not even stave off Pakistan's attempt to seize Kashmir by force in 1965. His non-aligned policy could not restrain Pakistan from joining CENTO and SEATO, the two cold war military alliances. Consequently, cold war reached at the doorsteps of India. Nehru was also criticized for his Tibet policy. Even after Nehru, the circumstances forced India to sign quasi-military alliance with Soviet Union in 1971 as the two states entered into a long term treaty called "treaty of peace and friendship". Critics have argued that Nehru's non-alignment in reality carried a pro-communist and anti-western bias and the implementation of Nehru's philosophy and policy appeared to carry double standards.

However, Nehru's policies were global-pragmatic-real politic. This is because he recognized correctly the need to form relations with powers at international level. The real politic because Nehru sought to creatively use the animosities among U.S., USSR and China to India's diplomatic advantage in difficult circumstances. India was militarily and economically weak and two communist states and Pakistan, a potentially hostile power, occupied India's neighbourhood. In fact, Nehruvian approach was an integrated one, a blend of idealism and realism, of internationalism and nationalism, and of short-term and long-term objectives. His concept of security constituted, political stability, economic steadiness, freedom and integration.

His perception was pragmatic because it was linked to the notion of Indian interests. Nehru used available means to achieve his ends. His policy was to immunize the region from external domination, to avoid the development of hostile preparations against India, and to escape forcible interventions. He also visualized a security zone for India, especially in Himalayan area below Tibet. He never aspired Indian domination over her small neighbours, the poor unprivileged states who had nothing to offer and whose absorption would add to Indian political, economic, and social problems India was faced with. The prize was the attainment of a greater power status that he achieved.

His idea of world federation seems to be an idealist, utopian, in fact unrealistic, and can be perceived as the outcome of his experience of integrating princely states in Indian union, of course with self-determination and freedom as the basis of federating units. The major policy plank of anti-colonialism and radicalism had not only its roots in the history of colonial experience of the past but also in the eradication of future remnants of Portuguese and French colonial spots in India. The agreements establishing Durgapur, Rourkela, and Bhilai steel plants in generous terms with Germany, Soviet Union and British reveal the economic content of his security designs for India.

Jawahar Lal Nehru was the main architect of Indian Foreign Policy. Nehru's continuing until the very end as his own Foreign Minister has only one significant parallel in modern times. In 1949, Chou-En-Lai became the Prime Minister of China and carried on for 7 years as a full time Foreign Minister. Even before independence, J.L. Nehru exclusively managed the congress party's foreign office. In Viceroy's Council too, he preferred to handle foreign affairs, whereas Muslim League leader held finance. His participation in the Brussels Conference of Oppressed

Nationalities, the visit to Moscow and discussions with representatives of freedom movements from Asia and Africa also enriched his global viewpoint. This became evident through his work "Glimpses of world history" in the early thirties when he began to saw the re-occurring of rise and decline of great powers. In twenties, he was worried about the expansionism of the British Empire. In the thirties, he diagnosed the evil of Nazism. He was also aware of Roosevelt and the New Deal. Ethiopian and Spanish Civil Wars were major developments to him.

The non-aligned policy was conceived by Nehru when he was in jail during the Second World War. He preferred to avoid taking sides in the struggle of European powers although, the clear choice was of rejecting the greater of the two evils: Nazism and Fascism's as against British imperialism. However, for colonized nations of the time, the better choice was not to get involved in these rivalries since these were not the struggles of African and Asian states. Although, the peaceful co-existence was the preferred Indian foreign policy posture, yet this did not stand for isolationism. First, India's national interest should dictate the choice of friends and enemies, and not power struggle in Europe. Second, India perceived a natural affinity and empathy with non-white Asian countries than with white European powers and would be determined to pursue closer ties with the former groups.

To quote him, "in particular we thought of close friends without neighbours in East and West, like China, Afghanistan, Iran, and Soviet Union. Even with distant America we wanted closer relations for we could learn from United States as also from Soviet Union."[1] After Indian independence although Burma, Ceylon also got freedom yet other two European empires in Asia, the French and the Dutch chose not to depart gracefully. Portuguese and French colonial posts in India also shaped Indian foreign policy objectives. The presence of Indians in Singapore, Malaysia, East Africa and Eden which continued to be parts of British Empire also determined the mode of exchange with these states. Therefore, the world federation, co-operation with U.N.O., friendship with all countries, peaceful co-existence, nuclear dis-armament, economic equality and freedom became main bases of Indian foreign policy.

The emergence of U.N.O., the end of Second World War after Hiroshima, emergence of Cold War, Berlin crises, Fulton speech, Marshal Plan, the war in Greece, terrible communal riots and the emergence of Kashmir problem are the backdrops in the light of which Indian foreign policy was framed. Nehru was first person to perceive that if cold war was not stopped, it would turn into hot war. He said, "we are living an age of contradictions and paradoxes. We talk of peace, but prepare for war. We talk of internationalism, but narrow nationalism govern us".[2] Thus importance of non-alignment was because of Nehru's distrust of European style of global politics with its changing military alliance formations and balance of power system. Here he exhibits the influence of Gandhian philosophy of non-violence and pacific settlement of disputes.

The philosophical interpretation of Panchshil and non-alignment suggest that such policies are inherently superior-even politically and morally too, against the alternative of military alliances and confrontations that keep the fear of war alive. According to this perspective, non-alignment and panchshil may not always prevent wars, but may make it less likely through a spirit of tolerance and co-operation. Nehru concluded that military weakness did not necessarily imply diminished security or political influence abroad. Instead, greater security could be achieved through non-involvement in military blocks. "The normal idea is that security is protected by armies. That is only partly true; it is equally true that security is protected by policies. A deliberate policy of friendship with other countries goes further in security than almost anything".[3]

Nehru's yard-stick of good policy was: "Does it hold forth the promise of early liquidation of poverty and illiteracy and bring better living conditions."[4] Thus first, he had concluded that India's interest lay with Asian and African nations. Such interests were to be determined not by prevailing global strategic considerations dictated by the western/European powers but the common, history, geography and political experience under imperial rule. Second, there was little to chose between the two rising powers, the United States and the Soviet Union. Third, primary objective of these emerging nations was to be the eradication of economic and Social justice at home.

Nehru saw both Soviet Union and United States as likely to take up the mantle of old European imperialism with the latter more expansionist than former. Of Soviet Union he wrote, "Soviet Union is showing expansionist tendency and is expanding its territories more or less on the basis of Tsar empire. How far this process will go is difficult to say".[5] In regard to United States, he wrote; "Whatever the future may hold, it is clear that the economy of USA after the war will be powerfully expansionist and almost explosive in its consequences. Will this lead to some kind of imperialism? It would be yet another tragedy if it did so, for America has the power and opportunity to set the pace for future. Concerning this impending global struggle between United States and Soviet Union, Nehru advised nations of Asia and Africa to ask themselves these questions: "Does it help toward our liberation? Does it end the domination of one country over another? Will it enable us to live freely the life of our choice in co-operation with others? Does it bring equality and equal opportunity for nations as well as groups within each nation".[6]

How prudent Nehru's integrated approach was: "We shall take full part in international conferences as free nation with our own policy not merely as satellite of another nation .... we propose, as far as to keep away from politics of groups, aligned against one another which have led in the past to world wars...... We are particularly interested in emancipation of colonial and dependent countries, and in the recognition for the theory and practice of equal opportunities for all races. We do claim equal and honourable treatment for our people wherever they may go and we can not accept any discrimination against them.........The world moves mentally toward closer co-operation and the building of commonwealth. It is for this "one world" free India will work. We send our greetings to the people of United States of America to whom destiny has given major role in international affairs. To that other great nation of modern world the Soviet Union that also carries a vast responsibility for shaping the world events, we send greetings. They are our neighbours in Asia and inevitably we will have to undertake many tasks. We are of Asia, India is so situated, she is pivot of Western, Southern and South East Asia. China that mighty country with mighty past, our neighbour, has been our friend through the ages and that friendship will endure and glow".

The co-operation with U.N.O. or World Federation stems partly because of this integrated approach. India has taken role in San Francisco Conference, and was among the signatories of charter of U.N.O. Pt. Nehru said: "U.N.O. was kind of bridge from the past and the conflicts of today and to the hopes of future. Nehru has faith in U.N.O., he synthesized idealism with realism. The British philosopher, Bertrand Russell haunted by nuclear nightmare, declared that Pt. Nehru stood for sanity and peace in critical movements of human history, it would be he, who would lead us out of the dark night of fear in to happy days.[7]

Nehru took Kashmir dispute to U.N.O. because of his firm faith in U.N.O. Not only this, Nehru contributed a lot during Korean war, Vietnam crises, Suez crises, Hungary crises, UNCTAD, all liberation movements, eradication of apartheid policy, Cuban crises, disarmament etc. India mediated between Washington and Peking on the release of U.S. airmen in China and the Chinese students in the

U.S. The failure of Indian security policy during the Nehru years may be viewed not so much as policy of conception and formulation, but as failure in policy implementation. Since Cold War division as seen by United States, was between the free world and communist states, and since the Indian political system appeared to fall within the former category, the idea of non-alignment had to be directed at the communist states rather than western democracies.

Aside from India's quarrel with Pakistan over Kashmir, if military threat to India did exist in the prevailing bipolar alignment of states, than this would probably come from communist block. In that case it was the two major communist states with whom tolerance and friendliness had to be the objective of foreign policy. India's foreign policy towards free world was to resist all attempts at drawing India in to western fold. Second, for Nehru non-alignment did not mean neutralism. Nehru said, " We have proclaimed during the past years that we will not attach ourselves to any particular group. That has nothing to do with neutrality or passivity or anything else. We are not going to join a war if we can help it, and we are going to join the side which is to our interest and when the time comes to make choices".[8] Non-alignment, therefore, implied a long term policy which did not preclude temporary and perhaps quasi-military arrangements under particular short term situations that affected Indian security. The policy when handled adroitly was expected to improve India's security against her neighbours and against the super powers. All this while minimizing the defense expenditure also retained the ability to conduct an independent foreign policy. The problem with this belief and approach that eventually led to military debacle of 1962 was that excessive dependence was placed on principles and faith without an adequate military back up.

Nehru's decision to adopt the policies of non-alignment and Panchshil was primarily motivated by desire to concentrate on India's economic development without the sacrifice of independence. Nehru said, "we do not want at this critical moment in the history of our respective countries that war should upset the plans we have laid and the dreams we have dreamed. [9] Until, 1962, the policy appeared to have succeeded. The new Indian nation enjoyed thirteen years of peace and averaged an economic growth rate of 4.5 per cent if compared to 3.5 per cent in the decade thereafter when three wars were fought and major arms build up was undertaken.[10]

In the Himalayan region, Nehru kept the parts of British policy and rejected parts of it. He saw no use in trying to maintain Tibet as a buffer as did British, but saw utility in maintaining special relations with Nepal, recognizing it as a vital part of Indian security zone. He kept the British view of the Mac Mohan line but did not see the use of policy of interference in buffer zone. Nehru failed to adequately measure the intensity of Chinese reaction to Indian stand on Tibet and Indian efforts to assert its version of the disputed boundary between the two countries. He also failed to take sufficient precautions to counter the American decision to arm Pakistan under the SEATO and CENTO Pacts.

If we take into consideration the situation in 1950's and the observation of Nehru that he made that: "the fact is and it is a major fact of middle of the 20th century that China has become a great power united and strong".[11] If Nehru had refused Chinese claim to Tibet, this would have led to Sino-Indian confrontation calling for vast Indian defence build up or alliance with one of the power bloc, thus terminating the ideas of non-alignment, independent foreign policy and rapid economic growth. Moreover, the army was reluctant to take on China in 1954 as well as in 1962. Take into account the words of General K.S. Thimaya, former Chief of Army Staff: "whereas in the case of Pakistan I have considered the possibility of a total war, I am afraid I can not do so in regard to China in an open conflict on its own. It must be left to the politician and diplomats to ensure our security.[12]

On Pakistan, Nehru recognized the problem of Hindu Muslim divide, but after 1948 and especially 1953-54, Nehru's policy was driven by strategic designs (managing Kashmir defence, curbing US-Pakistan link up and consequent militarization and internationalization of the Kashmir issue and Indo-Pakistan affairs) and not merely religious concerns. In regard to Kashmir problem Nehru observed, "well we deliberately did not war with Pakistan. So we went to Security Council. So long as we belong to United Nations we have to function as member of United Nations. So long as we believe in the processes of Charter of United Nations we have to function that way. Since India was modeled on western political ideas and institutions, there would be no question of parliamentary democracy being subverted from this direction. Though 1971 Indo-Soviet Treaty came under severe criticism for compromising with NAM but the subsequent regimes proved that India's non-aligned policy continue to be an inseparable part of Indian foreign policy.

The end of Cold War in 1990 with its bipolar military confrontation between East and West would appear to suggest that Prime Minister Jawahar Lal Nehru was right after all. The classical European style of 'balance of power politics' has been replaced by what seems to be a world system based on collective security under United Nations or at worst a unipolar world dominated by western capitalist states. Even before the cold war had ended countries such as Pakistan and Cuba were proclaiming themselves to be non-aligned nations despite their military ties with Untied States and Soviet Union respectively. Such declarations could be seen as demonstration of the fact that policy of non-alignment was desirable objective or necessary facade for states to achieve respectability in developing world.

Similarly, with President Richard Nixon's historic visit to China in February 1972, and subsequently to Soviet Union in May 1972, peaceful coexistence under names of rapprochement and détente were reflective of India's old penchant of Panchshil and non-alignment. Although, the power leverage enjoyed by non-aligned nations is debatable, yet even after 1990 the non-aligned nation are increasing in number because cold war was the condition not the cause of birth of NAM. Nehru's belief in impermanence of the cold war and the communist system of states are examples of his mental agility and innovativeness of thinking in the world dominated by super powers rivalry and stratagem.

No doubt, the current waves within globalization characterized by I T revolution, Corporate Governance and Information Capitalism are turning the traditional thinking extraneous yet the middle path preached by Nehru based on dynamic rational understanding of the global developments and maneuvers would keep on haunting the minds of statesmen, policymakers and thinkers alike.

NOTES

1. J.L. Nehru, *Discovery of India*, p. 337.
2. Quoted in Padma Srivastava, "Nehru, United Nations and Peace" *India Quarterly* p. 137, Vol. LII No. 1&2, Jan.- June, 1976.
3. J.L. Nehru, *India's Foreign Policy; Selected Speeches*, pp. 79-80.
4. Nehru, *The Discovery of India*, p. 400.
5. *Ibid*, p. 399.
6. *Ibid*, 399.
7. Quoted in J.L. Nehru, *India Foreign Policy Nehru's Speeches*, Govt. of India, Publication Division.
8. *ibid*, p. 24.
9. *The Hindu*, May 2, 1954.
10. K. Subrahmanyam, *Defense and Development*, Calcutta: Minerva Associates, 1973, pp. 2-3.
11. J.L. Nehru, *India's Foreign Policy: Selected Speeches*, p. 304.
12. S.S. Khera, *India's Defence Problem*, New Delhi: Orient Longmans 1968, p. 169.

12

NEHRU IN THE GLOBALIZED WORLD

HARISH K. THAKUR

In the era of globalization the voices that feel gravely estranged and subdued mostly belong to the socialist ilk. With the break up of the stringent state regimentations and the free flow of goods, capital, investment, technology and the world's becoming a battleground of the competing trans-national groups and multi-nationals the ideas of protectionism and welfare have suffered the most. In the current surge of events if the states are to witness immense increase in production and income the marginalized ones are to get further alienated and this is a matter of grave concern for the protagonists of the poor and the marginalized.

Globalization can broadly be defined as a compound of increased interrelations and interconnectivity among the actors—states, groups, societies and corporations and so on, each one having the potential to influence the others and vice-versa. "Globalization is the compression of the world and the intensification of the consciousness of the world as a whole".[1] It's a process that envisages interaction at socio-economic, political, technical, communication and cultural levels. It brings the tacit sense of salvation, satisfaction and prosperity for all but also the explicit rejection and discontent among the depressed and discriminated that punctures the over inflated boom of the concept.

From the perspective of globalization the modern liberal democratic state is often portrayed as increasingly trapped within the webs of global interconnectedness permeated by quasi-supranational, intergovernmental and trans-national forces and unable to determine its own fate. Globalization is frequently projected as a homogenizing force eroding 'difference' and the capacity of the nation-states to act independently in the articulation and pursuit of domestic and international policy objectives: the democratic territorial state seems to face decline and crisis."[2]

Obviously we are moving towards a borderless world, not strictly in the geographical sense but in terms of economic, trade and political relations. The concept of globalization envisages a world where national barriers wane away in favour of international ones and where people stand face to face in front of each other having direct reach and reciprocation with them. This surely doesn't mean that the state is going to loose its traditional role but a slash in its arena is visible. Also manifest in this surge of globalization that hinges upon the idea of 'Global Oneness', 'Global Village' or 'Global Interconnectedness' is the parallel idea of Nehru of 'One World' or 'World Federation' that he saw long back in 1930s and 1940s.

However, a big contrast is also discernible as Nehru's one world was guided by his philosophy of socialism and humanism. He envisaged a world where all the states would be equal in status and would have the magnanimity for the poor and the needy of the world. He would advocate socialism but again never at the cost of individual freedom, a socialism of different creed. However, in this phase of globalization, the ideas of Nehru have not lost their original gloss and his concern for the deprived and the idea of a welfare state where state planning and due ownership of natural resources by the state still carries meaning. Globalization is good to the extent it is homogenizing in effect and works for the uplifting of the all but if it creates further rifts and cleavages among people chiefly on economic grounds the socialist mode with due honour to individual freedom would never loose its relevance and so would Nehru. To understand the ideas of Nehru and their relevance in the new world order it is necessary to assess him as a socialist, planner, policy-maker, welfarist, humanist, internationalist and statesman.

A Socialist Unlike Socialists

While dealing with the immediate problems of India Nehru took into account the input from the international milieu, and rightly so, that had a direct bearing over the national events. 'In 1928 he presided over five provincial party conferences, was elected president of the All India Trade Union Congress, and addressed various gatherings of the nationalist youth. Everywhere he hammered on one basic theme—the twin goals of the nationalist movement must be complete independence and socialism. Action was essential he declared; even wrong action was better than no action at all. Industrialization was inevitable. Capitalism and imperialism must be eradicated. His attitude to imperialism was based on emotional antipathy to colonial rule, not on orthodox Marxism. From his speeches in 1928, it is evident as Brecher remarks, that Nehru had not yet worked out a coherent ideology and it is questionable whether he has ever done so'.[3] This holds good till day as there is no specific cult of socialist thought to which Nehru belongs and his socialism never became an 'ism' of sort rather became 'Nehruism' i.e. 'socialism graciously steered through the vitals of democracy'.

While addressing the Indian National Congress, session of Lucknow in 1939, Nehru remarked that I am convinced that the only right way of looking at our own problems is to see them in their proper place in a world setting. I am convinced that there is intimate connection between the world events, and our national problem is but a part of the world problem of capitalist imperialism. To look at each event apart from the others and without understanding the connection between them must lead to the formation of erratic and erroneous views.[4]

The socialist bent of Nehru's mind could be seen from his ideas over socialism that he expressed time and again. Once he saw a panacea in socialism for all the ills of the prevalent times when he held, "I am convinced that the only key to the solution of the world's problems lies in socialism, and when I use this word I do so not in a vague humanitarian way but in the scientific, economic sense. Socialism is, however, something even more than an economic doctrine; it is a philosophy of life and as such it also appeals to me, I see no way of ending the poverty and the vast unemployment, the degradation, and the subjection of Indian people except through socialism."[5]

Nehru further held that socialism was to be established within national boundaries and then eventually in the world as a whole with a controlled production and distribution of wealth for the public good. How this is to be brought out is another matter, but it is clear that the good of a nation or of mankind must not be held up because some people who profit by the existing order object to the change. He even went to the extent that if political or social institutions come in the way of such a change, they have to be removed.[6]

Planning

So far as the planning for India was concerned he was crystal clear over the apparent diversities of Indian society as well as its impoverished people and withered economy. No doubt, the prime objective was the elevation of the level of poor and upliftment of all the sections of the society.

The idea of economic planning was not unknown in India before independence. Nehru had preached its virtues since the late 1920s. The Congress socialists had embraced it wholeheartedly. The party's National Planning Committee under Nehru's inspiration had paved the way for its acceptance. During the second world war a spate of plans appeared. The Government of India's Planning Department did valuable preparatory work in the final years of the Raj. Nevertheless, as late as 1949 planning had not yet made a serious dent in the thinking of the Indian Government.[7] Nehru was also greatly influenced by the big leap that Russia had made in industrial development soon after the communist revolution. This in addition to his wide experience abroad helped him think for planning in India for which planned development and a Planning Commission was in his mind.

Nehru was also skeptical over the inner resistance within the organization because of the nationalist background of many of his colleagues with vested interests. He even sensed non-cooperation from them in the political struggle, obviously pointing towards certain important people in the party. Socialism for him was not merely an economic doctrine but was a vital creed. During his address at Lucknow he also held that "I should like the Congress to become a socialist organization and to join hands with other forces in the world which are working for the new civilization. But I realize that the majority in the Congress, as it is constituted today, may not be prepared to go thus far. We are against organization and we think and work only on the nationalist plane. It is evident enough now that this is too narrow even for the limited objective of political independence, and so we talk the masses and their economic needs. But still most of us hesitate because of our nationalist backgrounds, to take a step which might frighten away some vested interests. Most of these interests are already ranged against us, and we can expect little from them except opposition even in the political struggle".[8]

It was his love for the suffering humanity that socialism appealed to him and in it only he saw the means to bail out the state, not essentially in the doctrinaire cult of the term.

The objective resolution that he framed well ahead of the drafting of the Indian Constitution expressed this desire of him, though due to circumstantial limitations he gave it a more softer look. The political will to give India a socialist look and enact programme of socialist economy got translated into the Chapter IV of the Indian Constitution that contained certain directives to the state to be followed seriously so that the welfare of all could be ascertained. The state was directed to frame its policies as such that the common good of all the citizens could be secured, adequate means of livelihood could be provided to all, the concentration of wealth was to be checked, the means of production was to be directed for the common good and the ownership and control of the material resources was to be ensured in accordance with the common good.

In 1944 Nehru unequivocally advocated economic planning in the context of democratic freedom and with a large measure of cooperation of some of the groups who were normally opposed to the doctrine of socialism. He firmly held, "if class conflict was inevitable, it had to be faced; but if it could be avoided or minimized that was an obvious gain".[9]

The initial opposition from within the party that crystallized with the election of Tandon on to the top of the organization kept him bewildered from the prime objective. However, with the resignation of Tandon the organizational might was subdued and Nehru while preparing the party manifesto in 1951 stated, "The time has come for our struggle for emancipation to enter into the second phase of realizing those objectives without which the political freedom can have little meaning for most of us. Economic progress must therefore, be given first priority, subject only to the maintenance of the freedom and the integrity of the country".[10] He kept the rhetoric on though never at the cost of the virtues of democracy. He would address the Chief Ministers thus, "indeed I would say that there is an ultimate conflict between a democracy and an economic structure which doesn't lead to economic democracy".[11] He was the socialist theoretician of the most well organized conservative party of India. He preached socialism but never developed a socialist cadre or socialist group within the party. One of the Nehru's critics, Ram Manohar Lohia, said occasionally that Nehru was simultaneously India's Prime Minister and the leader of the opposition. He never moved too far in any direction to create a situation of civil war in the country.[12]

Nevertheless, he never closed the doors for the flow of capital from outside as it would shrink the vistas of rapid economic development, the dire need of the time. He sincerely confessed this when he remarked soon after independence that industrial development would not be possible without the foreign aid either in cash or in kind.[13]

Though, being a true democrat he was not averse to the idea of individual freedom and progress yet the good of many against the established gentry dictated him regularly and rightly so. Under the fervour of socialism he never got lost in to the deep fathoms of doctrinaire orthodoxy as this was again misleading and treacherous. Unlike the international counterparts turned into socialist regiments he kept due space for the free breathing of the common nationals.

In his own words even the complete nationalization of the industry unaccompanied by political democracy will lead only to a different kind of exploitation for while industry will then belong to the states, the state itself will not belong to the people'.[14] In Jaipur's AICC session of 1963 and Bhubneswar session of 1964 Nehru had deeper interest in defining India's socialist objective. He was of the view that concentration of economic activity should not be in the hands of the state but freedom of initiative and enterprise was necessary. 'He was too much an individualist and believer in personal freedom to like regimentation'.[15]

His adherence to the socialist society earned him a good number of dissidents such as C. Rajgopalachari and others.

The founding of Planning Commission was an old dream of Nehru realized soon after the implementation of the Constitution. This he could get done only after a long struggle against the intra-party elements. There was staunch opposition to the planning towards some major socio-economic reforms but it was his consistent approach that he succeeded in founding a planning commission of India, of which he remained Chairman till last.[16] Although it was an advisory body with decision-making powers remaining vested in the cabinet and parliament, it became increasingly powerful particularly in the mid-fifties. The functions and the boundaries between central government and it became blurred, and a small group of prime minister's hand-picked sympathizers dominated it under his leadership, with the assistance of an elaborate secretariat and technical experts who gathered detailed information on which policy cold be based. Outside it, in Congress, in Parliament and in the states few had the expertise to challenge it.[17]

Aware of the myriad of challenges he had to go for agriculture on the priority bases in the first five year plan. But as he would say that industrialization is the key to the quick economic development and rapid progress the Second Five Year Plan scored a point over the first and crystallized Nehru's objective of 'socialistic pattern of society', a phrase floated most probably for the first time at the Awadi Session of Congress held in 1955. 'For Nehru the role of public sector was desirable as well as compulsion. It was desirable in the sense that progressive state ownership of the means of production as enunciated in the industrial policy resolution of 1956 was necessary for the fulfilment of the objectives of socialistic pattern of society. It was equally a compulsion in that private sector was both shy and inadequate to meet the financial and technological requirements of the massive capital intensive infrastructure and heavy industry projects. Growth of the public sector was also necessary to prevent the dominance of private capital and the profit motive which promoted individual interests at the cost of societal needs. Driven by the economic philosophy the share of the public sector investment rose from 46 per cent in the First Plan to 56 per cent in the Second Plan and to 61 per cent in the Third Plan. The Annual investment in the public sector rose from Rs. 200 crores in 1950-51 to Rs. 450 crores in 1955-56 and Rs. 800 crores in 1960-61'.[18] Here he didn't shut the doors for the private investors as according to him there was plenty of room for private enterprise.

However, it didn't envisage a total nationalization of industries rather a mixed economy in which private sector was to exist side by side, of course to trigger rapid development. As capital investment was the need he will not shut the doors to the private companies of India or abroad. It was a time when the private sector grew in enormous proportions in India and it was no more looked down upon as a socialist protégé.

When asked about the criticism that was being levelled against him about India going the totalitarian way under his leadership, Nehru deplored the fact that his critics were ignorant of the modern international trend which was neither totalitarian in nature nor of the laissez faire variety of the nineteenth century. He further pointed out that the world trend today was a via media between the laissez faire of the nineteenth century and the totalitarianism as represented by some countries in the twentieth century; as the evils of the both these extremes had been realized by people in different countries. Nehru than gave the examples of the USA and USSR and pointed out that in the former, which was essentially a democratic country the sphere of state action was progressively enlarging, whereas in the latter a gradual relaxation of the governmental hold over the people was noticeable. In a totalitarian set-up the individual was sacrificed at the altar of the state, the individual therein was for the state and not the state for the individual. Nehru was very allergic to the idea of a state, wherein the individual lost his identity and became a mere tool in the hands of the state. He believed implicitly in the view that the state was intended primarily to advance the welfare of the individual; at the same time he was also aware of the fact that the individual could not be looked at in isolation and that his obligations to the society should correspond with his rights.[19]

Notwithstanding the attraction towards socialism Nehru saw some fundamental lapses in communism of the day. Neither he approved of the means of communists nor the tight regimentation of the state that took individual as a mere instrument to establish equality among unequal. It also ignored the vital aspect of human life, faith in religion and morality, bereft of which man falls into the web of disillusionment. In the words of Nehru "communism comes in the wake of this disillusionment and offers some kind of faith and some kind of discipline. To some extent it fills a vacuum. It succeeds in some measure by giving a content to man's life. But in spite of its apparent success, it fails, partly because of its rigidity, but even more so, because it ignore certain essential needs of human nature. There is much talk in communism of the contradictions of capitalist society and there is truth in that analysis. But we see the growing contradictions within the rigid framework of communism itself. Its suppression of individual freedom brings about powerful reactions. Its contempt for what might be called moral and spiritual side of life not only ignores something that is basic in man, but also deprives human behaviour of standards and values. Its unfortunate association with violence encourages a certain evil tendency in human beings".[20]

However, the welfare of all is the ultimate goal of all the systems. Every system whether capitalist, socialist or communist accepts the ideal of welfare state. Capitalism in a few countries at least, has achieved this common welfare to a very large extent, though it has far from solved its own problems and there is a basic lack of something vital. Democracy allied to capitalism has undoubtedly toned down many of its evils and in fact is different now from what it was a generation or two ago...the forces of capitalist society if left unchecked, tend to make the rich richer and poor poorer and thus increase the gap between them. Various democratic processes interfere with these normal trends. Capitalism itself has, therefore developed some socialistic features even though its major aspects remain.[21] Thus Nehru stood for a queer mixture of the two - capitalism and socialism as the two at their own extremes were not flawless. His idea of going for a planned economy paid the results and it was due to this balanced approach that India could face the difficult patch of time. The idea of planning would, in future too, remain as relevant as it is in the past. People can't opt for a free inflow of global forces as this would subdue the political and cultural bounds of the states and a whole lot of global mix can create a mess.

Foreign Policy and NAM

Today the groundwork done by Nehru for the foreign policy of India still works as the chief fabric of it no matter the slight shift that the last decade has witnessed in the area of political and strategic fields. His ideals of internationalism and peaceful coexistence still carry weight and have become part of the political culture of India which substantially derives from our rich past.

Nehru, a true child of the times, and the head of the interim government was the first to be looked for about the future course of events. Being at the helm of affairs and having a wide experience of international developments he took special interest in foreign relations of India. He kept the portfolio of Foreign Affairs with him till 1964 for about 17 years.

"Non-alignment despite the negative form of the term, is a positive concept, and we do not propose to have a military alliance with any country, come what may. The moment we give up the idea of non-alignment, we loose every anchor that we hold on to and we simply drift".[22]

This principle of NAM was quite clear from his words as Head of Interim Government in September, 1946, "We propose, as far as possible, to keep away from the power politics of the groups, aligned against one another, which have led in the past to world wars and which may lead again to disasters on an even vaster scale...the world in spite of its rivalries and hatred and inner conflicts moves inevitably towards closer cooperation and the building up of a world commonwealth. It is for this One World for which India will work, a world in which there is the free cooperation of free peoples, and no class or group exploits another".[23]

Today the solidarity of Indo-Russian relations don't show the kind of vehemence and enthusiasm it used to show a few decades back and Indo-US relations have reached a landmark point, a stage least visible in the past. With the new nuclear deal between India and United States a new pattern of relations and cooperation is emerging in South Asia.

Recently, the statement of US Secretary of the State Condoleeza Rice at the US-India business meet advising India to dump NAM seems to be guided or issued with inadequate knowledge about the idea. The External Affairs Minister, Pranab Mukherjee, rightly remarked that NAM has contemporary relevance. NAM is still relevant even after the end of the Cold War. India is founding member of the NAM. And since its birth NAM has been playing a very active role in fostering cooperation among nation particularly among developing countries. The relevance of NAM lies in promoting north-south dialogue, south-south cooperation and new international economic order. NAM members have a voice in almost all the international matters and NAM countries, which are mostly developing countries, have been playing a very active role in international bodies like United Nations. Increased memberships of the NAM over the years also signify the increasing relevance of NAM even today. Still those factors are prevalent which were responsible for the emergence NAM like corruption, transnational organized crime, hegemony of US, apartheid etc.[24] So it is wrong to say NAM has become irrelevant toady.

If we take NAM as a strategy and a means against the global alignments then it might have lost the edge but if we perceive it as an ideology or philosophy of peace, love, justice, equality, friendship, and cooperation at international level, as preached by Nehru it would never loose the gloss.

Internationalist

No doubt that Jawaharlal Nehru was a true nationalist from the core but his nationalism never stood in the way of his love for humanity, dignity of every individual and country. His ultimate objective was to found a world order where every nation would respect the sanctity of the honour of the other and peace would be the zeitgeist of the global life. Once he observed, "nationalism has a place in each country and it should be fostered, but it must not be allowed to become aggressive and come in the way of international development".[25] Mahatma Gandhi once observed of him that 'be it said to his credit that Jawaharlal Nehru will consider it beneath his dignity to purchase freedom at the price of any other country. His nationalism is equal to his internationalism'.[26] On several occasions in his autobiography Nehru speaks of higher ideals and objectives instead of getting confined to the bounds of narrow parochial vision. He was a true patriot from the heart and he strongly reacted against the allegations that he and Congress considered themselves as the only patriots. For him patriotism was not the monopoly of any group or person rather 'patriotism was no longer enough; what was required was something higher, wider and nobler'.[27] He found in Gandhi also a true internationalist in whom according to him met the ideas of a nationalist and internationalist.

For Nehru it was inherent in our culture to adapt with the foreign values and there should be no problem with us to accept the same today which, in fact has become the need of the hour. He held that because 'we march to the one world of tomorrow where national cultures will be intermingled with the international culture of human race, we shall therefore, seek wisdom and knowledge and friendship and comradeship wherever we can find them, and cooperate with others in common tasks, but we shall remain true Indians and Asiatics, and become at the same time good internationalists and world citizens'.[28]

His internationalism was more akin to the socialist oneness of the people of world. He wanted a setup in which everyone was equal, though not purely in economic sense, and that all get equal opportunities for development. This could be done only by eradicating the economic disparities which was feasible through the instrumentality of socialism. Charmed by the success of USSR he held with great expectations that 'if the future is full of hope it is largely because of Soviet Russia and what it has done, and I am convinced that, if some world catastrophe doesn't intervene, this new civilization will spread to other lands and put an end to the wars and conflicts that capitalism feeds'.[29]

Nehru also saw an imminent link between the nationalist struggles of different people and the global events shaping the world history. There was no use getting one adrift from such events which would only weaken the status of the state. If we want to solve our problems we have to study the struggles of the other people also and only after this we would be able to understand our problems in the right perspective.

Thus Nehru's ideas over international peace, cooperation and brotherhood together with his ideas on planning, non-alignment and mixed economy would remain relevant in times to come.

NOTES

1. George Ritzer & M. Ryan, "Globalization of Nothing", in Samir Dasgupta, (Ed.), *The Changing Faces of Globalization,* (N. Delhi: Sage Publications 2004), p. 300.
2. For details see S. Brown, *New Forces Old Forces and the Future of World Politics,* (Boston: Scott/Foreman, 1988).
3. Michael Brecher, *Nehru: A Political Biography,* (New Delhi: Oxford University Press, 1959), pp. 59-59.
4. Presidential Address at the Indian National Congress, (Lucknow, 1939).
5. J.L. Nehru, *India and the World,* (London: George Allen & Unwin Ltd. 1934), pp. 82-83.
6. Jawaharlal Nehru, An Autobiography, (Delhi: Oxford University Press, 1985), p. 523.
7. Brecher, *op.cit.,* p. 196.
8. Nehru's Presidential Address at the Indian National Congress, (Lucknow, 1939).
9. Jawaharlal Nehru, *Discovery of India,* (Delhi,), p. 480
10. Congress Election Manifesto 1951, *SWJN* (2), Vol. 16 ii, p.4
11. Nehru to Chief Ministers, 16 January 1956, *LCM,* Vol. 4, p. 337.
12. K. P. Karunakaran, *The Phenomenon of Nehru,* (New Delhi: Gitanjali Prakashan: 1979), pp. 22-23.
13. Jawaharlal Nehru's Speeches, Vol. II, 1949-53, p. 49.
14. Shriman Narayan, *Towards a Socialist Economy,*(Bombay: Asia Publishing House, 1964, p. 7.
15. Saroj Malik, "Socialist Ideas of Jawahar Lal Nehru", in Suneera Kapoor, (Ed.), *Thought and Vision of Jawahar Lal Nehru,* (New Delhi: Anamika Publishers, 2005) p. 79.
16. See F.R. Frankel, *India's Political Economy 1947-77, The Gradual Revolution,* (Delhi: Oxford University Press, 1978).
17. Judith Brown, Nehru: Profiles in Power, (London : Longman, 1988), p. 123.
18. S.K. Bedi, "Nehru's Economic Philosophy in the Context of the Contemporary Liberalization in India", in D.S. Chaudhari, (Ed.), *Nehru and Nation Building,* (New Delhi: Rawat Publisher, 2005), p. 42.
19. N.G. Rajurkar & Narhar Kurundkar, *Jawaharlal Nehru: The Thinker and the Statesman,* (Rohtak: Manthan Publications, 1985), pp.
20. Jawaharlal Nehru, All India Congress Committee, 15 August, 1958.
21. *Ibid.*
22. Speech in Rajya Sabha, May 4, 1959.
23. India's Foreign Policy, (New Delhi: Publication Division of Govt. of India, 1961), p. 2.

24. Deepak Kumar, *NAM Still has Contemporary Relevance*, July 1, 2007.
25. Independence and After, (New Delhi: Publication Division, Govt. of India, 1949), p. 300.
26. Nehru, *Abhinandan Granth*, (Birthday Book), p. 127.
27. J.L. Nehru, *An Autobiography, op. cit.*, p. 414
28. Jawaharlal Nehru, *The Discovery of India, op. cit.*, p. 540.
29. Presidential Address at Indian National Congress, (Lucknow, 1939).

13

NEHRU'S INTERNATIONALISM

NARINDER KUMAR GUPTA

The qualities of Nehru as a man which stand out and which still elicit our admiration are his genuine humanism, burning patriotism, his liberal internationalism, his rational and scientific approach to problems, his authentic secularism, his concern for poor and oppressed, his solicitude for the minorities, his freedom from narrow chauvinism and obscurantism, his absolute integrity and honesty, his tolerance of other men's ideas, his respect for the opposition, his understanding of incipient nationalism in many part of Asia and Africa, his fearlessness, his attempt to synthesize the old and new, the material with the spiritual and traditional with the modern.[1]

Nehru was one of the freedom fighter and struggled for about three decades and made many sacrifices for the freedom of the country. He was a great nationalist. He was also very much concerned with the humanity also and because of this reason he was more identified with internationalism. He never tried to sacrifice national interest in internationalism. However, he tried to reconcile both.

At present, despite globalization there is threat of arms race. When Pundit Nehru was on national and international political scene, he had his views on internationalism. His some views are still relevant.[2]

Nehru never wanted that the independence of any country should endanger the right of the freedom of another country. Thus, even during the freedom struggle, he kept an eye on internationalism. He visualized that freedom of any country must be a milestone towards international cooperation and brotherhood.[3]

Nehru felt that like nationalism, internationalism was also inevitable phenomenon. He was of the view that the entire world was a single unit and no division of humanity were possible. Thus, he could not separate India from the rest of the world and could not think of India without taking into account the well-being of other countries. The day India got freedom he said, "these dreams are for India but they are also for the world, for all nations and people are too closely knit today for any one of them to imagine that it can live apart. Peace has been said to be indivisible; so is freedom; so is prosperity now; and so also is disaster in this one world that can no longer be isolated fragment."[4] The realization of the bond between man and man was the fundamental cause of his internationalist ideas. He could not think of independence of India to be utilized only for limited purpose to pursue selfish motives of nations only without having regard for internationalism. He expressed the view, "Nationalist as I am in regard to Indian freedom, I do not look upon contacts with other people from narrow nationalist view point. My very nationalism is based on internationalism, and I am very conscious of the fact that the modern world with its science and world trade and swift methods of transport, is based on internationalism. No country or people can isolate themselves form the rest of the world, and if they attempt it, they do so at their peril and the attempt is bound to fail in end."[5]

Nehru was of the view that Indians should develop an international bent of mind so as to exist in the international world. He felt that isolation from world affairs would mean backwardness and decay. He observed that it was India's way throughout the history to welcome and absorb other cultures. He advised to use this habit to accept new idea of internationalism too. That is much more necessary today. He further said, "for we march to one world tomorrow where national cultures will be intermingled with the international culture of human race. We shall, therefore, seek wisdom and friendship and comradeship wherever we can find them, and cooperate with others in common task, but we shall remain true Indians and Asiatics, and become at the same time good internationalists and world citizens."[6]

Nehru's ideas of internationalism were greatly influenced by Gandhi which were acknowledged by him in his book *Discovery of India*, wherein he quoted Gandhi, "My idea of nationalism is that my country may become free, that if need be the whole of the country may die, so that human race may live. There is no room for race hatred here. Let that be our nationalism."[7]

Nehru had the vision to see unity in diversity. He expressed this vision in his presidential address to All Bengal Student's Conference, he said, "We are told of vital differences of race and character. So differences there undoubtedly are but . . . you will find common bond and more vital than the differences, though many of us may not realize the fact."[8]

Nehru's philosophy of internationalism was not adversely affected by power politics. He practiced his philosophy and said, "a free democratic India will gladly associate herself with other nations for mutual defence against aggression and for economic cooperation. She will work . . . for progress and advancement of humanity."[9]

Nehru tried to harmonize his nationalistic and internationalistic ideas. He was committed to work for national interest but tried it to balance with the interest of other nations. In this context, he said, "I have naturally looked to the interest of India, for that is my first duty. I have always conceived that duty in terms of larger good of the world."[10]

After independence Nehru worked to implement his ideas of internationalism. He opined that peace and freedom must not remain wishes for most of the countries of the world rather entire humanity may be allowed to enjoy freedom as their right. He said, 'Every intelligent person can see that if you have a narrow national policy it may enthuse the multitude for the moment . . . but it is bad for the national and it is bad internationally because you loose sight of the ultimate good and thereby endanger your own good. Therefore, we propose to look after India's interests in the context of world cooperation and world peace, in so far as world peace can be preserved."[11]

In order to promote world peace Nehru propounded five principles of international behaviour known as Panchsheel. These principles were : respect for each other's territorial integrity and sovereignty, non-aggression, non-interference in each other's internal affairs, equality and mutual benefit and peaceful co-existence.[12]

His vision of internationalism went ahead in the direction of world state where individuality of the nation state will be respected. The nation will continue to exist but "giving up only part of independence to the world order."[13]

It was under Nehru's leadership that India joined common-wealth. He was determined to use the commonwealth forum to preserve world peace. Nehru urged migrants Indian living in other commonwealth countries to behave with decorum in their host countries and to work with local people to resolve the tensions.[14]

Nehru emphasized the need for peace, and India's own wish to live in peace with all nations, in countless speeches at home and abroad . . . Nehru's support for commonwealth was in part because he felt it could be an institution through which to work for peace and mutual understanding. But the principal institution through which he hoped for a more peaceful world order was the infant United Nations.[15]

Speaking to the United Nations General Assembly in November 1948 he pledged India's commitment to the principle purposes of the United Nations Charter, and talked about throwing aside many fears which generated conflicts, invoking the teaching of Gandhi, which we hoped could be exported from the Indian situation as a means of dealing with world problem.[16] He supported United Nations constantly as a vehicle for peace.

Non-Alignment

Nehru's most significant strategy for prevention of war in the 1950's was the policy of non-alignment, which for him had profound significance as well as a realistic and pragmatic way of protecting India's Interest in the Cold War situation. Looking back from the perspective of the ends of Nehru's century and the ending of a world order demarcated by blocs raged against each other in the fear and hostility, it is perhaps difficult to recognize quite what an innovative and visionary stance India took under Nehru. It would have been far easier to shelter under the protective umbrella of one or other alliance structures, but Nehru was determined that India would be contained into such mould, would stake a claim for a moral stance which might serve and unite many Asian and African countries, seeking a genuine independence of policy, and would work for peace by preventing the building up of antagonistic power blocs.[17]

He spoke several times, mainly on the need for Asian and African countries to take a positive stance to secure world peace which in his eyes mean adhering to a policy of non-alignment and peaceful co-existence.[18]

Thus Nehru represented a combination of ideas as dictated by the imminence of contemporary times and the necessities of national interests of India. He gave due place to the ideas of human welfare, peace, cooperation and universal brotherhood and at the same time preached a middle path via non-alignment—a rational and pragmatic way out to the ferocious currents of cold war. His alternative of mixed economy governed by the tenets of socialism and welfare of all would keep on working at the mindscapes of people in general and statesmen in particular.

NOTES

1. Mehrotra, S. R., *Jawaharlal Nehru : A Reassessment, Thoughts and Vision of Jawaharlal Nehru*, (2005), p. 27.
2. Bhardwaj, Saroj, "*Nehru on Nationalism and Internationalism*", *Thought and Vision of Jawaharlal Nehru*, (2005), p. 127.
3. Selected Works of Jawaharlal Nehru, (1972), Vol. III, p. 191.
4. Shiva Rao, B., *India's Freedom Movement : Some Notable Figures*, (1972), p. 146.
5. Nehru, Jawaharlal, *Eighteen Months in India 1936-37: Essays and Writings*, (1938), p. 184.
6. Nehru, Jawaharlal, *Discovery of India*, (1951), p. 540.
7. *Ibid.*, p. 397.
8. Supra note 3, p. 189.
9. *Ibid.*
10. As quoted by Frank Moraes, *Jawaharlal Nehru : A Biography*, (1956), p. 416.
11. Constituent Assembly of India, (Legislative) *Debates*, Vol. II, Dec. 4, 1947.
12. Das, M. N., *The Political Philosophy of Jawaharlal Nehru*, (1961), p. 207.
13. Jawaharlal Nehru Speeches, Vol. V, (1968), p. 202.
14. Brown, Judith M., Nehru, A Political Life, (2003), p. 25.
15. *Ibid.*, p. 256.
16. *Ibid.*
17. *Ibid.*, p. 257.
18. *Ibid.*, p. 261.

14

NEHRU'S PERSPECTIVE ON GLOBALIZATION

DASARATHI BHUYAN

Jawaharlal Nahru's global perspective and internationalism based on peace, good will and co-operation among nations raised him to the stature of a statesman and world leader. He took great interest in world affairs and was almost the sole architect of India's foreign Policy.

After Independence, Nehru became the first Foreign Minister. He was clear in his mind that the foreign policy of a nation must be rooted primarily in enlightened national interests. He insisted that national interest was not enough and that India, even though in political bondage, must see her struggle in the larger context of global developments. He was in favour of a reasonable balance between nationalism and internationalism. Nahru's foreign policy as B. Pradhan remarks, "stood on a quadrangular ideological foundation, the four cornerstones of which were provided by scientific humanism, the flair for freedom, passion for peace and universalism and world view".

Nahru was a firm believer in the ideal of a world community, few had shown greater faith and allegiance to the character of the United Nations than Nehru. Nehru had a deep sense of cosmopolitanism. His vision of the future embraced the whole humanity. He was in the words of Kingslay Martin, "a symbol to all the world, a symbol of the world we look for, all hope for, which is yet to come".

Till very recently we have been frequently using the term internationalism to refer to the process of increasing connections and relations among nations. It denotes the concept of increasing social, economic, cultural and political co-operation among nations. Now instead of advocating internationalism, we have started advocating globalization which refers to a broader and integrated process of transformation of the world into a global village characterized by free world trade, freedom of access to world markets and increased social, economic and cultural linkages and relations among the people of the world.

Whereas internationalism stands for increasing scope and intensity of co-operation among nations, globalization refers to a free and integrated world system. Globalization neither is a purely economic process nor is related to communications only. It is a broad process of increasing social-economic-industrial-trade-cultural relations among the people living in all parts of the globe. It refers to the process, which is considered essential for transforming the world into an interrelated and inter-dependent global village. It is aimed at securing the benefits of free trade, open access to markets and equal participation in securing sustainable development for all the people. It involves the attempts aimed at the development of rules and procedures for making and enforcing all decisions required for securing globalization. In simple words, the aim of globalization is to secure socio-economic integration and development of all the people of the world.

The concept of globalization is not far away from the internationalism of Nehru. Globalization does not admit of easy definition, because it involves several processes some of which are overlapping. Some, time some of these processes also become contradictions or opposites.

Globalization, no doubt, relates to the globe or world. But it is much more than this. This implies that in an ideal regime of globalization, there are no national borders. There is free flow of information, ideas, capital, products, services and even governance across the border. Nehru had also the same vision. According to him, "Internationalism demands that each country shall take an intelligent interest in world affairs and give up the desire to live in isolation from the rest. In this age of atomic weapons and sputniks the only way to avoid the destruction of human civilization is the free association of all the nations in some type of world federation. Nationalism and internationalism must be balanced and harmonized in the interest of world peace and world unity".

Nehru believed that India's freedom struggle was a part of the global struggle. He had all the sympathy for the oppressed nations and he supported their cause. He supported the struggle for independence in Afro-Asian countries.

Nehru believed that the modern world with its science, 'trade and transport was based on internationalism'. No country could remain in isolation because that might lead to its own destruction. He was optimistic of a world federation. In 1947 at the Asian conference he said, "we have arrived at a stage in human affairs when ideal of one world and same kind of a world federation seems to be essential, though there are dangers and obstacles in the way".

In the past, there were a number of colonial empires. These empires had been established by several European Powers including Britain and France and the empires including colonies in the far away places like Asia, Africa and America. The colonial powers were capitalist ones and colonialism was transformed into imperialism. This prompted Lenin to argue that 'Capitalism' is the highest form of imperialism. The old colonialism crossed national barriers, sought to transplant some elements of culture of the mother-country (Colonial power) in the soil of the colony and forged some administrative linkages between them. Thus, old colonialism, to some extent, reflected globalization.

But when we speak of globalization today, we have mainly in mind that phenomenon or process of tremendous power and far reaching implications which has appeared in the aftermath of the end of cold war during 1989-92.

Even before the cold war, the leaders and experts of the west had been pleading free trade between nations so that being economically dominant, they would control and dominate that economics of developing countries. They wanted their free and unrestricted access to the markets and resources of developing countries. They advocated dismantling of protectionist barriers raised by developing countries, though they themselves practice protectionism to defend the interests of their own industrialists, workers and farmers. During the cold war, they were trying to persuade developing countries to accept their demand. But, with end of cold war, they are trying to impose, their views on the latter. US is aggressively pursuing the globalization agenda. Many developing countries, while appreciating same aspects of globalization, have strong reservations about its other aspects. But they find it difficult to oppose and check globalization. Slowly and gradually they have started to fall in line.

In the above context Nehru's concept of nationalism was not contradictory but complementary to internationalism. He condemned expansionism, imperialist desires and humiliation of one nation by another. He was a liberal and broad-minded leader of the world order. He did not favour any chauvinistic feeling or aggressive nationalism. He believed in and worked for world peace.

M.C. Chagla writes, "Nehru was a nationalist because he wanted his country to achieve the full status of nationhood, but in the heart of his heart, he was an internationalist, and the whole world was the stage on which he wanted to play his part. P.B. Gajendragadkar once said, "with all nationalism, Nehru was basically an internationalist. His life is a saga of valour, sacrifice, dedication; but its ultimate goal was the establishment of one world. Nehru never forget that ultimate destiny of human race is the formation of one brotherhood where friendship and comradeship will prevail and every citizen of the world will be enabled to enjoy life, liberty and happiness".

The concept of globalization also seeks to cut across national borders and dismantle national barriers. It has, as its ideal, a world without borders. Jawaharlal Nehru's dream of 'one world' has been really materialized today into a 'borderless world'.

The term globalization has been used in a multiplicity of senses. Concepts like "the global interdependence of nations", "the growth of world system", "and accumulation on a world scale", "a global village" and many others are rooted in the more general notion that the accumulation of capital, trade and investment is no longer confined to the nation-state. In its most general sense, 'globalization' refers to cross-national flows of goods, investment, production and technology. Many protagonists of globalization believe that the scope and depth of these flows have created a New World Order with its own institutions and configurations of power that have replaced the previous structures associated with the nation-state.

In 1937 Nehru wrote, "my very nationalism is based on an internationalism and I am very conscious of the fact that the modern world with its science and world trade and swift methods of transport, is based on internationalism". He further observed, "No country or people can isolate themselves from the rest of the world, and if they attempt it, they do so at their peril and the attempt is bound to fail in the end".

Nehru did not like the idea of supernational states. In 1944 he wrote, "I don't like the division of the world into a few supernational areas, unless they are tied together by some strong world bond".

Nehru attended the congress of oppressed Nationalities at Brussels as the sole representative of the Congress party in 1927. This conference broadened Nehru's international outlook. Nehru was a socialist and for him internationalism had a natural appeal. In the year 1933, Nehru said, "The struggle for Indian Freedom is essentially a part of the World struggle for the emancipation of the exploited everywhere and for the establishment of a new social order". In the subsequent years Nehru saw the possibility of a world federation. He himself said, "If a World federation comes, that will be welcomed". Nehru always advocated for the creation of a world federation. In his speech at the Asian Conference in 1947, Nehru said, "we have arrived at a stage in human affairs when the ideal of one world and some kind of a world federation seems to be essential, though there are many dangers and obstacles in the way". He further observed that, "Internationalism demands that each country shall take interest in world affairs and give up the desire to live in isolation from the rest. Nationalism and internationalism must be balanced and harmonized in the interest of world peace and world unity". Thus, Nehru advocated a sort of balance or reconciliation between nationalism and internationalism.

Nehru did not want internationalism at the cost of nationalism. He said, "in a contest between nationalism and internationalism, nationalism was bound to win. That had happened in every country and in every crisis, and was an inevitable and unavoidable consequence". During 1920's and 1930's, Nehru observed that free nations betrayed the cause of internationalism for national gain. He saw England and France playing false to the republican Spain and Czechoslovakia and thereby sacrificing internationalism for their own national interests. This view of Nehru is relevant in the present context too. The United States of America, the sole super power is ardently pursuing the globalization agenda for its own national interests and this is true of other states too. The preference for the national interests over the global and general human welfare will keep on challenging the dream of Nehru.

The end of the cold war marked the victory of capitalism over communism. Capitalist democracy has decisively won and communism has accepted defeat. Globalization is capitalism in a new form. In fact, capitalism enriches itself only when it makes the globe or a number of countries its field of operation. For the time being capitalism has come to stay, and there is no alternative to capitalism. Those who until the other day bitterly criticized capitalism have willy-nilly accepted it. Now the choice is between neo-liberal capitalism, advocated by neo conservatives of the West and regulated capitalism, advocated by liberal democrats of many developing countries. Globalization will be universally acceptable only when it brings freedom, rights, peace, security and economic benefits to the vast number of people across the globe who have remained poor weak and deprived. To Pandit Nehru, culture and civilization are not the monopoly of any one or more nations, and the hope of peace in the world is not just a pious aspiration but also a vital necessity.

The progress of industrial revolution in the 20th century was accompanied by a replacement of the 'Police State by a Welfare State'. The state came to be an active actor in the economic life of the society. In the socialist states, state ownership of means of production and distribution became the rule and state controlled command economies were operationalized and regarded as the best means for rapid socio-economic development. In many other countries, nationalization of key industries and enterprises was undertaken with a view to provide goods and services to the people. State began performing several socio-economic functions. In true sense of the term Nehru was not a socialist and what he favoured was a socialist pattern of society, which is not a rigid or set formula. He wanted to solve the economic and social problems of India without being a doctrinaire. He was a great democrat and was not in favour of sacrificing democratic values for socialism. Socialism in true sense of the term was against democracy, liberalism and capitalism. But Nehru had a weakness for both. Thus, he tried to combine both democracy and socialism in order to evolve a new concept known as democratic-socialism. His ambition was that, while individual freedom, initiative and enterprise would be allowed to function; at the same time state control would be there. There would be private sector and the public sector working together for national development. But the state would control the major means of production and distribution. While socialism does not allow privatization, democracy does not believe in excess state control. But democratic-socialism assimilates both into one. Nehru's socialism was in favour of mixed economy. That means both public and private sectors would grow simultaneously. The public sector or the state enterprise would take care of the major means of production like heavy industries and the areas where there are less margin of profit or where private sector lacks interest besides undertaking high order public utility services. The private sector would have to be left with other areas particularly the agricultural industry, which is very vital for India. He combined the free enterprise of U.S.A. with the state controlled economy of Soviet Union. Free India under the leadership of Jawaharlal Nehru adopted a mixed economic model. Ownership and control over key industries was entrusted to the public sector. Even insurance and banking were nationalized for securing a better mobilization of resources and consequently for rendering better services to the people. State regulation of economy and industry was practiced and the public sector was patronized by the state as the sector committed to provide essential goods and services to the public. The state, acting in the name of checking monopolies, undue concentration of wealth in some hands and economic inequalities, formulated and enforced strict regulation and control systems.

However, the experience with the working of mixed economic model, with a distinct leaning in favour of public sector was found to be inadequate slow and unproductive of desired results. Around 1985, Indian economy began showing big strains. Indian public sector became a liability and foreign exchange reserves came to be in very bad shape. Industrial growth became regressive and inflation was assuming alarming proportions. Around this time the world was heading for several big changes. The socialist economies, in particular the soviet economy and political system, were collapsing. Even 'perestroika' and 'glasnost' of Gorbachev could not save USSR. It collapsed as a state. The weaknesses of the socialist economic model became fully clear. All the socialist countries of Europe began witnessing a process of overthrow of socialist systems. All countries of the world began realizing the merits of the market economy, free trade, privatization, liberalization, delicensing and deregulation of trade, industry and business. In July 1991 the Government of India decided to go in for liberalization of economy. A new economic policy was formulated and implemented with an emphasis upon economic reforms. These were governed by the principles of liberalization, privatization, market economy, free trade, degeneration and delicensing. These reforms paved the way for initiating the process of liberalization and globalization of Indian Economy. It began with the aim of linking, integrating and unifying domestic economy with world economy. The role of state began emerging as that of a facilitator and co-coordinator, in place of an owner and controller. However, this does not in any way mean re-adoption of Laissez Faire or reversion to the principles of Police state. Under Globalization, the state still continues to be a welfare state. The economic activity of the state aims at providing social services such as education, health, social security etc. to the people. It acts as a facilitator and coordinator and refrains from acting as an owner and regulator. It continues to be a welfare state performing all the protection functions as well as several social functions. His decision to adopt a mixed economic model is not irrelevant in the process of globalization, which involves a change in the role of the state. Globalization constitutes a natural extension of the principles of international interdependence. It is a natural extension of the ideology of internationalism favoured by Jawaharlal Nehru.

References

Acharya. A.K., Nehru : The Non-Marxist salesman of Marxism in S.N. Rath (ed.) *Nehru : The Maker of Modern India,* Kalinga Publishers, Bhubaneswar (1989).

Brecher, M. Nehru : *A Political Biography,* Orxford University Press, London, (1959).

Baral, J.K. Hazary, S.C. & Padhy, AP, *Foundation of Politics and Government,* Kalyani, Ludhiana (2004).

Das, M.N., *The Political Philosophy of Nehru,* Allen & Unwin, London (1961).

Dutta, R.C., *Socialism of Jawaharlal Nehru,* Abhinab, Delhi (1981).

Ghai, K.K., *Foundations of Politics and Government,* Kalyani, (2004)

Gopal, K.K., *Jawaharlal Nehru : A Biography,* O.U.P., Delhi,(1985).

Hazary, S.C., The Nehru's Model of Development for India : An appraisal in S.N. Rath (ed) *Jawaharlal Nehru,* Annu Books, Meerut (1993).

Hazary, S.C., Democratic Socialism: A Critique of Indian Experiment in P. Bose (ed.) *Contemporary Socialism : An Analysis,* Harman, Delhi (1993).

Hazary, S.C., Jawaharlal Nehru, edited by Jugal Kishore Mishra, Sabdaloka, Cuttack,(1995).

Hazary, N., Democratic socialism and Jawaharlal Nehru in *Indian Journal of Political Science* (Conference Number).

Joshi, P.C., Nehru and Socialism in India, in B.R. Nanda (ed.) *Socialism in India,* Vikas, Delhi (1971).

Mohanty, M. Value Movement and Development Models in Contemporary India in Teaching Politics (1979).

Nayak, Gourang Charan, *Indian Political Tradition*, Kalyani, Ludhiana (2004).

Nehru, J., *The Discovery of India*, Signet Press, Calcutta (1946).

Pradhan B., Ideological Cornerstones of Jawaharlal's Foreign Policy in S.N. Rath (ed.), *Nehru : The Maker of Modern India*, Kalinga, Bhubaneswar (1989).

Rout, B, C. *Indian Political Traditions*, Panchashila, Cuttack (1996).

BIBLIOGRAPHY

Acharya, A.K, Nehru: "The Non-Marxist Salesman of Marxism", in S.N. Rath (ed.), *Nehru : The Maker of Modern India*, Bhubaneswar: Kalinga Publishers, 1989.

Ahluwalia, Montek S.,"India in a Globalising World", *27th Jawaharlal Nehru Memorial Lecture*, London, 20 April, 2005.

Akhilesh, Kumar Singh, "Groundwater is poison in U.P", *The Times of India*, October 24, 2006.

Alston, P., (Ed.), *The United Nations and the Human Rights*, (Oxford: Clarendon Press, 1992).

Andrew Heywood, *Key Concepts in politics*, (London: Macmillan Press Ltd, 2000) April-June 2000.

Appadurai,Arjun, *Modernity at Large, Cultural Dimensions of Globalizaion*, (Minneapolis University of Mineaswota Press, 1998).

Arat, Z. E., *Democracy, Human and Rights in Developing Countries*, (London: Lagneia Rainier Publishers, 1991).

Aruni Mukherjee, University of Warwick, *www.mkgandhi.org/articles/globalisation/htm*.

Aziz, Nikhil, "The Human Rights Debate in an Era of Globalisation: Hegemony of Discourse". *Bulletin of Concerned Asian Scholars*, Vol. 27, No. 4, Oct-Dec., 1995.

Badr, Alam Iqbal, "Globalization and Multinational Corporations in South Asia", *SARID Journal*, Vol. 1, Issue 1, 2000.

Bande,Usha,"Women and Peace", *pib.nic.in/feature/feyr2003/f030320031.html*

Baral, J.K,. Hazary, S.C. & Padhy, AP, *Foundation of Politics & Government*, (Ludhiana Kalyani, 2004).

Barnet, Richard and Cavenagh John, *Global Dreams: Imperial Corporations and the New World Order*, (NY: Simon & Schuster, 1994).

Basu, D. D., *Introduction to Constitution of India,* (New Delhi, Prentice-Hall of India, 2002).

Bedi, S.K., "Nehru's Economic Philosophy in the Context of the Contemporary Liberalization in India", in D.S. Chaudhari, (Ed.), *Nehru and Nation Building* (New Delhi: Rawat Publisher, 2005).

Benudhar Pradhan, *The Socialist Thought of Mahatma Gandhi*, Vol. II, (Delhi: GDK Publications, 1980).

Bergstaon, Fred & Randal, Henning, *Global Economic Leadership and the Group of Seven,* (Washington D C: Institute for International Economics, 1996).

Bhagwati, Jagdish, *In Defense of Globalization,* (New Delhi: Oxford University Press, 2004).

Bhaskaran, R., "The Philosophical Basis of India's Foreign Policy", in Misra, (Ed.), *Foreign Policy of India,* (New Delhi, 1984).

Bjorn, H., Inotia, A. & Sunkel, O., (Eds.), *Globalism and the New Regionalism,* (London: McMillan Press, 1994).

Boulder, Elise, "What is A Peace Culture?", http://www.globaleduc.org/whatisa.htm.

Boulding, Elise, "Feminist Inventions in the Art of Peacemaking", *Peace and Change,* Vol. 24, No. 4, October 1995.

Brecher, M., *Nehru : A Political Biography,* (Orxford University Press, London, 1959).

Brecher, Michael, *Nehru : A Political Biography,* (New Delhi: Oxford University Press, 1959).

Brecher, Michael, *India and the World Politics : Krishna Menon's View of the World,* New York, 1968.

Bregman, Ahron, *Israel's Wars: A History Since 1947,* (London: Routledge, 2002).

Brian, Mc Arthur: *Penguin Book of Twentieth Century Speeches,* (London, Penguin Viking, 1992).

Brooks, Chris W., "Globalization—A Political Perspective", www.bi.ulaval.ca/Globalization-Universities.

Brown, Judith M., *Nehru, A Political Life,* (London: 2003).

Brown, Judith, *Nehru: Profiles in Power,* (London : Longman, 1988).

Brown, S., *New Forces Old Forces and the Future of World Politics,* (Boston: Scott\Foreman, 1988).

Budhoo, D., "IMF-World Bank Wreak Havoc on Third World", *Third World Resurgence,* July 1992.

Burnell, Peter J., *Economic Nationalism in the Third World,* (Brighton,

Wheatsheaf Books, 1986).

Cammack, Paul, *Capitalism and Democracy in Third World*, (London: Leicester, 1997).

Carole, Collins, "A World in Mutation", *WSCF Journal*, December 1995.

Chakravarthi, Raghvan, "South May be Trapped into New WTO Round", *Nai Azadi Udghosh*, Vol. 6, No. 3-4, May-April, 2001.

Chatterjee, Somanath, "The Developmental Challenge in Rural India", *The Hindu*, 4 April, 2007.

Chauhan, Rajinder S. and Thakur, Harish K., *Globalization and Human Rights*, (New Delhi: Radha Publications, 2007).

Chawdhary, B.D. Nag and Bhatt, S., *The Global Environment Movement, A New Hope for Mankind*, (New Delhi: Sterling Publishers: 1994).

Congress Election Manifesto, 1951, *SWJN* (2), Vol. 16.

Constituent Assembly Debates, Vol. II, Dec. 4, 1947.

Crawford, J., (Ed.), *The Rights of People*, (Oxford: Oxford University Press, 1988).

Crook, S., J. Pukulski and M. Waters, *Postmodernism*, (London: Sage 1992).

Danilo, Turk, "How World Bank - IMF Policies Adversely Affect Human Rights", *Third World Resurgence*, May 1993.

Das, M.N., *The Political Philosophy of Nehru*. (Allen & Unwin, London, 1961).

Dasgupta, Samir, (Ed.), *The Changing Faces of Globalization*, (New Delhi: Sage Publications, 2004).

Dikshit, *Jawahar Lal Nehru : Centenary*, Volume, New Delhi, OUP, 1989.

Douglas Allen, "Gandhi, Contemporary Political Thinking and Self -Other Relations", in B.N. Ray, (Ed.), *Contemporary Political Thinking*, (New Delhi: Kanishka Publishers, 2000).

Dunn John, *Western Political Theory in the Face of the Future*, (Cambridge: Cambridge University Press, 1979).

Dutta, R.C., *Socialism of Jawaharlal Nehru*, (Delhi: Abhinab, 1981).

Elliott, Larry, "Warming Will Cost Trillions", *The Hindu*, October 14, 2006.

Engberg, Jan and Svante Ersson, "Illiberal Democracy in the 'Third World': An Empirical Enquiry," in Jeff Haynes (ed.), *Democracy and Political Change in the Third World*, (London: Routledge, 2001).

Field, J., in *Murm vs. Illinois,* 1994.

Frankel, F.R., *India's Political Economy 1947-77, The Gradual Revolution,* (Delhi: Oxford University Press, 1978).

Friedman, Thomas L., *The Lexus and the Olive Tree: Understanding Globalization,* (Cairo: International Publishers), 1999.

Friedman, Thomas, *The World is Flat: A Short History of the Globalized World in the 21st Century,* (London: Allen Lane, 2005).

Fukuyama, Francis, *The End of History and the Last Man,* (New York: The Free Press, 1992).

Gandhi, M.K., *Hind Swaraj and Other Writings,* (Cambridge University Press, 1997).

Gandhi, M.K., *India of my Dream.*

Gandhi, M.K., *Democracy: Real and Deceptive,* (Ahmedabad: Navjivan Publication, 1961).

Gandhi, M.K., *Socialism of My Conception* (Delhi).

Garfield, Simon, "Polar Bears on Climate Change", *The Hindu,* 6 March, 2007.

Ghai, K.K., *Foundations of Politics and Government,* (Ludhiana: Kalyani, 2004).

Global Issues, *Causes of Poverty, http://www.globalizationissues.org/Traderelated/Facts.asp.*

Gopal, K.K., *Jawaharlal Nehru, A Biography,* O.U.P., Delhi,(1985).

Gopal, S., (ed.), *Selected Works of Jawaharlal Nehru,* 2nd Ser., Vol. 13, (New Delhi: Jawaharlal Nehru Memorial Fund, 1992).

Haynes, Jeff, "Introduction: The 'Third World' and the Third Wave of Democracy,".

Hazari, S.C., in Jugal Kishore Mishra, (Ed.), *Jawaharlal Nehru,* (Cuttack, Sabdaloka ,1995).

Hazary, S.C., "The Nehru's model of Development for India : An Appraisal" in S.N. Rath (ed) *Jawaharlal Nehru,* (Meerut: Annu Books, 1993).

Hazary, S.C., "Democratic Socialism: A Critique of Indian Experiment", in P. Bose (ed.) *Contemporary Socialism, An Analysis,* (Delhi: Harman, 1993).

Hazary, N., "Democratic Socialism and Jawaharlal Nehru", in *Indian Journal of Political Science* (Conference Number).

Hensman, R., "Minimum Labour Standards and Trade Agreements: An Overview of the Debate", *Economic and Political Weekly,* 20-27 April, 1996.

Higgott, Richard, *Globalization and Regionalization, New Trends in World Politics* ,(The UAE :Emirates Centre for Strategic Studics and Research, 1998).

Hines, Colin, *Localization : A Global Manifesto,* (London: Earthhscan, 2000).

Hirst, Paul & Grahame Thompson, *Globalization in Question.*

Hufbaur, Gray C., *Globalization: Facts and Consequences,* (Institute for International Economics, 2001).

IMF, *World Economic.Outlook,* May, 1997.

Independence and After, (New Delhi: Publication Division, Govt. of India,1949).

"India High on Indoor Air Pollution": *WHO Report, The Hindu,* March 24, 2007.

International Labour Resources and Information Group, "Getting to Grips with Globalisation", *Workers World,* No. 3-4, January-February, 1996.

IPCC Report.

Jawaharlal Nehru Speeches, Vol. V, (1968).

Johnson, "Gandhi and Feminism : Towards Women-Affirming Cultures of Peace", *Gandhi Marg.*

Joshi, P.C. Nehru and Socialism in India, in B.R. Nanda, (ed) ,*Socialism in India,* (New Delhi: Vikas, 1971).

Kapoor, Suneera, (Ed.),*Thought and Vision of Jawaharlal Nehru,* (New Delhi: Anamika, 2005).

Karunakaran, K. P., *The Phenomenon of Nehru,* (New Delhi: Gitanjali Prakashan, 1979).

Kehar Singh vs. *Union of India,* AIR 1989 S.C. 6531 paragraph 7.

Khera, S.S., *India's Defence Problem,* (New Delhi: Orient Longmanns 1968).

Kochler, Hans (ed.): *Globility Versus Democracy? The Changing Nature of International Relations in the Era of Globalization,* (Vienna: International Progress Organisation, 2000).

Kothari, Rajni, *Footsteps into the Future,* (New Delhi: Orient Longman, 1974).

Kumar, Deepak, "NAM Still has Contemporary Relevance", July 1, 2007, *http://www.merinews.com.*

Lall, Arthur, "*Change and Continuity in India's Foreign Policy*".

Leake, Jonathan, Warming Sparks Extinction Fears, *The Times of India,* April 2, 2007.

Lechner, F.J. and Boli, J. (eds), *The Globalization Reader,* (London : Blackwell, 2001).

Louis, W.M., *The British Empire in Middle East: Arab Nationalism, the United States and Post-War Imperialism,* (OUP, 1986).

Malik, Saroj, "Socialist Ideas of Jawahar Lal Nehru", in Suneera Kapoor, (Ed.),*Thought and Vision of Jawahar Lal Nehru,* (New Delhi: Anamika Publishers, 2005).

Manfred B. Steger, *Globalization A very short introduction,* (London: Oxford University Press, 2003).

Manifesto, 2000, *IYCP UNESCO,* Paris.

Marsden, Richard, *The Nature of Capital, Marx after Foucault,* (Routledge Studies in Social and Political Thought 20, London, Routledge, 1999; Lenin, Vladimir, *IMPERIALISM, The Highest Stage of Capitalism,* (London:Lawrence and Wishart, 1948).

Maslow, Abraham, *Towards a Psychological Being,* 2nd Ed., (New York, D. Van Nostrand, 1968).

Mcqualis, D. Mcquail, *Mass Communication Theory,* (London : 2000).

Mehrotra, S. R., "Jawaharlal Nehru : A Reassessment", *Thoughts and Vision of Jawaharlal Nehru,* (2005).

Mehta, V.R., *Foundations of Indian Political Thought,* (New Delhi: Manohar Publishers, 1996).

Mishra, A.D., *Globalization: Myth and Reality,* (New Delhi: Concept Publications, 2006).

Mishra, Girish, "Globalization and Culture: Some Aspects", *Mainstream,* August, 16, 2003.

Mohanty, M. *Value Movement and Development Models in Contemporary India in Teaching Politics,* (1979).

Moraes, Frank, *Jawaharlal Nehru : A Biography,* (1956).

Mukerjee, Aruni, "Gandhi and Globalization", Article on Internet, www.mkgandhi.org/articles/globalisation.htm).

Murphy Craig N., "Political Consequences of New Inequality", *International Studies Quarterly,* 2001.

Nagraj, Adve, "Implications of Climate Panel Report", *Economic and Political Weekly,* March 24, 2007.

Nayak, Gourang Charan, *Indian Political Tradition,* (Ludhiana: Kalyani, 2004).

Nayar, Baldev Raj, *India's Globalization Evaluating the Economic Consequences,* (New Delhi : Vistar Publications, 2007).

Nehru, *Jawaharlal : An Autobiography,* (Delhi: Oxford University Press, 1985).

Nehru, J.L., *Nehru to Chief Ministers*, 16 January 1956, LCM, Vol. 4.

Nehru, J.L., *Abhinandan Granth*, (Birthday Book).

Nehru, J.L., *India and the World*, (London: George Allen & Unwin Ltd., 1934).

Nehru, J.L., *Nehru's Presidential Address at the Indian National Congress*, (Lucknow, 1939).

Nehru, J.L., *Nehru's Speech at the Concluding Session on April 24, 1955*.

Nehru, Jawaharlal, *Discovery of India*, (1951).

Nehru, Jawaharlal, *Eighteen Months in India 1936-37; Being Further Essays and Writings*, (1938).

Nehru, Jawaharlal, India's Foreign Policy: Selected Speeches.

Ohmae, Kenichi: *The End of the Nation State*, (New York: The Press, 1995).

Palmer, Norman D., "Foreign Policy of the Indian National Congress", in Misra, K P: *Foreign Policy of India*, (New Delhi, Thomson Press, 1977).

Pantham, Thomas, "*Beyond Liberal Democracy: Thinking with Mahatma Gandhi*".

Parameswaran, M.P., *Another World is Possible: Thoughts about a Fourth World*, Circulated on Net; Rajinder Chaudhary, "Fourth World: Marxian & Gandhian".

Environmental...", *Economic and Political Weekly*, Vol. 42, Oct. 15-21, 2005.

Parekh, Bhiku, *Colonialism, Tradition and Reform: An Analysis of Gandhi's Political Discourse*, (Delhi: Sage, 1989).

Parmeshwary, Dayal, *Gandhian Theory of Social Reconstruction*, (New Delhi: Atlantic Publishers, 2006).

Pasrichia, A., Gandhi, Boston.com/news/world/asia/articles/mahatma_legacy.

Paul, L.S.J., *Education for Globalization*, (America : America Press, 2002).

Powar, P.F., "Indian Foreign Policy: The Age of Nehru", *The Review of Politics*, Vol. 26, No. 2, April 1964.

Pradhan, B., "Ideological Cornerstones of Jawaharlal's Foreign Policy" in S.N. Rath, (ed.), *Nehru : The Maker of Modern India*, (Bhubneswar: Kalinga, 1989).

Pyarelal, *Mahatma Gandhi : The Last Phase*, Vol. 2, (Ahmedabad: Navjivan Publication, 1958).

Rajurkar, N.G. and Kurundkar, Narhar, *Jawaharlal Nehru: The Thinker and the Statesman*, (Rohtak: Manthan Publications, 1985).

Ramesh Babu, B., "Globalisation and the Indian Nation-State", in *Interpreting Globalization*, (New Delhi : Rawat Publication, 2004)

Ramjee Singh (ed.), *Gandhi and the Twenty First Century*, (New Delhi: Peace Publishers, 2005).

Ramjee Singh (ed.), *Gandhi and the Future of Humanity*, (Varanasi : Manak Publication, 2004).

Rao, Shiva, B., *India's Freedom Movement : Some Notable Figures* (1972).

Ritzer, George and Ryan, M., "Globalization of Nothing", in Samir Dasgupta, (Ed.), *The Changing Faces of Globalization*, (New Delhi: Sage Publications, 2004).

Robinson Richard and Goodman David S.G.(eds). "The New Rich in Asia: Economic Development, Social Status and Political Consciousness", *The New Rich is Asia*, London: Routledge, 1996.

Roerich, Nichola, > *http://www.pathwaystopeace.org/culture.htm.*

Rout, B.C., *Indian Political Traditions, Panchashila*, (Cuttack, 1996).

Rusett, de Alan, "An Understanding of Indian Foreign Policy", in Mishra, 1977.

Sanghaas, Dieter, "Modernity and Anti Modernity-Facing Cultural Globalization", *www.boell-meo.org/en/web/268.htm;* David Rethkop, "In Praise of Cultural Imperialism? Effects of Globalization on Culture", *www.globalpolicy.org/globaliz/culture.*

Schumaker, in, Weber, "Gandhi and Buddhist Economics, www.mkgandhi.org/ budhist.htm.

Seabrooke, Jermey, "Internationalism *versus* Globalisation", *Asia-APEC Internet message*, September 11, 1996.

Selected Works of Jawaharlal Nehru, (1972), Vol. III, September1946-April 1961, New Delhi, Publication Division, Government of India, 1961.

Sethi, J.D., *International Economic Disorder*, (Shimla, Indian Institute Advanced Study,1996).

Sethi, Nitin, "$5 Billion Worth Crops Destroyed Annually", *The Times of India*, 4 April, 2007.

Sharma, Rashmi, *Gandhian Economics: A Humane Approach*, (New Delhi, Deep & Deep, 1997).

Sharma, Jai Narain, "Globlising Swadeshi", in Mishra, A.D.(ed.) *Challenges of 21st Century*, (New Delhi, Mittal, 2003).

Sharma, Jai Narain, *Alternative Economics of Mahatma Gandhi and Globalisation*, (New Delhi: Deep & Deep, 2003).

Sharma, Jai Narain, "The New Economic Policy: Myth and Reality" in Radhakrishnan, N. and Vasudevan, N. (eds.) *A Nation in Transition, India at 50,* (New Delhi: Gandhi Media Centre, 1998).

Shiva, Vandana, "Violence of Globalization", *The Hindu,* March 25, 2001.

Shriman Narayan, *Towards a Socialist Economy,* (Bombay: Asia Publishing House, 1964).

Smith, Diana, "What Does Globalization Mean for Health?", *Third World Network,* 1999.

Srivastava, Padma, "Nehru, United Nations and Peace" *India Quarterly,* Vol. LII No. 1 & 2, Jan.- June- 1976.

Steger, Manford, *Globalization: A Very Short Introduction,* (Oxford University Press, 2003).

Stiglitz, Joseph E., *Making Globalization Work,* (Oxford University Press, 2003).

Stiglitze, Joseph, *Globalization and its Discontent,* (New Delhi : Penguin Books India, 1998).

Subrahmanyam, K., *Defense and Development,* (Calcutta: Minerva Associates, 1973).

Terchek, Ronald J., "Gandhi and Democratic Theory", in Thomas Pantham and Kenneth L. Deutsch (ed.), *Political Thought in Modern India,* (New Delhi: Sage Publications, 1986).

Terchek, Ronald J., *Gandhi Struggling For Autonomy,* (New Delhi : Vistar Publications, 2000).

Thakur, Harish K., and Chauhan Rajinder S., *Globalization and Human Rights,* (New Delhi: Radha Publications, 2007).

Thakur, Ramesh and Collin Bradford, "Climate Change and Global Leadership", *The Hindu,* February 10, 2007).

"The Challenge of Slums", *UN- Habitat Report, 2003.*

The Collected Works of Mahatma Gandhi, (New Delhi : 1963),Vol. 10.

The Collected Works of Mahatma Gandhi, New Delhi Publications Division. The Ministry of Information and Broadcasting, Government of India, 1980, Vol. 13.

Thomas Pantham and Kenneth L. Deutsch (ed.), *Political Thought in Modern India.*

Verzola, Roberto, "Globalisation : Its Third Waves", Nai *Azadi Udghosh, A Journal of Azadi Bachao Andolan,* Allahabad, Vol. 10, No. 5-6, September-December, 2003.

Visvanathan, Shiv, "Shop Till you Drop", *The Times of India,* 25 Oct. 2006.

Walfens, Paul, J. J. (*et. al*): *Globalization, Economic Growth and Innovation Dynamics*, (Springer Publishers, 1999).

Weinstern, Michael M., *Globalization What's New*, (New York: Columbia University Press, 2005).

Werner, Levi, "India Debates Foreign Policy", *Far Eastern Survey*, Vol. 20, No. 5, March 1951, pp. 49-52.

Wolf, Martin: *Why Globalization Works*, Yale University Press, 2004.

Xabier, Gorostiga, Jeremy Brecher, (ed.), *Latin America in the New World Order in Global Visions: Beyond the New World Order*, (Bostan, MA: South End Press, 1993).

Yurlov Felir N., "Globalization, Inequality and Threats to Sustainability Development", *World Affairs*, 5(1), Jan-Mar, 2001

INDEX

Accountability, 116
Accountability between ordinary people and public officials 18
Adam Smith, 66, 68
Advance technology, 105
Advani, Lal Krishna (Home Minister), 173
Afghanistan, 182
issue of, 13
Agri-business, xiv
Agricultural commodities, 39-40
Agricultural economies, 48-49
Agro-based industries, 168
Ahimsa, 27, 71
All India Congress Committee, 159
All India Trade Union Congress, 193
America's socalled war against terriorism, 13
Americanization, 83, 95
Anguliman, 35
Antarctica, 52
Anti-colonialism, 160, 181
Anti-corruption, 108
Anti-democracies, 126
Anti-fascist, 161
Anti-globalization, 24, 143-45
Anti-imperial nationalism, 161
Anti-modernization, 126
Anti-Nazi, 161
Aparigrah, 96
Arora, Anil, xxvi, 93
Asian-African Conference, 162, 218
Asian rivers, 87
Asian tigers, 154
Attlee (Korean Prime Minister), 162
Autonomy, 5, 14
Axix power 107
Azia, Nikhil, 147

Backlash against globalization, 121
Bande, Usha, 23
Bangladesh, 131
Bardhan, C.P., (Communist Party of India), 173
Barner, Richard, 146
Bell, Daniel, 11
Berlin Wall, 93
Bhagwati, J., 79, 117
Bhuyan, Dasarathi, xxxiii, 213
Blood, Mary, 33
Boulding, Elise, xxii, 24, 29-32
British East India, 94
Brussels Conference, 181
Budhoo, Davison, 132
Business Conglomeration, xvii
Californization, 151
Call, E.H., xiii
Cambridge University, 107

Capital corporatism, xvii
Capital flows, 138
Capital monopolis, xxvi, xxxii, 49-50, 94-95, 140, 200
Capitalist democracy, 219
CENTO Pact, 187
Chagla, M.C., 26
Challenges, xxix, 166-69, 198-99
Chandel, Kulbhushan, xxv
Cheap imports, 66
Chemical agriculture, 40
Chhachchi, Amrita, 130
Chiang-Kai-Shek, 162
Child labour, 65
Child mortality, 145
China, 180, 182, 185-87
Chomsky, Noam, 80, 143
Chou-En-Lai (Prime Minister of China), 181
Chouhan, Rajinder Singh, xxx, 179
Civil disobedience, 6
Cold War, 138, 160
Cold war between capitalism and communism, 93
Colonial bureaucracy, 38
Colonial power, 38-39
Commercialization, 26, 108
Commonwealth Forum, 210
Commonwealth Prime Ministers' Conference, 162
Communication, 214-15
Communism, 200-201
Communist Party of India (M), 15
Communist revolution, 195
Competition, 5
Computer Hardware and Software industries, 43
Comradeship, 209, 217
Consumerism, 24, 87, 106, 110
Controversis, xvii, 15
Corporate Governance, xxx
Corporate Globalization, 141
Corruption, xxv, 77
Cosmopolitanism, xxx, 213
Cottage industries, xix
Crisis, 41, 174
    kinds of, 49-50
Cuban Missile crisis, 174, 185
Cultural aggression, 39
Cultural faminism, 34
Cultural imperialism, 28
Cultural internationalism, 28
Culture, 44-45
    mechanization of, xxii, 24
Culture of Peace, 23
Cyberlords, economic powers of, 48
Czechoslovakia, 218

Decentralization, 13, 14, 67, 71-72, 101, 103
Deforestation, 103
Democracy, xx-xxii, 3-6, 101-2, 196-97, 201, 219-20
    categorizations of, 18
    Gandhian vision of xxi, 12-20
Democratic decentralization, 71
Deprivation, 125, 134
Developing countries, 216
Dharma, 9
Diana Smith, 127
Dictatorship, 18, 30
Dignity of Labour, 69-70
Drinking water, 26
Dutch East India, 94

Eco-feminism, 34

Ecological disaster, xiv
Economic crisis, 76
Economic decentralization, 15, 72
Economic equality, 71-72
Economic globalization, xvi-xvii, 50, 59-60, 137-42, 148-50
Economic inequality, 80-81
Economic liberalization, 167, 174
Economic nationalism, 39, 51-52
Economic reforms, 174, 221-22
Economic structuralism, xviii
Economics and Ethics, 68
Education, 26
Eisenhower, Dwight D., 28
Electoral democracies, 8, 17-18
Emigration, 138
Employment, 26, 116, 152-54
  growth of, 65-66
  opportunities, 69
Environmental catastrophe, 30
Environmental challenges, 85-86
Environmental crisis, 79-80
Environmental hazards, 106
Environmental issues, 61-67
Environmental pollution, problems of, 87
Equality between men and women, 31
Ethical accountability, xxv
European imperialism, 184
Exploitation, xxv, 77
Export quotes, 39
Export-imports, 166

Farmers, demonstration, 131
  suicides, of, 66, 84
Fascist manifestation, xxvi
Feher, Ferenc, 11
Five Year Plans, 169
Foreign competition, 53, 99
Foreign Direct Investment (FDI), 163
Foreign Investment, xxiv, 40, 63
Foreign exchange market, 147
Foreign policy, 201-02
Fourth World Conference, 14, 31
  political structure of, 16
Free Trade Policy, 166
Free World Trade, 214, 221
Friedman, Thomas L., 82, 93
Frustration, 12, 30
Fukuyama, Francis, 98, 107
Full employment, 68-69

G-8 nations, 94, 121
Gajendragadkar, P.B,, 216
Galbraith, J.K. (Ambassdor), xxiv, 49, 174
Gandhi, M.K., xviii-xx, 26-28, 96-100, 203, 209-12
  criticism towards industrialization, 103
  reaction against industrialization, 100
  spirituality of xviii
  Vision of peace and justice, xxii
Gandhian economic model, 66-67, 77-78
Gandhian philosophy, xxii, 14
Gandhian political orientation, 107
Gandhian Vision of *Swadeshi*, 83-84
Gandhigiri, 108
General Agreement on Tariff and Trade (GATT), 53, 58
  Final Act, 131
Geneva, 58
Geneva Conventions, 115

Giddens, Anthony, 79
Gita, 76
Global competition, 64
Global Corporations, 41, 141
Global Culture, myth of, 82-83
Global economic liberalization, 138
Global homogeneous culture, xxvi
Global information economy, xxiv, 42-46
Global warming, 85-86
Globalization, xxviii-xxv, xxix-xxx, 23-25, 48-50, 57-60, 79-80, 116-20, 124-26, 128-30, 137-40, 152-54, 163-65, 169-72, 191-95, 216-20
  contradictory, 103
  dynamics of, 53-54
  implications of, 62-63
  Nehru's perspective on, 213-22
  phenomenon of, xiii
  second wave of, 40-41, 47-48
  third wave of, 47-48
Goodman, David, S.G., 150
Gorbachev, 221
Green house gases, 85
Gross Domestic Product (GDP), 96
Gupta, Narinder Kumar, xxxii, 207

Handicraft industries, 5
Hahn, Thick Nhel, 30
Haynes, Jeff, 17, 18
Health Care, 26
Heller,Agnes, 11
Himalayan glaciers, 87
Himsa, 27
Hind Swaraj, 24
Hiroshima, 183
HIV/AIDS, 122-24, 127
Horse-trading, 4
Huang, Ho, 87
Human Development Report, 154
Human rights, overproduction of, 120
Human Rights violations, 126-27
Humanitarianism, xxii, 24
Hungary crisis, 185
Hussain, Syed Iqbal, 87

Illiberal democracy, 17-18
Illiteracy, 101, 84
Immigration, 138
India, Foreign policy of, xxx, 160, 179-80, 182, 186, 213-14
Indian National Army, 107
Indian National Congress, xxix, 174, 193
Indian National movement, 166
Indian nationalism, 105
Indian, quality of life, 76-77
Indira Gandhi, 173
Indo-Pakistan relations, 13
Indo-Russian relations, 202
Indo-Soviet Treaty, 188
Indoor Air pollution, 87
Industrial countries, 40-42
  economic programmes of, 58
Industrial cyberlord, 98
Industrial economies, xxiv
Industrial revolution, 52, 219
Industrialization, xxii, 24-26, 67-68, 100-02, 106-110, 193-94, 198-200
  evils of, 74-75
Inequality discrimination, 77, 125
Information capitalism, xxx, 189-90
Information economies, 42, 45-46
Information monopolies, 43-47
Information technology, 43-44, 61-62

revolution of, xxx, 189-90
Integral democracies, 18
Intellectual Property Rights (IPR), 46, 123
International Bill of Human Rights, 115
International Competition, 168
International dictatorship, 50
International disputes, 160
International economies monopolies, 50
International Labour Organisation (ILO), 129
Inter-Governmental Panel on Climte Changes (IPCC), 85
International Monetary Fund (IMF), xxiii, xxv, 41, 58, 61, 62, 70, 76, 94, 98, 132, 139, 144, 146, 166, 168-69, 172
International Year of Culture and Peace (IYCP), 28, 31
Internationalism, xxxii, 203-04, 208-10, 213-15

Jain, Mohini, 118
Japanese economies, xxvii
Jay Mazur, 80
Jesus, 25, 108
Jewesh illegal immigration, 162
Johnson, Richard, 34

Karl Marx, 164
Kashmir 180
problems of, 183
Kashmir dispute to UNO, 185
Kashmir issue, 188
Khadi and Village industries, 73-74
Khalid, Mohammed, xxviii, 159
Krishnamurti, J., 29
Kuldip Singh, 118
Kyoto Protocol, 103
Liberal democracies, 19
Liberal internationalism, 159
Liberalisation, 54, 94, 221
policy, 149
Lord Buddha, 35
Lohia, Ram Manohar, 197

MacMohan Line, 187
Mandes, Jerry, xiii
Manmohan Singh (Prime Minister), 13, 99, 173
Margaret Thetcher (British Prime Minister), 149
Market economy, 221
Marquand, David, 11
Martin, Kingslay, 214
Maslow, Abraham, 26
Mcquil, D., 83
Migration, 83, 138
Milamoric, Baraniki, 59
Military aggression, 39
Military technology, 37
Mind-boggling progress, xxiii
Missionary Conference, Madras, 52
Modern technology, 12, 16
Monbriot, George, 80, 86
Monopolies, 44-45
Monopolistic prices, 40
Mukherjee, Aruni, 25
Mukherjee, J., 118
Mulford, David (US Ambassador), 173
Mullin, Francis Coralic, 117
Multinational Corporation (MNCs), xxv, 16, 61, 63, 66, 120, 171-72

NAM, 201-02
NATO, 169
National Planning Committee, 195
Nationalism, xxxiii, 203, 214-15
Nationalization, 111
Nehru, Jawaharlal, xviii, 84-85, 159-62, 165-68, 174-78, 180-83, 185-88, 190-94, 198-200
    economic ideology, 170-72
    economic policy, 168-70
    economic thinking, 167
    idea of mixed economy, xxxiii
    ideas over international peace, 204
    international outlook, 218
    internationalsm, xxxii, 207-11
    mixed economic model, 220-21
    philosophy of internationalism, 209-10
New International Economic Order (NIEO), 58
New World Order, 217
Nicaraguan Scholar Xabier Gorostiage, 147
Nominal democracies, 8
Non-alignment, xxx, 160, 180, 186,, 211-12
    policy, 180-82
Non-economic context, 60-61
Non-violence, xxi, 107-08
Non-violent action, campaign for, 27

Obligation, 6
Obscurantism, xxxii, 207
OECD, 133
Ohmae, Kenichi, 149
Old colonialism, 215

Pakistan, 131, 180, 188
Pakistan-India People's Forum for Peace and Democracy, 33
Palestine issue, 161
Panchayati Raj Institutions, 110
Panchayati Raj System, 72, 76
Panchsheel, xxx, 161, 186
    philosophical interpretation of, 183
Papola, T.S., 61
Parameswaran, M.P., 14
Parekh, Bhikhu, 27
Participatory democracy, 15
Pasricha, Ashu, 107, 115
Pathak, C.J., 117, 118
Peace-culture, 28-32, 34
Physical violence, 32
Place of Machinery, 74
Planning for India, 194-95
Planning Commission, 195, 198
Pluralist model, 10
Political decentralization, 15, 72
Political democracy, xxxi, 5
Political economics, 32
Post-cold war, 174
Post-colonial development, 39
Post-modernity, xix
Poverty, xxv, 69, 77-78, 124, 184
    problems of, 67-68, 74-75
Pradhan, B, 213
Pranab Mukherjee (External Affairs Minister), 202
Privatization, 44, 125-26, 220-21
Protest against war and injustice, 30
Publishing industries, 43
Purna Swaraj, xxi, 8

Push-pull migration, 30

Quasi-democratic, 17

Radicalism, 181
Raghavan, Chakravarty, 41
Rajan, Manoj, 137
Rajiv Gandhi, 173
Rajgopalachari, C., 197
Rajni Kothari, 11
Ramrajya, xxi, 8
Rapid industrialization, 99, 165
Ray, Barati, 25
Reconciliation between nationalism and internationalism, 218-19
Richard Nixon, 189
Robinson, Richard, 156
Roerich Nichola, 27
Ruskin, 25, 108
Russell, Bertrand, 184
Russian revolution, 98

Sambhava, 76
San Francisco Conference, 185
Sanjay Dutt, 107
Sarva Bhavantu Sukhina, 24
Sarvodaya, xxi, 9, 67, 102, 108
Satyagraha, 103
 movement, 33
Schumacher, E.F., xvii, 112
Science and Technology, xix, 167
SEATO Pact, 187
Second Five Year Plan, 198
Second World War, xxvi, 51, 94, 129, 152, 182-83
Secularism, 167, 207
Self-sufficiency, 73, 99-103
Sensationalism, 4
Shakespeare, 119
Sharma, Jai Narain, 37
Sharma, Vijay, xix, 3
Shiva, Vandana, 25
Simple living high thinking, 69-70
Sino-Indian Conflict, 161, 174
Slithaporaya, 35
Small Scale and Cottage Industries, 74-75
Socialism, xviii, 109
Soras, George, 95
Spiritualism, 24, 66
Stockhome Conference, 88
Structural Adjustment Programme (SAP), 132, 148
Subsidies, 66, 171
Suicides by farmers, 66
Suez Crisis, 185
Swadeshi, xxiii, 52-53, 67, 70-72, 111-12
 movement, 99
Swami Ram Krishna Parmhansa, 54
Swaraj, 8, 72, 99

Tagore, Rabindranath, xviii
Telecommunication, facilities, 164
Terchek, Ronald, J., xix, 10, 13, 14
Terrorism, 13, 153
Thakur, Harish K., xxviii, 105, 191
Thoreau, 25, 108
Tibet policy, 180
Tigerhood, 134
Toffler, Alwin, xxiii
Tolstoy, 25, 108
Toxic pollution, 42
Trade liberalization, 122
Treaty of Peace and Friendship, 180

True democracy, 7, 9
Trusteeship, xxvii, 7, 13, 67, 75-76, 97
principle of, 76
Turk, Danilo, 132

UN General Assembly Resolution, 162
UN Millennium Summit, 85
UNESCO, 31
UNICEF, 133
Unemployment, xxv, 12, 63, 67, 74-75, 77, 125, 152
problems of, 65
Universal Declaration of Human Rights, 116, 119, 122
United States, 76
Unorthodox internationalism, xxxii
University Grants Commission (UGC), 167
Unsustainable technologies, 38
Uruguay Round, 58
USSR, 15

Vasudhaiv Kutumbakam, 35
Vienna Declaration, 122
Vietnam, 131
crisis of, 185
Village Centric development, 83-84
Village Communities, 72-73
Village Swaraj, 67
Violations of Human Rights, 127-28
Violence, xxv-xxviii
Voice against Violence, 33
V.P. Singh, 173

Washington Consensus, 93
Water pollution, 87
Westernization, 106
Wolf, Martin, 79
Women and Culture of Peace Programme (WCP), 31
World Bank, xxiii, xxv, 41, 58, 61, 62, 76, 94, 132, 145, 146, 166-69, 172
World Economic Crisis, xxv
World Federation, 192
World Conference on Human Rights, Vienna, 121
World Trade Organization (WTO), xxiii, xv, 41, 43 46, 61, 62, 76, 94, 98, 99, 121-22, 127, 131, 133, 149, 169, 172
agreement of, 66
World Wars, 93

Yangtze, 87
Yechury, Sitaram (CPI(M) Polit buro), 173
Yurlov, Felix, 81, 96

Zakaria, Farid, 17